To my parents, John and Priscilla, and my brother, John, for their support and encouragement.

Acknowledgments

Thanks first and foremost go to God for blessing me with this opportunity and putting so many extraordinary people in my life. I'm grateful for the love, support, and encouragement of my parents, John and Priscilla, my brother, John, and the rest of my family, friends, and colleagues.

I realize how lucky I am to be able to work in this industry and as a writer. It is through the patience, professionalism, and direction of Course Technology PTR acquisitions editor Orren Merton and project editor Cathleen Small that this book has been published.

Thank you to my mentor, Jim Progris, longtime head of the music industry program at the University of Miami. I am grateful to have you as a teacher. You'll never know how much your wisdom and belief in me has meant.

My sincere appreciation goes out to all of the friends and colleagues who shared with me their wisdom and advice on MySpace, marketing, and the music industry at large. Thank you also to my good friends who let me use their words and faces as examples throughout the book.

This project wouldn't have been possible without the positive vibes and support of everyone mentioned here. My gratitude goes out to each and every one of you.

About the Author

Fran Vincent is the founder and president of Retro Island Productions, Inc., a social media, Web PR, and music-industry consulting firm. Before starting her own company, Fran spent six years as the marketing and public relations specialist for Warner Bros. Publications, a division of Warner Music Group. She has also authored articles for *Electronic Musician* and *InTune* magazines.

Fran has previously worked at some of America's most prestigious companies, including AOL Time Warner, General Motors, Campbell-Ewald Advertising (Chevrolet's agency of record for almost 100 years), and Independent Newspapers, and she is a former journalist and editor herself. She holds a master's degree in music business (a hybrid music and business degree) from the University of Miami and a bachelor's degree in journalism from Oakland University. Fran is also an accomplished musician, performer, and college instructor, and she taught music licensing, marketing, public relations, and management courses at the University of Miami.

Fran now resides in the Detroit area and continues to work with music, marketing, and social media clients around the world.

Contents

Chapter 5
Identifying Your Target Market   53

Chapter 6
Getting Started   73

Chapter 7
Signing Up and MySpace Profile Basics   93

Chapter 8
Customizing Your Page   107

Chapter 9
You Gotta Have Friends   149

Chapter 10
Comments, Anyone?   171

Chapter 11
Playlists and the Music Player   197

Chapter 12
Photos and Videos   217

Chapter 13
Apps and Widgets   227

Chapter 14
Bulletins and Event Invitations   241

Chapter 15
Blogging in the MySpace World   267

Chapter 16
Using Groups and Forums   287

Chapter 17
Contacting Your Audience   295

Chapter 18
Protecting Your Virtual and Physical Security   307

Chapter 19
Managing MySpace   315

Chapter 20
Now What? MySpace and Your Marketing Plan   329

Introduction

Social media and its applications are ubiquitous and ever-changing. Just a few short years ago, MySpace was the main player in social networking. Stories of the website's marketing possibilities, the millions it fetched when sold, and the unfortunate tales of predators' exploits dotted the print and broadcast media landscape almost constantly. It seemed that MySpace was firmly entrenched in today's popular culture as an icon of Web 2.0, the next generation of the Internet.

Flash forward a few years. MySpace is still a major player, but it's not the only game in town. Facebook, Twitter, and other up-and-comers have stolen a lot of the spotlight. Now MySpace must share. While other social media tools boast different strengths and offerings, MySpace still retains a place in the hearts of music lovers and artists everywhere.

It's no wonder, then, that so many people, especially those aged 13 to 34, can attest to the "magic" of MySpace. It's still the only social network that was really founded around music and nightlife events. Facebook and Twitter have their benefits, but they're not music portals. The beauty of MySpace is that it combines the ability to discover new music and keep up on favorite artists with other fun and useful tools. And while its market share may fluctuate depending on the tastes of the public and the needs of social media users, MySpace has something the others do not: the ears of music lovers.

But MySpace is not just a giant music-marketing machine. For some, it is an essential part of their social lives, the primary way they keep in touch with friends and customers, and their main method of meeting new people in their real lives.

And then there are those who see it as a way to reach out to others, to communicate beyond their homes, town, or even country. To say to both friends and strangers, "I am here. I am looking, and I want to be found."

What You'll Find in This Book

The flurry of activity on MySpace, with its millions of pages of user-generated content, is ever-growing and changing. The scope of it is overwhelming. There are almost 200 million profiles as of this day. Features and site offerings change regularly...one never knows what new trinket will pop up. It excels at reaching music consumers and industry types. That makes it a powerful marketing force for bands, and one worth learning about.

MySpace for Musicians, Second Edition will introduce you to MySpace and what you will find on the site, how you can manipulate it, and how to use the service to your promotional advantage as an artist and entertainer.

While the book attempts to be comprehensive, it cannot cover every possible aspect of the MySpace experience. The technology, the site, and its offerings are changing almost daily. Even when programmers the world over quickly catch up and develop more tweaks and new ways of manipulating the site, it changes yet again. The code recommendations and site links offered here worked at the time the book was written, but there's no guarantee they will work forever. MySpace develops code blocks and filters all the time, and third-party tweak and layout sites come and go. Therefore, this book is only a snapshot in time. The best way to use this book, since some information or the layout of MySpace's features may have changed since its printing, is to take the concepts and adjust them to what the site is right now, at the moment you are using it. If a link to a feature doesn't appear where it says in the book, it's likely still around, just moved in one of MySpace's reorganizations.

Despite the unpredictable nature of the site and its usage, this book will introduce you to what's possible, with the hope that you will continue to keep abreast of new developments on your own.

MySpace for Musicians will walk you through the maze of grassroots marketing using the MySpace site. You'll become a proficient MySpacer and hopefully an adept marketer.

One other note… This book is an independent commentary on MySpace and its usage. Requests to interview MySpace staff and even obtain comments, clarifications, and tips that would help you, the music marketer, were declined by MySpace.

Who This Book Is For

MySpace for Musicians, Second Edition is for every band, soloist, side musician, record label, publisher, music manager, and entertainment industry–affiliated company who wants to use MySpace to its fullest potential. It's for all those who are not sure what they should be doing with MySpace. Maybe you've thought of it, but you think it's only for teenagers, or you are too intimidated to get started. Perhaps all of your friends and colleagues are on it, and they're always asking you, "Are you on MySpace?" but you haven't made that first step. Anyone who is starting out on MySpace and is overwhelmed by the task at hand now has a guide to walk them through the process. You don't have to spend countless hours figuring it out on your own.

This book is also for those who have signed up but don't really know what to do with their profile now. You may be new to marketing or unsure of how to maximize your experience on MySpace.

For every artist who wants to hop on the MySpace bandwagon but doesn't think he or she is Web-savvy enough to do it, this book is for you.

How This Book Is Organized

MySpace for Musicians, Second Edition is organized logically from an introduction to MySpace and social media, to determining what kind of account to open, all the way through to customizing your profile, adding friends, leaving comments, crafting bulletins and blogs, and then onto the basics of email marketing, protecting your security, and even managing your experience. This book takes you on a step-by-step journey through the service in a way that makes sense for most people who have thought of joining the community but haven't yet jumped in.

Each chapter will first introduce the content, giving you the basics of the topic, then further break down the information so you learn how to accomplish each task yourself. The best way to learn is by doing, so you can follow along and try the pointers in the book right in your own MySpace account.

Throughout the book, you'll find references to other resources outside of MySpace, such as image hosting sites, code generators, and more. The appendixes at the end of this book offer even more resources, organized by category, such as music industry, music downloading, mobile marketing, and more. You won't have to spend an exorbitant amount of time web-searching to find the best sites. Most of what you'll need has been sourced and listed in the appendixes for you. However, that shouldn't stop you from researching on your own should you not find what you need here.

Are you ready? Fire up the computer. Make sure you're connected to the Internet, and let's get you turned on to MySpace!

1 Intro to MySpace and Social Media

In just a few short years, the terms *social media* and *social networking* have become common in the modern lexicon. Tweets scroll at the bottom of news stalwarts such as CNN and primetime dramas. People rush to enter status updates on their Facebook and MySpace pages through their iPhones and Blackberries. Celebrities and nobodies alike record their opinions in YouTube video blogs. Everyone's got something to say . . . from the useful and profound to the mundane and ridiculously unimportant. We're all connected 24/7 in a never-ending stream-of-consciousness-like blather.

This is social media . . . the connections of friends and networks, the comments on stories and products, the recommendations of fans, and the complaints of critics. It's the authentic opinions of users worldwide and the fabrications of shills who are paid to plug ideas and products in YouTube, blog, and news story comments . . . all in an attempt to sway public opinion and influence sales or even votes.

In the "old days," consumers could only write a letter to a company, complain to a manager, or simply tell anyone they encountered of their bad experience. A business had to guess how many dissatisfied customers any one complaint truly represented. Today, consumers have a global platform in which to vent their displeasure with a product or service, disseminate news in a war-torn country or during a natural disaster, or sing the praises of their new favorite song. Businesses and advertisers have taken notice in an unprecedented way. Never before has a brand, or a band for that matter, been able to monitor the conversations of the public in such an open way. People yell from the virtual rooftops, spreading their discontent like a wildfire amongst dry tinder in the desert. The commentary can be devastating to a company financially and can wipe away the public's good will.

By the same token, good news also travels fast. Numbers of people posting all over the Internet about a sublime new artist, an irresistible tune, or a hilarious video clip are hard to ignore. Their voices create a tidal wave of sentiment that can sway fans and tastemakers one way or the other. Social media is influential, and its power is undeniable.

While social media can be considered the great equalizer, with the people finally finding a direct platform to voice their opinions, it is also the great manipulator. All that buzz you've been hearing about a particular political issue, an entertainment hot topic, or the latest gadget

1

might not be the wave of independent thought and analysis it portends to be. In many cases, it is legions of street teams and publicists on the payroll tapping into the power of social media and networking to influence the public. Consuming social media—well, any media, really—requires a savvy eye for detecting BS and an interest in ferreting out the truth for oneself.

So what does this mean for you? As a band, you have a remarkable opportunity today that didn't exist 10 or even 5 years ago. You can now market yourself amongst networks of interest groups and friends who will promote you willingly. You can build awareness and influence opinion. And you have many avenues to exploit—from networks such as MySpace, Facebook, Twitter, and LinkedIn, to blogging, commenting, article syndication, book-marking, video marketing, and more. There's a lot to learn. Although we can't cover all the social media ground in this one tome, we'll focus on what you came here for—MySpace.

MySpace Today

Just a few short years ago, MySpace was the main game in town. It was a viral marketing phenomenon that even the least media-savvy among us knew about. It was hard to escape the hype and the not-so-subtle hoopla surrounding it—the numbers of business and friendship connections being made daily; the new music being discovered by consumers and labels alike; and unfortunately, like virtually all interactive sites, the sex predators and weirdos who plague every corner of both the real and virtual worlds. We were hearing MySpace-related stories on the nightly news; movie trailers and CD liner notes listed their MySpace page addresses prominently; and parents worried that their teenage daughters were posting pictures with too much skin. It seemed that all walks of life had an interest in MySpace.

MySpace slid into the forefront of new media marketing. It's a free site comprised of user-created profiles where the community views and shares content in a variety of interactive media (music, video, blogs) and links to others to form "friend" groups, all with powerful results (see Figure 1.1).

Hundreds of millions of people call MySpace home, a virtual hangout comprised of teenagers, urban hipsters, stay-at-home moms, yuppies, bands, businesses, and entertainers of every stripe. Imagine the force of marketing, advertising, and promotional possibilities that exists in a community of that size and with such a varied demographic. Media giant News Corp., owners of Fox Broadcasting, Fox News, 20th Century Fox Studios, and a cadre of media outlets, saw the potential and in 2005 purchased MySpace's parent company, Intermix Media, for $580 million. At that time, MySpace had about 20 million members, just a fraction of what it has at this moment. In just a few short years, it had cracked the Top 3 of websites in the U.S. and rivaled Internet heavyweights Google, AOL, Yahoo!, MSN, Amazon, and even eBay.

Times have changed, though. MySpace is no longer the main player in social media. Facebook has steadily punched out more market share and now occupies a spot in the Top 3 websites in the U.S., with MySpace dropping down to a respectable number 5 (see Figure 1.2). While

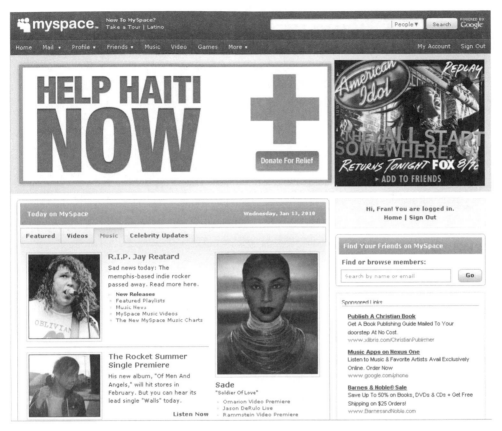

Figure 1.1   MySpace.com's home page.

everyone and their grandmother seems to have set up shop on Facebook, MySpace is still an important social media portal. Don't let anyone tell you differently. People gravitate to the place where their friends and family hang out. For many people right now, that place is Facebook. But you have to remember that just because your friends and family are on Facebook, addicted to Twitter, or frequenting MyYearbook.com, that doesn't mean your fans are hanging out there.

MySpace is still *the* place for independent and major label music (see Figure 1.3). Facebook is not usually where fans, journalists, booking agents, managers, and A&R executives go to hear your latest single. They go to your MySpace profile first to get a quick-and-dirty synopsis of what you're all about (see Figure 1.4). Your MySpace band profile is open and free, accessible by even non-MySpace members. It doesn't require one to become a fan, download an app, or do anything else to experience your music. MySpace music profiles are very much a staple of the music business and media community and are critical to your success—journalists often request an artist's MySpace page first. From there, they decide whether they want you to send in a CD or email MP3s based on what they experience on your profile. If you don't have a MySpace band profile, you're behind the eight ball.

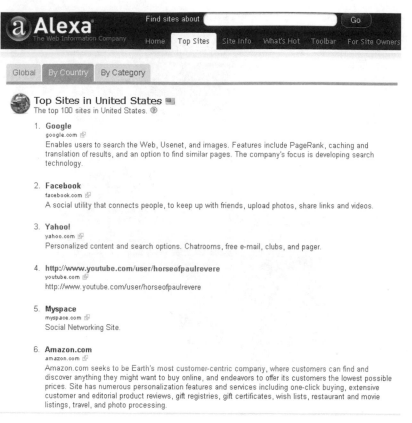

Figure 1.2 Alexa Internet ranks websites globally and by language, country, and other parameters. These results in January 2010 show the top six in the U.S. (www.alexa.com).

You may find that your target fan base is on both Facebook *and* MySpace. Facebook does have its place in the social media experience for fans. Facebook fan pages can be rigged out to include some of the information that is traditionally seen on a MySpace page, especially if artists link their iLike.com pages with their Facebook fan pages (see Figure 1.5). However, Facebook's unique benefit is the ease of carrying on an ongoing conversation with fans in an informal manner. As an artist, you post status updates, offers, gigs, and more on your Facebook, and it easily meshes with your fans' other updates from friends and family members. Fans can respond to your updates and even to other fan's posts on your page (see Figure 1.6). It's quite seamless. That's the advantage of Facebook . . . the interface is more about the conversation between friends and keeping that dialogue open (which Facebook does quite well—and, in my opinion, better than MySpace) than it is about creating a branded musical environment, which is what MySpace excels at. Both sites have their advantages. However, even if most of your fan base congregates on Facebook (or another social network), it is still critical for you to have a MySpace presence that showcases your best work and promotes your image to the music business and media industries.

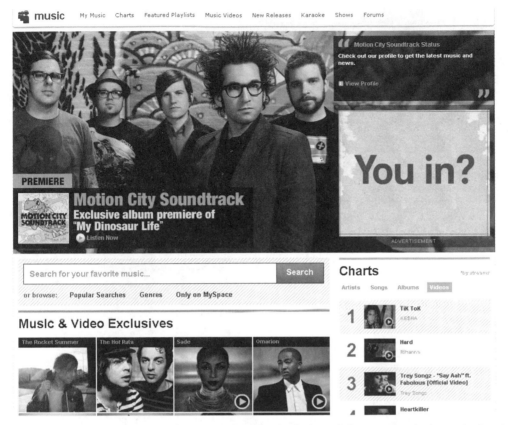

Figure 1.3 The main page of MySpace Music, the home of the community's musical artists.

Social Networking: An Old Concept

What was just an idea a few years ago has become a marvel of marketing, advertising, big business, and grassroots buzz. But what is social networking? One of the latest Internet and marketing go-to terms isn't a new term at all. It was invented in the 1950s by J. A. Barnes to describe a chart of the relationships between people and how they are connected to one another. In today's marketing-driven world, social networking denotes part word-of-mouth marketing and part Six Degrees of Kevin Bacon. It's turning others on to what you like and getting them in the groove with your friends. Whether online or in the real world, social networking has been an important part of building ties in the community, in business, and sometimes even in the dating scene. After all, many a match has been made when a friend of a friend's single cousin was introduced to the neighbor's daughter's accountant!

And so it is with MySpace and its contemporaries. People connect in virtual spaces, making friends, dates, and business contacts and turning each other on to favorite bands. They post blogs and videos, music, poetry, and photo journals of their vacations. They find old class-mates and discover new friends, adding these friends to their profiles. Amongst their group,

Figure 1.4   The profile of artist Katharine McPhee (www.myspace.com/katharinemcphee) makes it quick and easy to see her latest updates, listen to her new album, watch videos, and more.

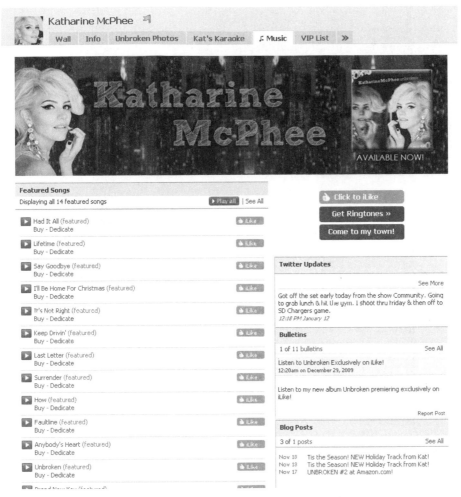

Figure 1.5   McPhee's fan page on Facebook (www.facebook.com/katharinemcphee). The default Music tab presents songs and artist info, but in a much more streamlined, less branded manner than in her MySpace profile (refer to Figure 1.4).

social media users are influencers and tastemakers, publicizing the newest and latest, and even the classic and underrated.

Notable Social Networking Sites   MySpace gets a lot of media attention, but it's not the only player in the world of online social networking. Following are just a few of the dozens of related sites making waves on the Internet.

- **Bebo.com.** Launched in 2005, Bebo's offerings are similar to many other social networking sites. It has become one of the most popular social networking sites in Ireland.

- **Facebook.com.** What started as a site for the college crowd has grown into the big dog in social networking, with noticeable growth amongst adults in their 20s through 40s, as well as business networkers.

- **Friendster.com.** Friendster was an early comer in the social networking scene, and the most popular until MySpace overtook it around 2004. Interest in Friendster has slowed down dramatically in the U.S. but is still big in some non-U.S. markets.

- **LinkedIn.com.** This heavy hitter in business networking sites is also regularly ranked among the Top 20 websites in the U.S. (according to Alexa.com) as of this writing.

- **MEETin.org.** A free grassroots site that connects people in various cities. Members plan events with the aim of building real-life friendships in their local metropolis.

- **Meetup.com.** Want to form clubs and groups in the real world? Meetup.com assists users in finding local people with similar interests. (This site is unrelated to MEETin.org.)

- **Multiply.com.** A new take, Multiply.com combines traditional aspects of social networking with photo printing and photo management software.

- **MyYearbook.com.** An innovative way to meet new people, this site is tied together by playing Games and Matches using virtual currency called *Lunch Money*.

- **Orkut.com.** Google's answer to social networking, Orkut has been a fairly quiet endeavor in the U.S., but it still has tens of millions of members and is growing.

- **SecondLife.com.** This *Sims*-esque 3D virtual world by Linden Labs allows users to create avatars and the environment around them and even hold virtual concerts and events.

- **TagWorld.com.** A site launched to compete with MySpace. It allows users to up-load up to 1 GB of music and other media.

- **Tribe.net.** Organized by geographic area, Tribe encourages discussion and inter-action amongst members who share tips on job leads, their favorite websites and activities, and more.

- **Twitter.com.** A social network and micro-blogging site. The short blurbs users send out are known as *tweets*.

- **Windows Live Spaces (spaces.live.com).** Microsoft's version of a social portal, Live Spaces users post profiles, blogs, and more.

- **Xanga.com.** Another popular networking and blog site, Xanga has tens of millions of members. It began in the late '90s as a portal for people to share book and music reviews.

For a list of music-based social networking sites, please consult Appendix A of this book.

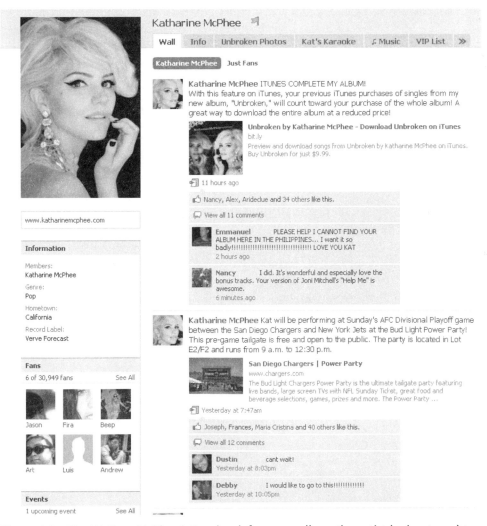

Figure 1.6   The Wall on McPhee's Facebook fan page allows the artist (or her team) to post updates and fans to comment and interact with each other. The ease of creating "conversations" is the primary benefit of Facebook over MySpace.

It's All About the Music

Unlike most other sites in the social networking category, MySpace's unprecedented growth can be attributed to its reputation as a must-stop for indie music. Once upon a time, you went into your local record store and chatted up the sales associates to find out what was new and groundbreaking. Their recommendations were gold, and you took them seriously and even based your purchases on the shoppie's list of must-haves. I'm sure some of you reading this remember those good ol' days. Unfortunately, the local record shop is largely gone now. With radio stations mostly playing the same 10 songs day in and day out, where is a person supposed to look for new music? The tradition of interfacing with the local music guru may be defunct, but the idea lives on in MySpace. Here, people recommend bands to each other and feature song clips and videos of their favorites on their profiles. If you like to browse and discover for yourself, the MySpace Music section is a directory of more than a million bands and solo artists in every genre imaginable, as well as a few that defy classification.

Unsigned and signed, major and indie—bands flock to MySpace to hock their wares in snapshot form. And by all accounts, they do so with quite a bit of success. There's no guarantee that you'll end up with a record deal, but you will have gained more exposure than the day before you signed up with MySpace. At the end of the day, that's really the purpose—getting your music out there to the masses who are waiting to discover you. This direct-to-consumer model has changed the face of music industry sales and promotion forever.

For all its hype, MySpace is not a perfect environment. It has its share of problems. Although it's a design-it-yourself community in many ways, the basic layout fields can be restrictive. Anyone who has been a member for more than a week will tell you that there are times it slows to a crawl and often a dead stop. The overwhelming amount of traffic, especially after work hours, is taxing on the servers. Errors and bugs pop up enough to try the patience of even the most low-key of Type B personalities (see Figure 1.7). And browsers crash when presented with profiles by overzealous MySpacers who are sure everyone wants to wait for 50 pictures and 10 videos to load.

Figure 1.7   MySpace's tech team posts info about bugs and twitches that are in the process of being resolved.

That's just from a functional perspective. You're not competing with tens or hundreds of bands anymore. Now you're competing with millions, all living in the same place. That's a lot of promotional noise to sift through, a task not lost on users and musicians alike. My-Spacers are inundated with requests from bands to listen to their songs. Never before has there been this level of musician/consumer interaction. Bands put themselves out there, and not just passively. They're vying for attention on a one-on-one level.

At this point you may be wondering, if there's so much competition, why bother? You really could say that about anything in life, but should that stop you from getting in the game? It *is* possible to differentiate yourself and break through the noise. But it takes consistency, patience, and a willingness to devote your time and energy to it. You shouldn't neglect your music, of course, but making money by making art doesn't happen by accident. Like any business, your music is a product, and if anyone's going to buy it, they have to be aware of it first. You want people to listen, talk, and recommend. And that's where MySpace can help.

In Chapter 2, we'll explore the impact that MySpace has had on the music and entertainment industry.

2 The Impact of MySpace on Music and Entertainment

Music industry insiders and watchers note MySpace's impact on music and entertainment as the millennium's one-stop shop for indie and major label artists. The old models of the music industry—record deal, mass radio play, major distribution—have been turned on their ears a bit. That's not to say that the standard business model is irrelevant. It's still vital in achieving mass-market penetration. But now there's a change in how musicians can get their songs heard. They're no longer solely reliant on terrestrial radio as a means of reaching consumer cars, nor are they dependent on a record label for selling music. Instead, artists can market themselves directly to consumers, who in turn pass the word on to their friends. The web in general has made a direct-to-consumer approach possible for a long time now, but not until the proliferation of MySpace users who love music was there a ready-made community just sitting there waiting to hear the next big music star.

In this chapter we'll take a brief look at how MySpace has affected the landscape of the entertainment industry.

In the Beginning . . .

The generally accepted story of MySpace's founding is that two guys from California, Tom Anderson and Chris DeWolfe, created the site in 2003 along with a small group of programmers. It may have started as a new way to keep people in the know about local Los Angeles bands and club gigs, but it grew into a place to meet new friends and keep in touch with old. Artists of all stripes, including poets, filmmakers, and especially bands, flocked to the site, and it got a reputation as *the* indie music portal (which it still maintains today). There are some who dispute this story and the founders' accounts, including Brad Greenspan, former head of parent company Intermix, who claims to be the real founder of MySpace.

Nevertheless, it's hard to believe that a few short years ago, MySpace was just a fledgling creation. In 2005, only two years after its founding, Rupert Murdoch's News Corporation bought Intermix for a whopping $580 million. More than $300 million of that is said to be for the MySpace properties alone, which easily draw in the coveted 16-to-34 age demographic.

The Evolution

Today, nearly 300 million profiles later, MySpace can brag about its desirability. Every time you visit the home page MySpace.com, you'll see another major label, movie studio, or TV network advertising its latest project or launching its newest product (see Figure 2.1). And we're not just talking banner ads, either (although MySpace has no shortage of those). Entertainment heavyweights look to MySpace to showcase fabulous customized profiles that fit the label, studio, or network's branding like a well-programmed glove (see Figure 2.2). And while other social media sites (such as Facebook) have gained ground, MySpace is still king when it comes to music and attracting massive amounts of music-lover traffic.

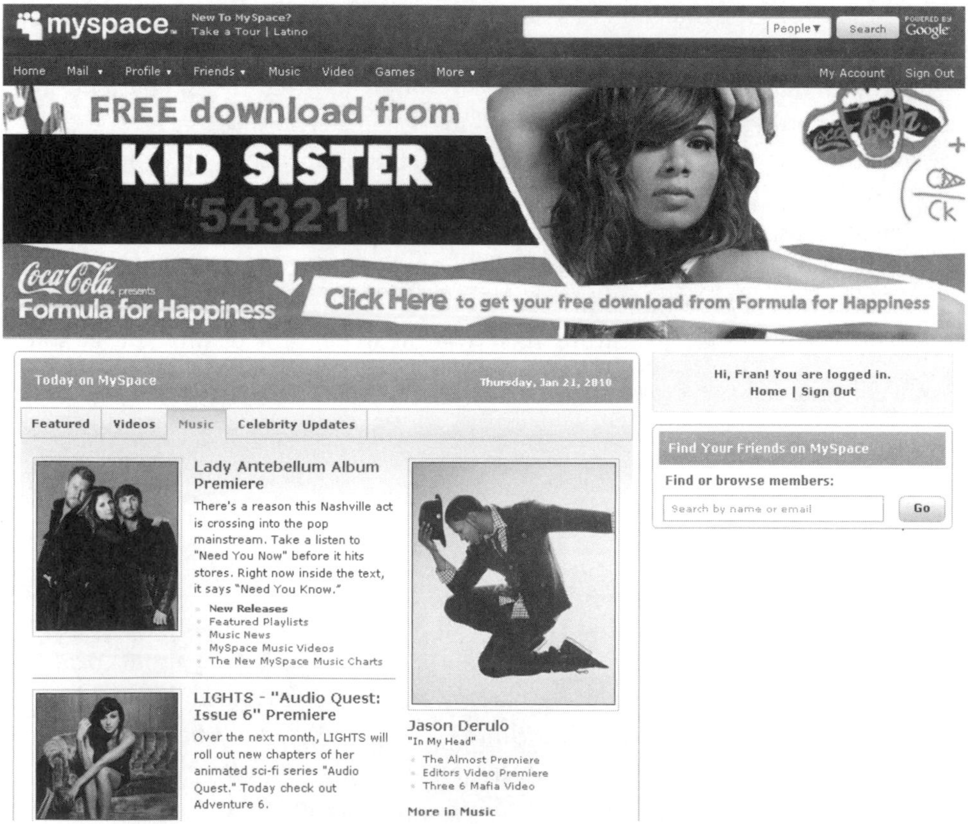

Figure 2.1 This portion of the MySpace home page shows featured music artists, movies, videos, and other paid promotions, as well as editorial features. In this example, you can see both a paid banner ad promotion for Kid Sister and Coca-Cola's Formula for Happiness, as well as featured music artists likely chosen by editors.

Those of you who aren't on MySpace yet may wonder why the industry sees it as an essential marketing venue. Why not just use a regular website, as people have been doing for years?

Figure 2.2   This MySpace profile for the movie *X-Men Origins: Wolverine* is a great snapshot of the movie and its brand.

It's not enough anymore. With MySpace, your audience is built in. Millions of people are going to the home page to log in and check their e-mail and peruse their friends' profiles anyway. Each and every one of them will see a home page promotion, and they'll click and find more than just some static advertisement. They may find select video clips, contests, posts from artists and actors themselves, music, giveaways, free videos, and downloads. They're interacting with the product and their communities in a quicker, more efficient way than by visiting a website. Not only will you see a movie's or an artist's official website address on a trailer, ad, or CD, but you're also likely to see the MySpace address, too.

Matt Crossey, creative director for Working Class Records in the UK, sums up the beauty of a MySpace profile like this: "People's attention spans are so minute. [MySpace] is bite-sized—a brief summary for most people is all they need."

You may not be promoting your music on the home page like major record labels and movie studios do, but you are still a MySpacer with music to market. The same mentality about it applies. I, too, find myself seeking out artists' MySpace pages more than their websites now.

I eventually get over to the website, but sometimes I find the profile much nicer to deal with. It all loads on one page, including music clips, and that's that. If I want a few extras, I hop over to the official website, and once in a while I sign up for the official mailing list. But when I want to check quickly for tour dates or news, I click on the artist's profile. You'll find this is true of many MySpacers. Do a web search on your favorite artists, and you're likely to see their MySpace page pop up pretty close to the top of the search results.

Don't think you don't need an official website, your own dot-com. You *do*. The key is to marry the two and realize that they are used differently. Remember that old saying about putting all your eggs in one basket? MySpace has been hot for a while (and at one point, it was the top of the social media food chain), but who's to say it will stay a marketing stalwart forever? What if they start charging for access? What if another site usurps its popularity and users jump ship (which has already happened to some degree with the rise of Facebook)? If all you've got is a MySpace profile and nothing else, you're in trouble. Use MySpace to build your own marketing list by getting people over to your website, too. You're not just building a profile or a site—you're building relationships with your customers and fans.

And it's not just about your fan base, either. The industry is using MySpace as the ideal virtual artist kit for press, touring/booking, publishing, and licensing. Back in the old days, magazines and even online reviewers expected artists to send in a hard-copy press kit with photos, a CD, a bio, and other info for editorial consideration. Today, it's quite common for many media outlets to simply say, "Send us the MySpace address. If we're interested, we'll let you know." That's true for publishers, record labels, managers, agents, and other entities looking for artists. This reality makes it even more critical for your MySpace page to be up to par with others in your genre and to really showcase your music and image. More than just fan viewership, you're there to impress the industry as well.

How to Be Successful

The number of artists who were discovered through MySpace is growing all the time, from Ingrid Michaelson (see Figure 2.3)—an indie singer/songwriter from Staten Island whose music reached the ears of *Grey's Anatomy* music supervisors through MySpace, launching Michaelson's professional career—to the tale of the Arctic Monkeys (see Figure 2.4)—a UK band promoted by fans on MySpace and beloved by the underground way before they were ever offered a record deal.

Then there's the discovery of the 43-year-old father of two from North Carolina. Tommy DeCarlo, a Home Depot manager, loved to sing karaoke to his favorite band, Boston. So when the classic rock band lost its lead singer Brad Delp to suicide in 2007, DeCarlo's daughter created a MySpace page featuring tracks of her dad singing Boston songs as a tribute to Delp. Boston managers came upon DeCarlo's MySpace page—and hired him to be

Figure 2.3 Artist Ingrid Michaelson's music has been featured on ABC's hit drama "Grey's Anatomy," and subsequently in Old Navy commercials and other TV spots. Her debut album, Girls and Boys, has sold more than 400,000 copies.

their new lead singer. DeCarlo, who sounds a lot like Delp, had never even sang with a live band before in his life. "I've never dreamed this big.... Never in a million years [had] I thought this could happen," said DeCarlo in a 2008 ABC News story.

It's true that people are finding their own way more and more, circumventing the initial need for label support, developing their own images, recording and manufacturing their own albums, and even selling them to customers without a distributor. But let's be honest with ourselves. Stories like that of Ingrid Michaelson, the Arctic Monkeys, Tommy DeCarlo, and others like them are not going to happen for everyone. MySpace, for all its positive attributes, is not a panacea for artists. Some of those who have remarkable MySpace stories are the bands who got in on the ground floor, when the site was new, shiny, and had a lot less competition. And a few just got lucky.

And while situations of this magnitude don't happen every day, smaller successes do take place. From pumping up audiences locally to securing touring partners, licensing

Figure 2.4   The Arctic Monkeys' profile has evolved over the years, and they still attract new fans.

deals, and more—the list goes on. It's important to remember that if you don't get in the game, then you'll have zero chance of making a dent, getting a licensing or record deal, and getting more exposure. Now, a MySpace profile is not just an option for the serious artist. It has become a required tool in the normal course of industry marketing, something that cannot be said about the zillion other possible social media profiles available out there. "If someone didn't have a MySpace page, I'd think they weren't very clued up," states Crossey. "The novelty is past. Now it's part of the standard marketing portfolio."

Internet aficionados and recording execs alike do indeed see MySpace as a standard marketing element now. Even consumers are surprised if their favorite major label artists don't have profiles. Unless it's part of your anti-marketing plan, sort of thumbing your nose to all things commercial, Crossey notes, you have to have one if you want to be taken seriously.

Marketing companies are popping up all over the web, swearing that they can inflate the number of hits your profile receives, making you more desirable to labels. One even claims that a record label won't look at you unless you have at least 75,000 hits on your profile, meaning that many people have visited your page. But is that true? Does the number of hits, friends, or music plays you have determine your appeal to a label? "No. If it's a low number of people [who have accessed your profile], then that's brilliant. I would be excited because I'd think I'd discovered you early," says Crossey. "Record labels are competing over the same artists once they get big."

Crossey also doesn't take notice of the number of music plays, because the player usually starts automatically when you visit an artist page. Therefore, it's not a true indicator of the song's popularity. And, the numbers can be inflated by companies who, for a fee, can load your profile over and over again to bump up the numbers. As for friends, the numbers are not that important unless you have 50,000 friends or more, which is an intriguing amount. What's even more indicative of the dedication of fans and the quality of that fan base is the number and sincerity of fan comments, feedback, and interaction.

It may surprise you that Crossey looks for the kind of traffic you get on your main artist website, not on your MySpace profile. This is where your analytics come in: How many hits is your website getting daily and monthly? How many visitors lingered there, and for how long? And how many migrated from your website over to your MySpace profile and vice versa? Do you have a custom social network on your artist website, and what kind of fan interaction are you experiencing? These factors, along with the quality of your music, the professionalism of your demo songs, and your photos (are they artsy and glossy-looking?) are what labels look at more and more. Very few record companies want to spend much time or invest much money developing an artist nowadays. You're more desirable if you're ready to go "out of the box," so to speak.

Over the past couple of years, MySpace has not only been a music portal, but it has become a record label itself (www.myspace.com/myspacerecords; see Figure 2.5). Culling talent from among its members, MySpace Records' distribution is through Universal Music Group's Fontana Distribution, and its marketing is through Universal's Interscope Records.

No matter where you are headed in your career, MySpace is really useful for getting exposure and creating hype (though not necessarily great for generating record sales). Your profile is quite like a little online press kit. It's much easier for people to take in who you are and what you're about by visiting that one page. You want to sell records and get people to shows, of course, but you have to get into their consciousness first. Getting on the radar is what MySpace helps you do best, which is why you bought this book in the first place.

Crossey continues, "Before MySpace, people would always have a mailing list. But now, if a band has buzz, with MySpace the buzz can get around much faster."

It's time to get started. First, let's decide what type of MySpace account is for you. Chapter 3 will take you through the kinds of accounts and who should use them.

Figure 2.5   MySpace Records finds talent among the MySpace ranks.

3 Which MySpace Is for Me?

When you first hop onto the MySpace.com home page, the natural inclination of an enthusiastic music marketer is to click on that enticing Sign Up! tab and just start filling in the fields. But wait! MySpace offers several types of user accounts, and before you jump in feet first, you should know what they are so you can make the right decision (see Figure 3.1).

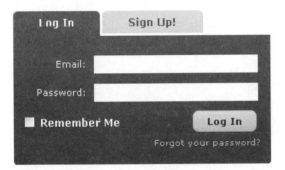

Figure 3.1 The Sign Up! tab beckons would-be MySpacers, but consider other types of MySpace accounts first.

That Sign Up! tab on the home page leads to a form-field-filled page that will allow you to create a regular MySpace account only. Musicians will want to steer away from a regular account because it won't allow you to upload and market your music—which of course won't do a musician any good. The other types of available accounts—Musician, Comedian, and Filmmaker—can be found by looking to the right of the regular form on the Sign Up! page (see Figure 3.2). In Chapter 6, "Getting Started," we'll cover exactly how to open an artist (musician) account.

For now, we will cover all the types of accounts offered by MySpace and which ones might be appropriate for the various categories of potential users.

I'll Just Have the Regular

The regular MySpace account is the bread and butter of the biz, so to speak. It's what most MySpacers use, and it is ideal for the non-entertainer. This type of account has all the bells

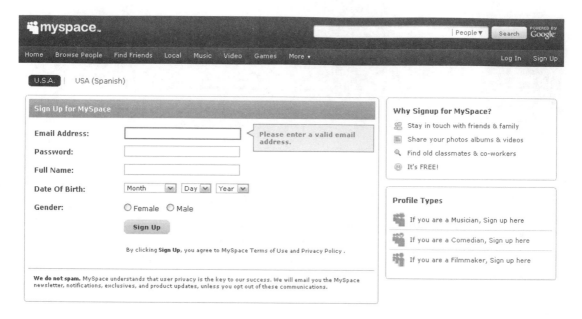

Figure 3.2   To the right of the main sign-up form, you can choose which type of specialty account you prefer.

and whistles the average netizen would want. Your basic profile (see Figure 3.3) allows you to:

- Create a customizable profile with a distinctive URL

- Fill out information fields for: Basic Info (Gender, Birthdate, Occupation, Location, Ethnicity); About Me; Who I'd Like to Meet; Interests (General, Music, Movies, Television, Books, Heroes); Background and Lifestyle Details (Relationship Status, Reason for Being on MySpace, Sexual Orientation, Religion, Children, Hometown, Body Type, Drink/Smoke, Zodiac Sign, Education, Occupation, Income); Schools Attended; Companies; and Networking

- Enter a profile headline

- Send and answer e-mail messages

- Upload videos and photos and create albums and slideshows

- Use and display applications (programs you can add onto your profile)

- Create and add music and video playlists to your profile

- Add friends, create a Top Friends list, view Friend Updates, and comment on your friends' pages

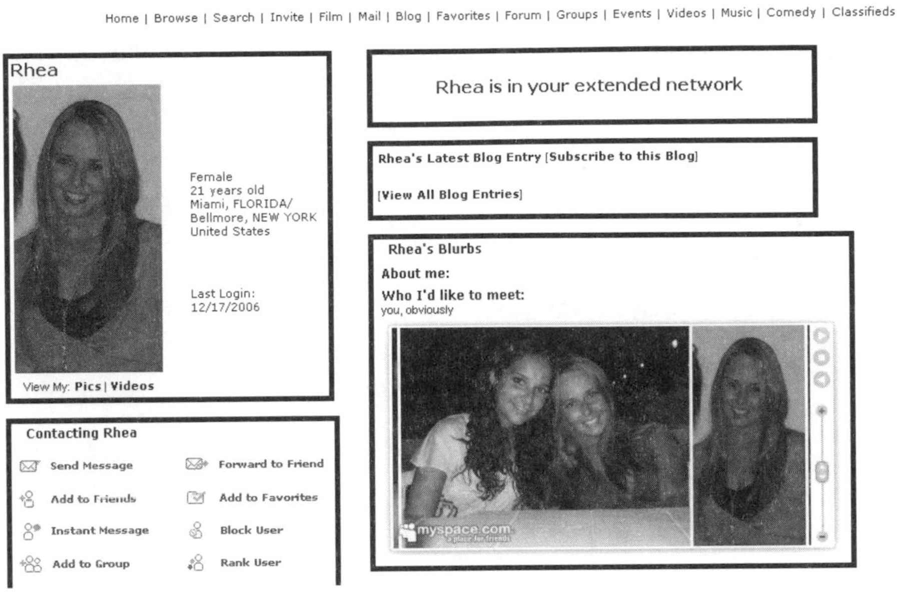

Home | Browse | Search | Invite | Film | Mail | Blog | Favorites | Forum | Groups | Events | Videos | Music | Comedy | Classifieds

Figure 3.3   A basic profile created by signing up for a regular MySpace account.

- Search for users
- Create a blog
- Chat using the IM feature
- Generate an address book
- Manage a public calendar
- Invite people to join MySpace
- Implement privacy and mobile settings
- Block users
- Save favorite profiles
- Post bulletins and event invitations
- Start and join groups
- Access classifieds
- Participate in forums

All MySpace accounts—whether regular, artist (musician), comedian, or filmmaker—offer at least these basic features, with the exception of the information fields. Those for a regular account are much more personal than fields you would find in an artist, comedian, or film-maker signup, such as relationship status, sexual orientation, body type, occupation, income, and so on (see Figure 3.4). All of these are optional, and you don't have to fill in any field with which you are uncomfortable.

Chris's Details	
Status:	Single
Orientation:	Straight
Hometown:	Hendersonville, NC
Zodiac Sign:	Aries
Smoke / Drink:	No / Yes
Children:	Someday
Education:	Grad / professional school

Figure 3.4 A sample of the personal information fields of a basic profile.

The regular account is probably for you if:

- You are joining MySpace to promote a business or organization that does *not* require you to upload sound, video, or appearance dates.

- You are *not* a musician, artist manager, record company, producer, music publisher, radio station, DJ, filmmaker, comedian, voiceover artist, or motivational speaker.

- You are only joining MySpace to keep in touch with your friends and maybe make some new ones.

The types of industries that may benefit from use of a regular account include:

- **Acting.** Embed your headshots and video reel clips; mention recent theatre, TV, commercial, or film appearances and positive reviews; link to your acting resume; and list your agent contact, union affiliations, and upcoming performances.

- **Modeling.** Post your modeling card and create a portfolio slideshow or post agency info, as well as most recent bookings/clients.

- **Real estate.** Put together a slideshow of virtual tours; list properties for sale plus recent successes; and offer home buying/selling tips and info about your expertise.

- **Law.** Tout your education and legal know-how and offer helpful blogs for your target audience.

- **Sports.** Whether you're a professional, amateur, or local team/league, build continued fan loyalty with player bios and blogs, exclusive photos, video clips, and updated stats.

- **Book and magazine publishing.** Showcase your latest publishing projects and issues, reveal centerfolds and photo essays, and post calls for submissions as well as subscription and order information.

- **Beauty and fashion.** Makeup artists, hairstylists, and fashion designers can boast about their newest clients, looks, styles, and more. Show off a portfolio, throw in beauty and fashion suggestions, and post where/how you can be booked.

- **Event and party planners.** From bridal bashes to corporate functions, event and party planners can brag about their triumphs in taming bridezillas, offer a guide on how to throw small (but fantastic) soirees, and entice new clients with photos of successful gatherings.

- **Printing and graphics.** Post your latest discounts for "friends," dazzle with retouching before-and-afters and graphic design projects, and include some helpful print promotion ideas.

- **Photography and videography.** With permission from your clients, use your profile to show the breadth of your work, such as headshots, modeling photos, wedding and engagement photography and videography, lifestyle work, and magazine or product work. Team up with a makeup artist and a fashion stylist to give would-be customers tips for making the most of their shoot.

You may also want to use a regular account if you are in an entertainment industry–affiliated business, but you don't rely on sound samples to sell your product or service. Examples may include:

- **Public relations, marketing, and advertising agencies.** Tell the world about how you've helped clients boost sales and product awareness; showcase your best work by posting ad campaign graphics, press releases, and video clips; and offer promotional tips and articles.

- **Booking.** Your profile is an excellent place to show visitors what your booking company does and how artists can be on your roster of acts. Be sure to list booking needs and any specialty genres.

- **Entertainment and sports law.** Focus on what you can do for entertainment or sports clients and keep "friends" up to date on the latest in licensing and industry trends. You may even have an introductory rate for new clients.

- **Licensing.** The world of music licensing and publishing changes quickly, with new court rulings altering the way the game is played. Consultants and clearing houses may offer licensing services, list fees, and even a primer in music copyright and the types of licenses artists may encounter.

- **Club promoter.** Build a list of savvy club-going friends, issue VIP invites, promote special events and guests artists, and even offer specials on bottles and cover charges.

- **Concert promoter.** Advertise shows, opening and feature acts, and ticket sales.

- **Talent agent.** Build a strong list of actors in your area and send out calls for castings as they come in or list new calls on your profile. Show off your clients and where they are booking.

- **Music writer, columnist, or photographer.** Your profile is the perfect place to link to your published stories, books, columns, and photos. Use it as a portfolio where you can send prospective publishers to view your work.

- **Graphic designer, animator, or illustrator.** All specialties, including CD packaging, band merchandise/poster design, and video animation, have a place to brag about their work, linking to clients' websites and profiles.

- **Stylist or fashion designer.** Many musical artists of all genres want help with their imaging. Stylists and designers can offer their consulting services for overall artist imaging and styling, as well as video- and photo-shoot styling.

- **Choreographer.** It isn't only dancers who need choreographers. Singers, rappers, and many other types of stage performers benefit from learning how to use the space around them. Promote new client packages, embed video of your performance work, and offer free consultations.

- **Venue.** No matter what kind of venue you have—nightclub, bar, theatre, or stadium—a profile will help you promote open mics, artist appearances, and drink specials.

- **Show producer or designer.** For the musical act that is taking it big time, a show producer or designer is a must. Someone has to plan out the sets, lighting, and more. Use your profile to brag about what you've done and what you can do to make big shows and festivals spectacular.

- **Educators and trainers.** This broad category encompasses musical and studio instruction, industry training, seminars and panels, and even university programs. Attract new students and keep current ones with a profile that gives all the details on upcoming events, cutting-edge curriculum, and free guides on making the most of a music career.

- **Music organizations.** What better way to grab the attention of new members than with a profile filled with useful information about the organization, benefits, membership costs, and other perks?

If you represent artists already on MySpace, you can create and display a profile playlist that links to their uploaded songs.

The Artist Signup

The artist account, also referred to as an *artist profile*, *band profile*, or *musician account* (see Figure 3.5), differs from the regular account in a few main areas, including the information fields that can be displayed on a profile and the crucial ability to upload music. Some of the ways an artist account is more tailored to the music community include the ability to:

Figure 3.5   The artist/musician account allows you to offer streaming music samples. (www.myspace.com/kesha)

- Upload up to 10 songs and album artwork to your profile. Users can stream the songs, download them for free (optional), and add your song(s) to their profile playlist.

- For artists with professional distribution, the music player automatically integrates a Buy icon for downloads sold through Amazon and ringtones sold through Jamster. Artists without major or indie distribution can still sell their music through their own links to outside stores, such as CDBaby.

- Fill out Artist Information fields: Basic Info (Band Name, Region), Genres, Bio, Members, Influences, Sounds Like, Website, Record Label, and Label Type.

- Promote upcoming shows and appearances, which are also searchable by ZIP code.

- Make your profile available in the MySpace music directory.

- Upload music videos, which are searchable by artist name and song title.

- Advertise your band with banner ads and MySpace's self-service advertising platform.

- Contend for spots in the Music Charts (formerly Top Artists lists).

The artist account also includes the same features as the regular account, plus the previous extras.

You should consider opening an artist account if:

- You are a music maker who wants to keep in touch with your current fans with MySpace accounts, and/or you want to expand your global audience.

- You are not yourself a music maker, but your desired clients are.

- You are not a music maker, but you are in another business in which sound clips are important, such as motivational or keynote speaking.

Artist profiles are useful for many types of musicians and music-related companies. The following lists explore the different uses.

The artist profile is made for you to gather an audience, build some marketing momentum, sell records, gain attention for a record or publishing deal, attract film/TV music supervisors, and get people to your shows. It is the ideal place to post music clips, bios, and appearance dates if you are in the following categories:

- Bands, musicians, and vocalists of all types and genres

- Spoken-word artists

- Performing songwriters

The profile is especially useful for networking; telling others what you do; finding collaborators, music jobs, and clients; disclosing union affiliations; and more. If you are in the following categories, you can post music clips, tidbits on whom you've worked with, and your specialties:

- Session players, background singers, and accompanists

- Non-performing songwriters and arrangers

- Producers and engineers

- Film and videogame music composers and music supervisors

- Sound effects, sampling, and audio loops creators

- Event/mobile DJs

- Voiceover artists

Trendsetters, such as those in the club scene, will also love a music profile to bring bodies into the venue or to the station, to hype new artists, and to tout their DJ-ing abilities. If you are in the following categories, just remember to only post music and spoken banter to which you have the rights:

- Club DJs

- Record pools

- Turntablists

- Remixers

- Radio stations and radio DJs

Companies and music-business types also use profiles to gain exposure for their artists, plug songs, and sell their music or artist services. These categories include:

- Record companies of all sizes

- Music publishers

- Artist and tour managers

- Recording studios

- Music-specific promotion and PR houses

- Mobile content and ringtone providers

Coaches and instructors who help artists can post audio tips and mini-lessons to help build their clientele. Examples include:

- Speech therapists and accent-reduction coaches

- Vocal coaches and singing teachers

- Recording-studio consultants who teach you how to use or set up gear

Even non-musicians who rely on sound as their bread and butter will find music profiles to be helpful in letting their audience hear what they have to offer. They can also couple this with other products and services, such as books, manuals, seminars, and maybe even votes. Examples of such categories include:

- Motivational speakers
- Audio-book publishers
- Political and activist speechmakers
- Voiceover artists

Comedian and Filmmaker Accounts

Like the artist accounts, comedian and filmmaker profiles (see Figures 3.6 and 3.7) have largely the same features offered by regular accounts, with a few modifications (noted in the following sections). However, unlike in artist profiles, comedians and filmmakers can also include the same personal information as regular account holders.

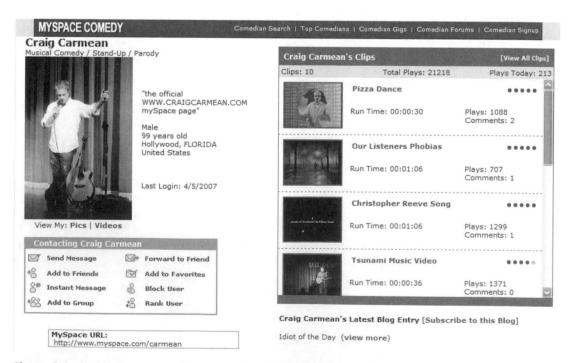

Figure 3.6 Comedian and radio personality Craig Carmean loads up his video clips onto his comedian profile.

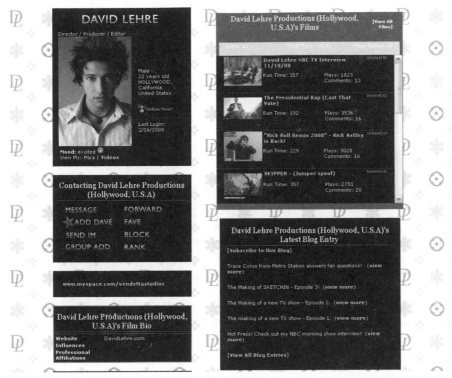

Figure 3.7   Young filmmaker David Lehre's short films appear in a scrolling box on his profile.

For the Funny Girls and Boys

Comedian accounts allow you to:

- Upload comedy video clips

- Fill in Comedian Information fields: Career Details (Bio, Members, Influences, TV Appearances, Film Appearances, Albums, Website); Basic Info (same as a regular account); Listing Info (type of comedy performed)

- Promote upcoming shows and appearances, which are also searchable by ZIP code

- Be searchable in the MySpace comedian directory

- Compete for the Top Comedians list

Comedian accounts are ideal not only for comedians of all types, but also for comedy venues that want to showcase upcoming performers, include show times and directions, offer drink specials, and provide links for people to buy tickets.

It's Time for Your Close-Up

Filmmaker accounts allow you to:

- Upload video clips

- Customize Filmmaker Information fields: Filmmaker Details (Roles, Status, Website, Influences, Directors, Awards, Festivals, Professional Affiliations) and Basic Info (same as regular accounts)

- Promote upcoming screenings, which are also searchable by ZIP code

Filmmaker accounts allow you to specify your field (options are included in the following list) and are also ideal for:

- **Directors, producers, screenwriters, and documentarians.** Your film clips, whether professional, amateur, or student, are the main draw for this kind of profile. Also, you can offer info on project help you are seeking, casting calls, as well as notes on upcoming release dates.

- **Cinematographers, lighting experts, and editors.** Examples of your work can be posted, but remember to give plenty of information on what you can do for a filmmaker. You can also include testimonials from previous clients and notices of any unions to which you belong.

- **Animators and special effects gurus.** Post shorts and B-roll video clips touting your expertise and the kind of work you've done for other clients.

- **Costumers and makeup artists.** Sketches, B-roll footage, actual film clips and photos of your work, plus any specialties you offer are all excellent fodder for a profile.

- **Set designers and location companies.** Feature photo slideshows showing off your design and location work, plus a list of films on which you've personally assisted, along with testimonials.

- **Archivists, historians, preservationists, and restoration experts.** Discuss your collections, any publications you've authored, and the importance of preservation. Offer before-and-after photos and video clips of films you've restored.

You can also specify whether you are a student, amateur, or professional filmmaker.

Have you narrowed down which type of account is for you? If so, it's time to become one of almost 300 million MySpacers!

4 Membership and Community Features

MySpace offers a host of features above and beyond music. You may wonder why a chapter that includes non-music site features would be included in a book designed to help musicians market themselves using MySpace. In order to be a good marketer, you have to be aware of the many opportunities around you ... including those that don't seem obvious. By knowing about some of the many other features and benefits MySpace offers, you may find or be inspired by avenues other than the music profile that will help you promote your songs, band, or other product.

MySpace is known for helping members network with others and keep in touch with friends. But it also offers many other things that make the community experience enjoyable and more interactive, including an ever-expanding photo album, video uploads, and much more. Lesser-discussed aspects designed to amuse and entertain the community are also a fun part of the experience. While additional features are being added all the time, this chapter will take a look at the better known—as well as the often overlooked but worthwhile—offerings of the MySpace community and provide hints on how you might use these in your marketing endeavors. Although we won't be able to do a comprehensive rundown of every MySpace trinket, I recommend you explore the site further on your own to see whether there are other things that strike your fancy and can be translated into promotion of your music or entertainment business.

MySpace Is Your Place

The most media-touted element of MySpace is the profile. Signing up for a free account automatically generates a profile for you, the body of which you populate by filling in fields about yourself—from your entertainment interests, to a bio, to descriptions of who you'd like to meet, and more. Those who are more web-savvy (or at least enjoy a challenge) can learn to change the look, layout, background and text colors, and fonts by adding customized code to their profiles. Learn how to embed photos, slideshows, videos, and other third-party bells and whistles. MySpace as a social networking vehicle encourages you to reach out to others, find old friends, and add them to your Friends list. This alone makes it a titan of user-generated content.

MySpace manages to get hundreds of millions of people to their servers to hang out and interact with one another. But it aims to be more than a virtual community of people who are seeking and those hoping to be found. It is also a place that merges myriad interests with corporate cross-promotions, bringing layer upon layer of entertaining and helpful modules to the masses that congregate there. It's more than banner ads and sponsored links, however. Even bookworms and fashionistas can get in on the action.

Because most of this book already focuses on the profile, pics, videos, and other means of promoting yourself, let's begin with some other offerings that make MySpace a pretty entertaining place for you and your potential audience to hang your hats.

More on MySpace

It's true: There's something for almost everyone on MySpace. If you can't find the entertainment you seek on someone's profile, you should try looking at the multitude of links and menus offered on the site. There's an inconspicuous little link at the top of the MySpace home page (as of this writing) hiding an array of goodies (see Figure 4.1) that could keep a netizen busy for a long while—or at least for a lunch hour.

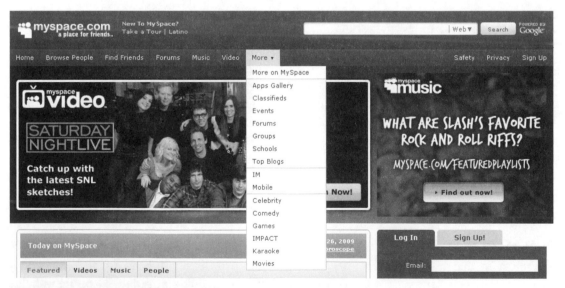

Figure 4.1   The More menu is the place to start your search for the many features of the MySpace site.

Clicking on the unassuming More menu transports you to a More on MySpace page where you can click to your heart's content (see Figure 4.2). This is our first stop in the MySpace Member Features Tour.

Figure 4.2   A page of entertaining and helpful links is linked from the MySpace.com home page. It changes now and again, so remember to inspect it once in a while to see what's new!

Portable Programs

Apps (short for *applications*) are embeddable programs that can be placed in one's profile to enhance the user's or visitors' experience. These profile apps include things such as games, polls, quizzes, and music and video players. Users pick the application(s) they want from the MySpace Apps Gallery (see Figure 4.3), install them onto their profile, and choose whether to allow visitors to view/interact with the program. Check out the Music section of the Apps Gallery for an array of interesting music programs, including those that allow users to rate and share your music, display your upcoming events, grab your favorite music videos, and more. You'll also notice that the Music apps section has many programs promoting specific artists (such as Taylor Swift, Lil Mama, and Coldplay). Companies like Nabbr can develop an artist app (also called a *widget*) that users can download and promote on their profiles. For more on apps, see Chapter 13, "Apps and Widgets."

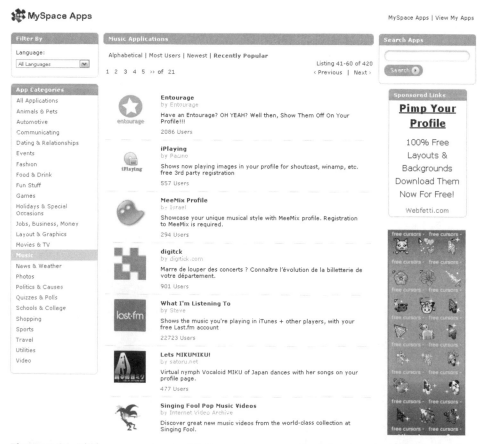

Figure 4.3   Click on over to the MySpace Apps area to delve into hundreds of nifty little programs that can run on your profile!

MySpacers Love to Write

Looking at the millions of profiles, it should be obvious that MySpacers are a gregarious bunch. But beyond that, there is an outlet for the most verbose among us. Every user gets space for a *blog*, an online journal of sorts where they can post musings on any topic. (See Chapter 15, "Blogging in the MySpace World," for more about blogs.) Millions of blog posts can be pretty difficult to sort through, unless you click on the Blog link. Here you'll find the Most Popular Blog Posts page (see Figure 4.4), which is updated daily, a blog search tool, plus a cacophony of blog categories about everything from photography, to sports, to movies, to the art of blogging itself.

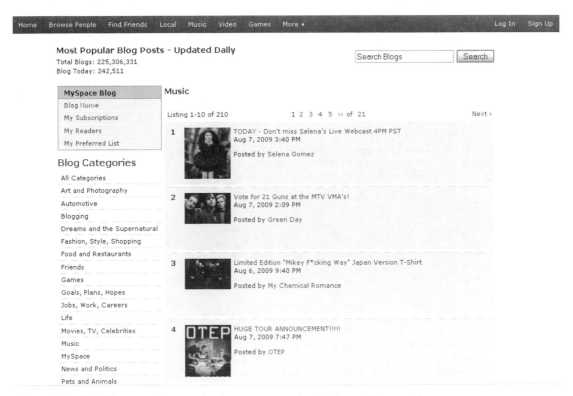

Figure 4.4   The Blogs section tracks the most popular MySpace blog entries.

Social Surfing the Events

Why mope at home when you can get out there and mingle? The Events area will help you do just that. Browse events in your area by city or Zip code, as in Figure 4.5. You'll see club promotions, birthday parties, live music, arts/crafts, and CD release parties. Click on the

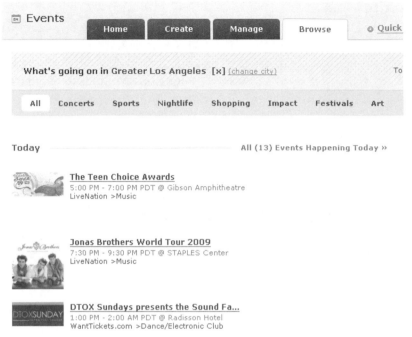

Figure 4.5   The Events area is the perfect place to find social gatherings, live music, and more . . . or to post your own!

event of your choice and RSVP or leave a comment. Events will come in handy when it's your turn to promote your performances. (See Chapter 14, "Bulletins and Event Invitations.")

Forums and Groups

Forums are one way to generate discussions with others (see Figure 4.6). Discuss music, let others know about your new release, and invite people to critique your music.

Groups are a little more specialized than forums and are user-created. You may be awed by the number of discussion areas, from pets and politics to sororities and science. Each group is categorized and searchable by keyword. Or browse through the category of your choice (see Figure 4.7). The sheer number of groups is staggering, so this is no easy task. At this time, music alone has almost 400,000 groups! When you find the one you want, you may need to join the group in order to view it. In some cases, you can only join a private group if you are invited by the moderator to do so. But once you're in, you may find some great resources and interesting rapport. You may also find that a group for a topic you want to discuss does not exist, in which case you can start it!

For more about forums and groups, see Chapter 16, "Using Groups and Forums."

MySpace FORUMS

♥ Saved Topics ☐ My Topics ✕ Settings

Choose MySpace Forum ▾   [   ] Music ▾ ✎Search

MySpace Forums » **Music**

Forums	Last Post	Topics	Posts
Acoustic	Cleveland 2009 update.... by Lew Bear 07-29-2009 5:45 PM	25,974	245,811
Alternative	Songs in Common by mark 07-29-2009 3:55 PM	35,359	347,825
Electronic/Dance	**** Advertise your Sh... by R -o- b- r- o 07-29-2009 5:35 PM	51,640	451,361
Emo	my chemicle romance by Lea 07-29-2009 5:13 PM	30,884	694,782
General	ACZONE THE MUSICAL by diANA 07-29-2009 5:42 PM	153,270	1,483,157
Hardcore	What really pisses me ... by Moxie Mommy 07-29-2009 5:41 PM	22,967	255,149
Hip-Hop	--->Promote Your Music... by Pedro R. Cabrera 07-29-2009 5:37 PM	214,780	1,865,520
Metal	CONVERSE HERE by Malum Aeternum 07-29-2009 5:45 PM	81,011	1,656,640
Punk	Promote your band/show... by Scary Cherry and th... 07-29-2009 5:45 PM	42,480	621,597
Rock	favorite 70s band? by Pattimelt 07-29-2009 5:44 PM	65,259	891,766

Sponsored Links

Create Your Band Website
Industry Level Features and Tools
Private Domain and Killer Designs
www.bandvista.com

Rock Musicians Wanted
Musician Jobs for Kinds of Musical
Instruments. Got it in Your Area.
www.ExploreTalent.com

Find Local Musicians
Free Profile - Bands & Artists
Over 300,000 Members - Pics, MP3
www.BandMix.com

Figure 4.6   Forums are MySpace-created discussion areas and can be used to promote your music or profile.

Groups Home   Choose Language: [English   ▾] [what's this?]

Groups by Category

Activities (379305 groups)
Automotive (59977 groups)
Business & Entrepreneurs (31227 groups)
Cities & Neighborhoods (46463 groups)
Companies / Co-workers (41968 groups)
Computers & Internet (20724 groups)
Countries & Regional (15507 groups)
Cultures & Community (94429 groups)
Entertainment (406031 groups)
Family & Home (61793 groups)
Fan Clubs (282800 groups)
Fashion & Style (92080 groups)
Film & Television (53258 groups)
Food, Drink & Wine (47407 groups)
Games (89503 groups)
Gay, Lesbian & Bi (47426 groups)
Government & Politics (38647 groups)

Health, Wellness, Fitness (34656 groups)
Hobbies & Crafts (40345 groups)
Literature & Arts (38198 groups)
Money & Investing (17779 groups)
Music (377779 groups)
Nightlife & Clubs (72827 groups)
Non-Profit & Philanthropic (26964 groups)
Other (1481601 groups)
Pets & Animals (44062 groups)
Places & Travel (23293 groups)
Professional Organizations (54983 groups)
Recreation & Sports (158115 groups)
Religion & Beliefs (126166 groups)
Romance & Relationships (76519 groups)
Schools & Alumni (208496 groups)
Science & History (11384 groups)
Sorority/Fraternities (35564 groups)

[Create a Group]

Keyword [   ] [Search] **Advanced Search**

Figure 4.7   The number of MySpace groups in each category is overwhelming. Together, there are a million-plus discussion groups in this community alone.

Making an Impact

The MySpace Impact page features people who are making waves in their communities and in the national media. Here you can find out about scene-makers in politics, philanthropy, business, the environment, medicine, and more. As a band or solo musician, you can find organizations and philanthropies in your area in which you want to be involved. Some charitable events may be open to you playing at their functions or lending some fundraising and promotional power to their cause.

Take MySpace with You

With the proliferation of smartphones, tons of users check MySpace while on the go. By logging into http://m.myspace.com from their phone's web browser, mobile MySpacers can download an application to install on their phones, giving them easy access to their MySpace accounts while away from their computers. The MySpace Mobile application works on most cell phones equipped with web browsers and Internet access. See Figure 4.8.

Figure 4.8   The MySpace Mobile section of MySpace shows users how to download the MySpace Mobile application, allowing them to access MySpace from their cell phones.

Get Local

A newer feature to the MySpace experience is MySpace Local (see Figure 4.9). Here you can browse listings and reviews of restaurants, bars, and nightclubs anywhere in the country. Search by city/state or Zip code. This can come in handy when you're trying to find new places to gig or when you're planning to expand to another area. After you play a bar, club, or restaurant, leave a positive review about your experience there. It's a nice way to build a relationship with that venue and introduce others reading that review to you as an artist.

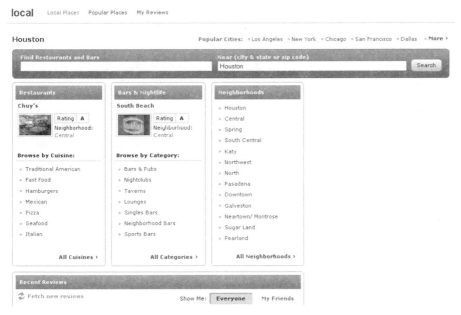

Figure 4.9   This snapshot of the MySpace Local page from Houston also shows surrounding neighborhoods or cities that you can check out as well.

Eye Your Favorite Celebrities

MySpace Celebrity is a fun section of the site where you'll find celebrity videos, status updates from your favorite bands, news from the entertainment world, plus highlighted photos and blogs all in one spot (see Figure 4.10). There is also an area for the current rising star (see Figure 4.11), where MySpace touts a new up-and-comer. For more on MySpace editorial decisions, check out Chapter 20, "Now What? MySpace and Your Marketing Plan."

Humor Is the Best Medicine

In Chapter 3, we discussed the different types of MySpace accounts and what they have to offer. One of those is the Comedy profile. And, like the Music section of MySpace,

Figure 4.10   MySpace Celebrity offers a quick, fun snapshot of new celebrity photos, blogs, videos, and more.

Comedy also offers one-stop browsing for your favorite funny men and women (see Figure 4.12). Check out the featured comedian blog, improv pick of the week, sketch comedy, and videos from your favorites and even find gigs in your area. Bummed out that you haven't gotten that big break in music yet? Mosey on over to the Comedy section to lift your spirits!

Fashion Forward

Are you a slave to fashion? Do you dream in accessories and color swatches? MySpace Fashion is for you. Check out trends, fashion news, special fashion programming exclusive to MySpace, interviews, and even exclusive MySpace discounts from fashion retailers (see Figure 4.13). MySpace Fashion is a great way for any artist or band to keep abreast of new looks to help keep their image fresh.

Kings and Queens of Karaoke

The Karaoke section is where you'll hear the good, the bad, and the tone deaf amongst America's shower singers and car radio virtuosos. Record right from your computer microphone straight into the MySpace site. Then users can rate your performance. MySpace adds new karaoke tracks regularly and often has special contests linked to a famous artist (see

Figure 4.11   The Rising Star section of MySpace Celebrity profiles an up-and-coming celebrity.

Figure 4.14). This might not have major significance to an indie musician or band, but it's an amusing musical component of the site.

MySpace Latino

This area of MySpace has a Latin flavor. Many of the featured artists and celebrities are popular throughout Latin America. Although not every section of the US/English side of the site is translated, MySpace Latino still offers some great content in Spanish.

Figure 4.12   The Comedy area rounds up the best and brightest in the laugh-making profession.

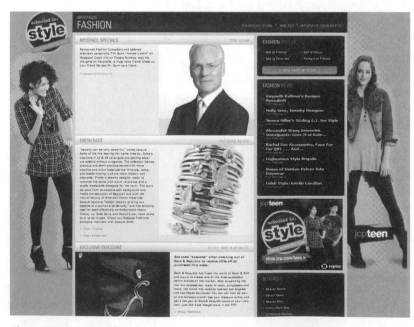

Figure 4.13   MySpace Fashion is a great space to keep up on the latest trends to help you keep your artist image fresh.

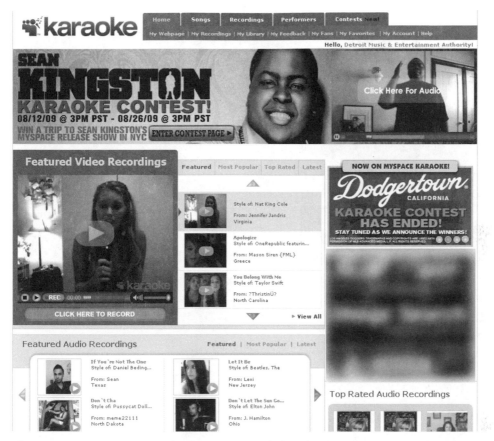

Figure 4.14   MySpace Karaoke features sound-alike (and sometimes sound-nothing-alike) recordings from around the community. There are also regular karaoke contests tied in with a famous musical artist (in this example, Sean Kingston), with trips and prizes at stake for the best karaoke performer.

Music for the Masses

MySpace Music, the crux of this book, is one of the major hubs of music news and featured content on the Web—from artist profiles and music news to exclusive videos and interviews, behind-the-scenes looks, playlists, and more. See Figure 4.15.

Music Videos

The Music Videos link takes you to a section within the Music area that is focused only on music vids (see Figure 4.16). Always a popular item with MySpacers, it's not just about the glossy promotional music video anymore. Today, viral videos and video blogs are also an incredibly important part of promotion. (See Chapter 12, ''Photos and Videos,'' for more information on videos.) In this section, you'll find exclusive and featured videos, recently uploaded videos, and MySpace interviews with artists.

Figure 4.15   Music lovers all over the world use this section to see what's new and happening in the major and indie label scene.

Viewing Videos

The Videos section (see Figure 4.17) acts as a catch-all area for MySpace videos in every category, from music, comedy, and filmmaker videos, to vids about sports, cars, and travel, and even clips from your favorite shows and movies. From this page, you can access your own videos, upload new vids, record right from your webcam to your MySpace account, and browse through everyone else's videos. The Search function will try to pin down your choices by keywords.

Ringtones

MySpace, in conjunction with Jamster, gives users a place to look up their favorite artists and download available ringtones (see Figure 4.18). In order for artists to have their ringtones included, they should check with their music distributor for the options available to them. See Chapter 20 for more information on selling ringtones through MySpace.

Figure 4.16   Music videos are an important part of imaging as an artist. This section showcases some of MySpace's originals and featured artists' videos.

You'll Have to Get on My Calendar

Found in your account home control panel, your calendar keeps you organized and can even alert friends to where you'll be any day of the week. A similar function appears in artist accounts, but there it is focused on gigs as opposed to personal appointments.

Click on Manage Calendar in your account. (The link appears next to your profile pic.) Add your appointments (as simple as Studying at the Library) with or without locations, as in Figure 4.19. Then set your options to remind you of your appointments through MySpace or to send an alert email to your regular email address (see Figure 4.20). You can make your calendar public to everyone, private for friends, or for your eyes only. However, unless you are using your personal calendar to let people know which business conventions or other non-public-accessible events you'll be attending, it's not a good idea to post your comings and goings for every would-be stalker to see.

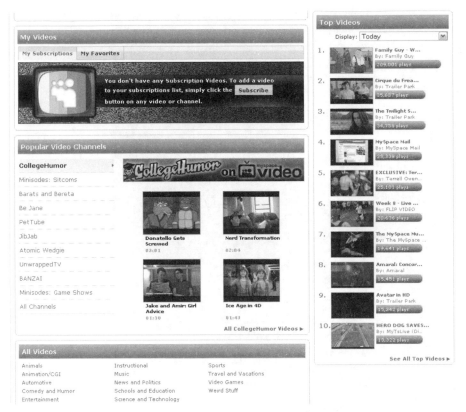

Figure 4.17 The Videos page is an easy way to search and access all the clips on MySpace, even your own.

Sponsored Profiles

Sponsored profiles and corporate promotions are peppered throughout MySpace, usually featured on the home page or on the Music, Comedy, and other section landing pages. It's becoming more and more commonplace for big-budget movie studios and major record labels to promote their flicks and high-powered artists to the MySpace world (see Figure 4.21). You may have already noticed that most music CDs have the artist's MySpace URL on the packaging, and MySpace addresses also sometimes appear on movie trailers. All of this is an effort to build a brand relationship with the coveted MySpace demographic, primarily ages 16 to 34. The promos come and go quickly, so enjoy the ones of interest while they're there.

Favorites

You can keep track of profiles of interest by adding them to your Favorites list (see Figure 4.22). Then, review your list either by clicking Favorites in the medium-blue navigation bar or by going into your account's home control panel and accessing your favorites from there.

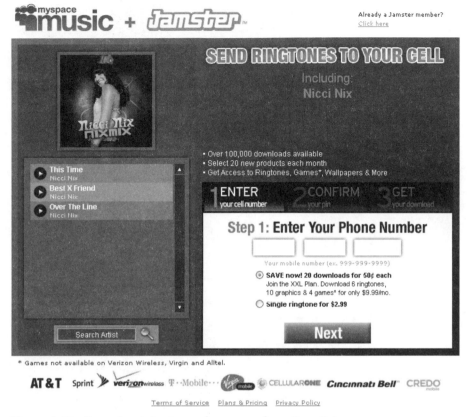

Figure 4.18   Download ringtones from your favorite artists.

You may not want to add everyone you encounter to your Friends list, but perhaps someone has something amusing or memorable on her profile that you'd like to go back to later. That's what the Favorites list is for. To add a profile to your list, click on the Add to Favorites link on the person's profile. The link is in the person's contact table, where you'll also find links to Send a Message and Add to Friends.

You may have already known about all the different treats described in this chapter, but you'd be surprised by how many people don't have any idea that much of this exists. They go straight to their profile, check emails, maybe leave a few comments for friends, and that's it. It's advantageous for MySpace to offer you many other options, however. The longer they can keep you within the community, the more time they have to expose you to their advertisers. It's similar to offering lots of content on your artist profile page . . . the longer you can keep fans engaged, the longer you have to build a relationship with them.

So enjoy the fun features, but just remember you're here to market yourself and your art, too! Let's learn how to get started . . .

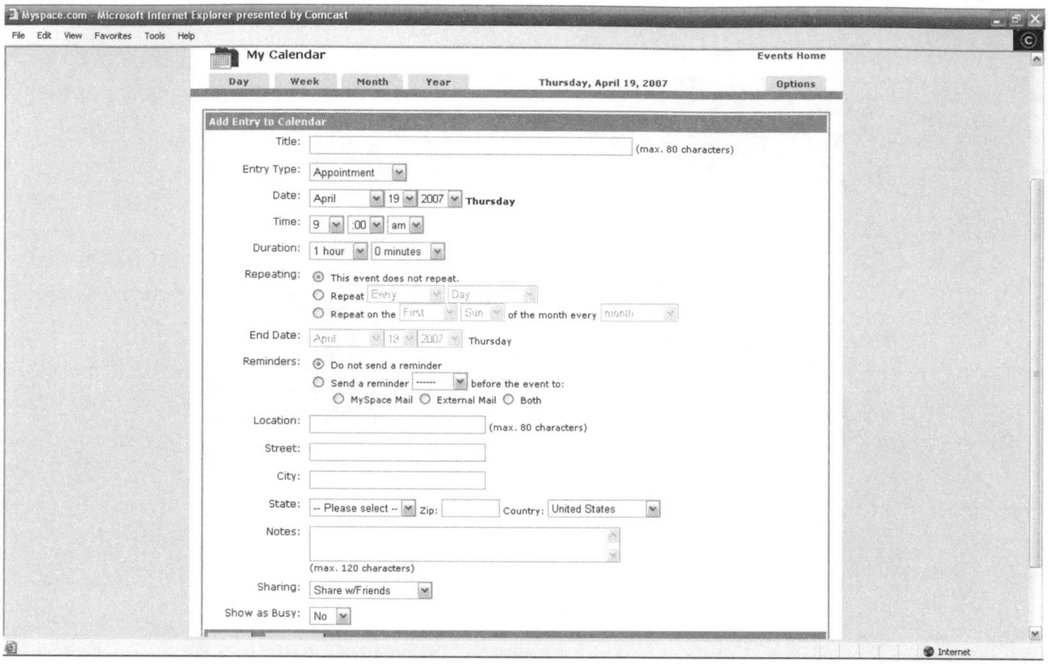

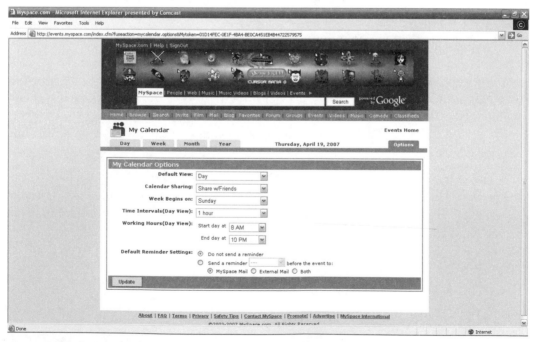

Figure 4.19   Enter your schedule into the calendar to help remind you of where you need to be.

Figure 4.20   Set calendar options to remind you of events via email.

UNRATED
The HANGOVER
JOIN THE AFTERPARTY AT
WWW.NATLHANGOVERDAY.COM
BUY IT ON BLU-RAY & DVD NOW!
ADD TO FRIENDS
FWD TO FRIENDS
ADD TO GROUPS
ADD TO FAVORITES
BUY IT ON BLU-RAY & DVD
Menu

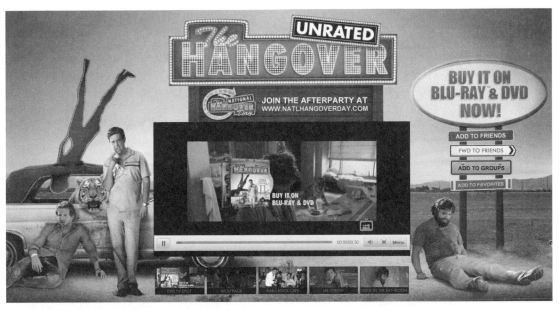

Figure 4.21 The movie *The Hangover* from Warner Bros. has its official profile on MySpace. Visitors can watch trailers, download wallpapers and photos, read the synopsis, and comment on the movie. Warner Bros. has updated the film's original profile with a refreshed design and new info on the DVD and Blu-Ray releases.

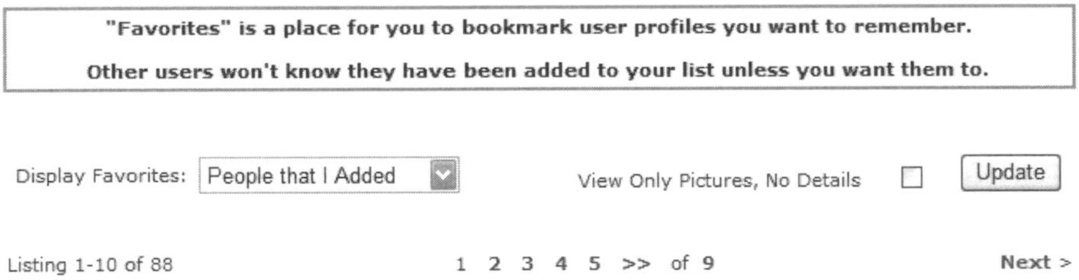
"Favorites" is a place for you to bookmark user profiles you want to remember.
Other users won't know they have been added to your list unless you want them to.
Display Favorites: People that I Added
View Only Pictures, No Details
Update
Listing 1-10 of 88
1 2 3 4 5 >> of 9
Next >

Figure 4.22 Keep track of interesting profiles in your Favorites list.

5 Identifying Your Target Market

All marketers must find out who their target audience is before they can hope to reach them. This is true whether you are a self-marketing artist or a record company executive. You may already have a preliminary idea of who your audience is based on the people who come to your shows and sign up for your mailing lists. But for those of you who are just starting out and who don't yet have a following, determining who will listen to your music, buy your records, and come to your shows can be a daunting task. In this chapter, I'll show you some tips for figuring out who your audience is and how to reach them. You'll find this useful not just for creating and marketing your MySpace presence, but for planning all your marketing, promotion, and publicity endeavors as well.

Who Are You?

Instead of wading through marketing theory and principles, let's take a homegrown approach to defining your product (you and your music) and learning about your target market. This is not a mental exercise; you must write down everything. The goal is to wrap up your brand and who your fans are in a concise paragraph or two.

If you've ever watched *American Idol,* you know that image and song choice are key to progressing in the contest. The judges say it over and over again to singers who don't shine in their performance: "That just wasn't the right song for you." Singing the wrong song for your voice and ability, trying to emote lyrics inappropriate for your age group, or not jiving your image with your music is the kiss of death on *Idol.* The same is true for the regular Joe and Jane Musician finding the right image to complement their talents.

First you must figure out, in a nutshell, who you are. Your MySpace profile, CD art, posters, emails, website, and more will be a reflection of you the artist. The "brand" you present at any given time must marry your music and image you wish to portray during any given album cycle in a way that makes sense to your fans and the public. Your imaging, look, and branded graphics may change a bit with every album, but they still need to be consistent and complement each other.

The following questions will help you pin down what you have to offer. New artists struggling to find their niche will find this helpful in their quest for identity. Seasoned artists will likely find that their answers flow more easily. The exercise is important for both.

- How do I describe my music?

- How do friends, fans, or business associates describe my music?

- If I had to put my music into categories, what would they be?

- Are there deficiencies in my music? (Be honest.) If so, what are they? (Examples include songwriting, lyrics, guitar skills, vocal range, production, and so on.)

- What kinds of people come to my show? What do they wear? How do they behave? How old are they?

- What kinds of places do I gig? What venues are appropriate for me?

- Who buys my music and where do they buy it?

- What kind of lyrics do I write (or prefer to sing)?

- Is there a common message, theme, or tone in my music?

- How do I see myself in terms of physical image? Is this compatible with my music and what people are hearing?

- What kind of image do I want to portray?

- Whom do I hope to reach with my music?

- What, musically, am I passionate about?

- What do I prefer to sing/play?

- What kind of voice do I have? What is its range and color?

- What kinds of songs really let my talent shine through? What do I absolutely love to play/sing?

- Who are my contemporaries? What other artists (signed or unsigned) are in similar categories to mine, and how would I describe them?

As in *Idol,* self-awareness can make or break a performance and a following. This means knowing what you're good at, what people want to see you play, and how you affect others. Gather the information you've just generated and roll it into an Artist Summary paragraph of about 150 to 250 words. Be concise and direct. Write in detached third-person, as if you are writing about someone else.

This is a snapshot of who you are as a musical talent—what kind of music you make, what you excel at, and what your image and musical message are. You don't have to plug in the answers to all the questions. Instead, take what you've learned about yourself and wrap up the highlights into your summary.

You may have holes in some of your answers. Perhaps the image you portray as an artist does not gel with what you envision or isn't compatible with your music in general. You may be aware of things you need to fix in your music, such as getting a great co-writer or producer. Make a note of what you have to change and work on. It is your roadmap for improvement. Write your summary wrap-up as if you have already fixed all these things. When you have a clear, written understanding of who you are *and* what you want to be, you will aspire to fulfill it.

Here is a sample of an Artist Summary written by the artist herself:

> Jane Vocalist is an award-winning singer/songwriter from Portland, Oregon. Her crystalline soprano voice radiates warmth into her songs and is coupled with ethereal and emotive piano playing. Her lyrics are sometimes considered impressionistic, with interpretations varying depending on the listener. Yet she admits her themes are often about relationships, including those between family members and even her relationship with God. While Jane writes most of her songs, she often indulges in creating new arrangements of favorite cover songs, mostly in the pop genres of the '60s and '70s, as well as jazz standards. This acoustic pop piano artist appears throughout the Portland area. Jane's fans describe her live shows as captivating and enveloping. She peppers her performances with poetry of favorite writers between songs. Jane is an urban songstress who is both sophisticated and down to earth in her music, style, and interaction with fans. She believes in the truth of the human being, both beautiful and sometimes ugly. And her music attempts to unveil the human spirit as optimistic and enduring, despite its downfalls.

As you can see, it reads a bit like a bio. It can certainly be the beginnings of your bio—you can make it longer and more encompassing. The more experience you have, the more you will have to say. Your Artist Summary, however, should be no more than one page long, no less than 150 words.

Take a look at the MySpace profile snapshots in Figures 5.1 through 5.3. How would you describe these artists, and do their profiles seem to be reflective of their music and image?

Your task is to clearly define who you are and what kind of music you offer. Believe it or not, that's the easy part. Read on to discover how to pin down your audience and craft your Target Market Summary.

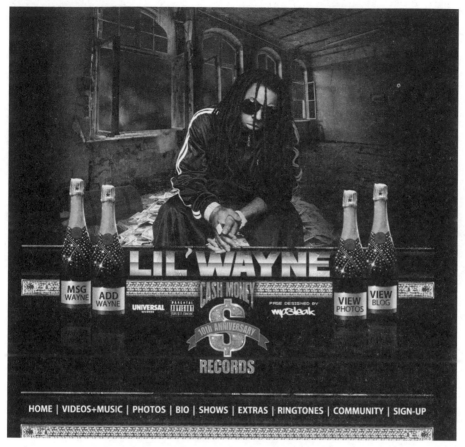

Figure 5.1   Lil Wayne's MySpace profile is similar in tone to his official website page . . . dark, urban, hardcore, with money and bling (www.myspace.com/lilwayne).

How and Where to Research

The next stage of identifying your target market entails researching who your would-be fans are. There are a lot of questions to answer, so before you get that deer-in-the-headlights look, I want you to be fortified with a guide for how to find all this information.

■   **Pay attention.** The first thing you need to do is tune in to what's happening in music, media, print, technology, business, popular culture, and consumer promotions. The best way to get a real sense of what your potential audience is experiencing is to look around. Get in the habit of knowing what's going on in the careers of other artists, in the lives of consumers in your country, and in sports and entertainment—and especially technology. If you saw this book and said, "Hmmm . . . what's a MySpace?" then you've been tuned out for too long.

Figure 5.2   Rock band Nickelback's image is tied in with their album Dark Horse, and their page and graphics have a dark, hard rock feel (www.myspace.com/nickelback).

- **Listen and watch.** As a musician, you probably already have a voracious appetite for music. But you can always listen *more*. It's easy to get into our little comfort zones and surround ourselves with only a certain type of music. You're not doing yourself any good. Listen to music that you never thought you would. Hate country music? Can't stand punk? Don't understand world music? Then go online and partake of the many free radio stations and streaming music video sites. You'll find them by using Rhapsody.com's player (see Figure 5.4) or visiting VH1.com (see Figure 5.5) or music.Yahoo.com (see Figure 5.6). And that is just the tip of the iceberg. There are so many music freebies out there that it'll make your head spin. Consume as much as you can until you think you've listened to darn near everything ever created. This is what musical greats do. They are inspired by others. And they know what kind of music is out there, what new and exciting things people are doing musically today, and what the legends have done in the past. They start to get in tune with the audiences of various types of music. They absorb the vibe and get a better understanding of what music consumers want across the board.

- **The tube is your friend.** It's very hip to say you don't watch TV. "Nah, I never touch the stuff," you balk. It makes you seem intellectual and mysterious. Seriously, you need to

Figure 5.3 Teen pop artist Miley Cyrus's profile mirrors her updated, edgier image while still retaining her approachability and teeny-bopper appeal (www.myspace.com/mileycyrus).

turn on the TV once in a while and absorb a little pop culture. If you're busy, at least set your DVR and watch some shows in your off time. Bands and records are being broken on commercials and TV shows all the time. The WhatsThatCalled.com forum allows users to post queries on which artist and song were featured on a particular commercial (see Figure 5.7), and the community answers. Adtunes.com tracks the top ad music (see Figure 5.8). Little-known artists are finding followings when their music is played on TV shows. Music is everywhere, not just on the radio or online—it's in movies, too. TuneFind.com (see Figure 5.9) breaks down the music featured in films and on TV and lists the most popular artists. Hearing all this music on the tube or in the theater should be giving you ideas. That artist who has a similar vibe as you is getting play on a teeny-bopper drama or maybe a primetime suspense series. What does that say about who your audience might be? They're using your genre of music to sell cars. And who buys these kinds of cars? Yep, you're seeing the connection now....

■ **Read, read, read.** Pull out a print magazine or a newspaper, and you'll see features, CD reviews, profiles, and more about musical artists of every stripe. Visit your local

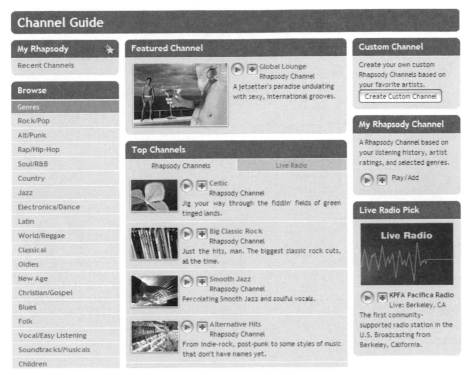

Figure 5.4   RealNetwork's Rhapsody player offers dozens of radio stations, or you can customize your own.

bookstore or library once a month and flip through pubs you might not normally read. Yes, guys, you can look at women's magazines. Absorb who gets coverage in which magazines. What audience does each magazine reach? What kind of music is appropriate for that publication? Artists in *Source* might not be in *Ladies' Home Journal*. Then again, maybe they are. Can you see how an artist might be appropriate for both? This is how you get familiar with the media and who fits in where and why. It's not just editorial, however. Look at the advertisements and observe which artists are endorsing or promoting which products. That says a lot about who their audience is. Beyoncé may be modeling hair color, but she's probably not endorsing athletic shoes. Also, get familiar with industry trade magazines, including *Billboard, Hollywood Reporter, Variety,* and *Rolling Stone,* as well as genre-specific titles, such as *Source, Downbeat, Country Weekly, Christian Musician,* and *Alternative Press.*

■ **Get out of the house.** Want to see what's out there? Go to live shows, both large and small—especially those of your contemporaries. Check out who's on tour and the reviews from layman and critic alike. What companies are sponsoring these tours?

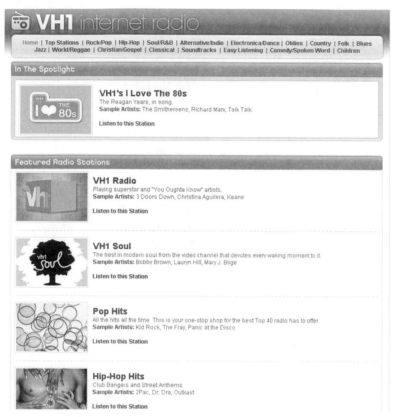

Figure 5.5   VH1.com's glitzy Radio page offers tons of stations in myriad genres (www.vh1.com/music/radio).

Pollstar.com keeps the pulse of the concert industry (see Figure 5.10). Take note of who goes to these shows and what they say. Chat with people. Find out what they do and don't like. Why are they there? Where do they buy their music? What other bands do they listen to? If you are also gigging around town, invite people you chat with to your show. Be casual and nonchalant. Attract, don't attack.

■ **Network like you mean it.** Going to shows was the first step; now you have to branch out. Attend some music business, film music, or songwriter seminars or panels. Go to a convention or two. Visit record stores (if there are any left in your area). Talk to people. But listen more. Ask people what they think of the industry, of your favorite musical artists, of the state of *[fill in the blank with your favorite genre]*, and so on. You may find out that coalitions of club DJs (record pools), popular in Atlanta, New York City, Los Angeles, and a few other urban areas, are breaking hip-hop unknowns and helping send them to the top of the charts. Someone may slip you the tip that an indie music supervisor he or she knows is looking for unsigned talent for a new project. Bring business cards and

Figure 5.6 Music.Yahoo.com showcases videos from top artists, as well as video premieres.

demos or even press kits. You never know who you'll meet. Take these people's cards and follow up with them.

- **Be a joiner.** So you're going to shows and seminars. While you're at it, get even further connected with your artistic community by joining some organizations. Not only do they provide opportunities for meet-and-greets, they may also offer resources, membership directories, discounts to conventions and seminars, and more. The National Academy of Recording Arts and Sciences (the Grammy people) is a great place to start. If you're a songwriter, you should belong to a performing rights organization, such as ASCAP or BMI. Also, look for artist coalitions, music unions, and songwriter groups in your area. Billboard sponsors events all over the country. Check out BillboardEvents.com for a complete calendar (see Figure 5.11).

- **Crawl the web.** Web research is a must in this day and age. Run web searches on musical genres, contemporaries, and even yourself to see what comes up. Look for press coverage of similar artists. Visit artist websites and check out how they are marketed. Comb

Figure 5.7   The WhatsThatCalled.com community helps you figure out what song you keep hearing on your favorite ad.

through music sites, such as AllMusic.com, Billboard.com, VH1.com, music.AOL.com; music and tech blogs (DigitalMusicNews.com, PopEater.com, and StereoGum.com are three favorites); and even the media search tool LexisNexis.com. Many local and state libraries also now offer magazines online. Of course, you'll want to pore through MySpace music profiles to get a feel for what's out there. Remember to visit the profiles of your favorite band's friends as well to see what kind of audience the band attracts.

- **Look for "intelligent" feedback.** Search for similar artists on sites and services such as Amazon.com, Rhapsody's player at Rhapsody.com (see Figures 5.12 and 5.13), Pandora.com, and Last.fm (see Figure 5.14), and these sites will kick back additional artists you might like. This will help you understand who shares a similar fan base. For instance, do you like The Black Eyed Peas? Last.fm suggests you might enjoy Flo Rida, The Pussycat Dolls, Ciara, Timbaland, and Rihanna as well. A fan of Miley Cyrus? Amazon says customers who like Miley Cyrus also bought music by Selena Gomez,

Top Ad Music of 2008

Adtunes presents the **Top Ad Music of 2008**. Here is our annual list of the most memorable ad music trends from the past year.

10. Justice is Served

U.S. cars and SUVs may have fallen out of favor, but luxury car maker Cadillac doesn't want you to forget about the Escalade. The band Justice (French DJ duo Gaspard Auge and Xavier de Rosnay) lent their electro house track "Genesis" as the theme for 2008 Cadillac Escalade commercials featuring actors Brian Bloom and Sofia Vergara. The track was also used in a commercial for Levi's 501 jeans and in the Punisher: War Zone movie soundtrack. Taken from the band's 2007 album Cross (album title "†" according to the band), Genesis imparts the crunchy techno that commercial producers love.

9. Mickey Mouse Club

The stars of the Disney Channel appeared in countless TV commercials throughout the year, making them the go-to talent pool for "tween" themed ads. The Jonas Brothers covered "Hello Goodbye" for retailer Target. *High School Musical* star Vanessa Hudgens sang for Sears and Mark Ecko. Ashley Tisdale performed wearing Degree Girl deodorant. The Disney movie High School Musical 3 got a bit of cross-promotion courtesy of a Sara Lee commercial. Songs by Disney artists including Miley Cyrus were featured in an Target holiday commercial.

8. Welcome to The Show

This year's "pop folk female singer-songwriter makes the big time via commercials" would be Australian singer Lenka (aka Lenka Kripac). Her song, "The Show", first premiered in an Old Navy commercial, later in an Ugly Betty commercial for ABC, and then followed by a trailer for the Renée Zellweger movie New in Town. Not bad for a former children's television show host. Lenka and her music are no strangers to television -- her songs have previously been featured in shows like *90210* and *Grey's Anatomy*.

Figure 5.8 Adtunes.com is a compendium of ad music news and info, as well as the top-ranked advertising songs.

Owl City, and Taylor Swift. So start typing in your contemporaries, and you'll begin to get a better idea of who their audience is.

■ **Get it from the horse's mouth.** You needn't rely solely on third-party research. You can ask your fans directly. Implement a mailing list form on your website and MySpace page that asks a few questions about your fans' interests and buying habits. Or try crafting a short survey by using PollDaddy.com or SurveyMonkey.com. You can even offer a freebie for their time, such as a coupon good toward music or merchandise, a free download, or an entry into a drawing for something small but cool (such as said

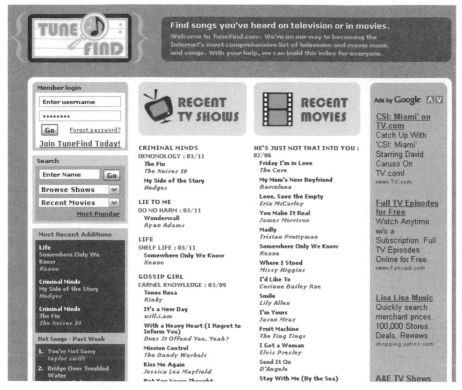

Figure 5.9   TuneFind.com is a comprehensive guide to TV and film songs, complete with top artist and song charts.

download or merchandise). Cultivate a good list, and you'll have people to come back to for future feedback.

Asking the Right Questions

Now that you know where to look for answers, it's time to ask the questions. Just as you had to ask yourself a litany of queries to get to the core of what you have to offer, you will do the same of your target audience. Some of the answers will be based on concrete research. Some will be anecdotal evidence and supposition. It's not all hard science. To find out more about your current and potential consumers and fans, try to answer these questions:

- How would I describe my first impression of my target audience?

- Where does my target market shop?

- What are their ages?

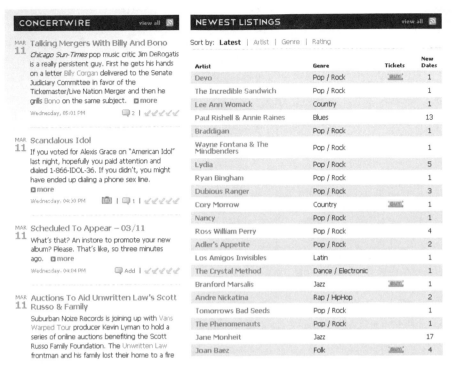

Figure 5.10 Pollstar.com is the concert industry bible and features the latest touring news.

- Where do they come from?
- What kinds of clothing do they buy and wear?
- Do they have any particular characteristics as a group?
- What magazines do they read?
- What radio stations do they listen to?
- Where do they live?
- What is their lifestyle?
- What are their views on life?
- What kind of education do they have?
- What is their income?
- What type of expendable income do they possess?
- What kinds of entertainment do they enjoy and purchase?

Figure 5.11   BillboardEvents.com is the place to go to find out about all the many Billboard-sponsored events throughout the year.

- What is the ideal way to reach these consumers?
- How do they prefer to be contacted?
- What kinds of products, in various categories, do they buy?
- What do they drive?
- What kind of movies and televisions shows do they enjoy?
- What websites do they frequent?

Figure 5.12 Rhapsody's player has a search feature that suggests similar artists. In this case, the searched artist was R&B legend Stevie Wonder.

- Where/how do they purchase their music?

- With what consumer brands do they identify?

- What other types of music, besides mine, do they listen to?

- What is their comfort level with technology? Explain . . .

You may think of other questions that are relevant. Our example artist, Jane Vocalist, answered a few based on her experience, online research, and a mailing list survey through her website:

Q: How would I describe my first impression of my target audience?

A: Mostly women in their late teens through early 40s. They seem to identify less with the saccharin pop female icons of the day and more with contemporary male and female singer/songwriters. Some dress in a sophisticated manner; others are more free-spirited types. All seem to be interested in personal empowerment, musical

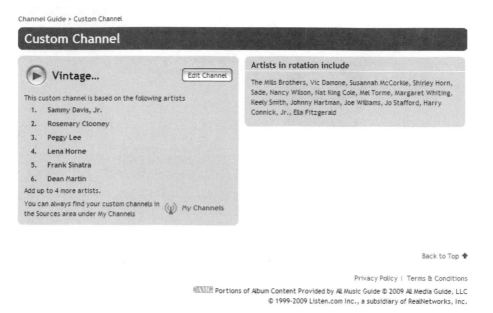

Figure 5.13   Also in Rhapsody, when you create a custom radio station, the system suggests other artists similar to those you listed.

quality, and intellectual pursuits. My listeners are both single and married. They are mostly college educated.

Q: What magazines do they read?

A: *Rolling Stone; Yoga Journal; O, the Oprah Magazine.*

Q: Where/how do they purchase their music?

A: The younger end of the target audience tends to be very web savvy and will likely download much of their music. The older spectrum (late 30s+) tends toward purchasing music at well-known retail outlets, such as Target and Best Buy, but they are not above learning how to download music. The older group especially tends to listen to music at work on their computers.

The quest doesn't end there. Looking at what others are doing and to whom they appeal is essential.

Researching Contemporaries and Competitors

One of the best ways to answer questions about your potential audience is to research how similar artists in the same or a similar category to you reach *their* consumers.

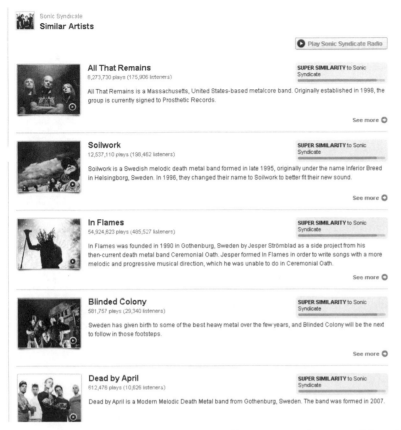

Figure 5.14   Last.fm has the ability to offer up a list of comparable artists. This gives the marketer a better look at what other artists in similar genres a fan might be interested in. The searched artist here was Sonic Syndicate.

List your contemporaries and find out:

■ What magazines are they featured in?

■ What products do they endorse?

■ With which other artists do they collaborate and how?

■ What TV shows and movies feature their music?

■ How does their record company position and market them?

■ Where is their music sold?

■ Who attends their shows?

- What are their website and MySpace profile like?

- What does their CD packaging look like?

- What kinds of publicity do they receive?

- Where do they play? (What kinds of venues and in what parts of the country/world?)

- What is their image like?

- What kinds of clothes do they wear?

- Who do they appeal to?

- What can you extrapolate about this artist's fans from this information?

- How might this info apply to you?

Now that you are up to your eyeballs in info, you are ready to trim it down into a usable paragraph or two, called your Target Market Summary.

Like your Artist Summary, you won't need to throw in every answer to every question. You're gleaning overall impressions and demographic information and rolling this into a concise blurb.

Jane Vocalist's sample Target Market Summary reads like this:

> Jane Vocalist's audience, although primarily female, is diverse in age and socioeconomic background. The group that will have the greatest interest in Jane is the 20- to 40-something age range. They are drawn to her unique, almost performance-artist style of acoustic pop alternative, with lyrics that touch upon their own life experiences. She tends to appeal to positive-minded, deep-thinking women who have an appetite for new and non-homogenous music, are opinionated on politics and world events, and read publications such as *Rolling Stone, Alternative Press,* the *New Yorker,* and even *O, the Oprah Magazine.* Her fans are both married and single and tend to be college educated. The target market also enjoys other contemporary artists, such as Tori Amos, Regina Spektor, Sarah McLachlan, and Ingrid Michaelson. Retailers apt to carry Jane's music are local and some regional record store chains, as well as online merchant eMusic. Appropriate radio stations include those in the alternative, top 40, and adult contemporary genres. Her audience is very web focused and download savvy, so particular attention will be paid to reaching out to a non-local fan base through sites such as GarageBand.com and Live365.com.

As Jane learns more about her audience and herself, she will be able to flesh out her Target Market Summary even further and narrow it down more.

Realize that your two summaries—one about you as an artist and the other explaining your target market—are dynamic in nature. They may change over time. You will need to tweak them as you grow and learn. This kind of focus is essential to your success. It keeps you from taking the "spaghetti on the wall" approach. (You know, throwing everything and anything out there and hoping something sticks.) Instead, your summaries will keep you on track. They are like your mission statements, guiding your activities toward the goal of reaching that coveted target audience. When opportunities come by that don't fit into your goal, you'll know they aren't right for you.

You, too, will be able to identify your target market in a concise paragraph. Doing this initial research and planning will help keep your message and marketing activities, both online and off, focused and on track.

Now that you've laid the foundation for your marketing efforts, let's learn how to get started on MySpace.

6 Getting Started

By this time you've already read about the pros and cons of MySpace, social networking in general, its impact on entertainment, what types of accounts are available, the features of the community, and how to pinpoint who your audience is. But before you jump in and sign up, let's come up with a game plan. This chapter will help you round up all the information and materials you should have in your arsenal to create a basic profile. Many of these details will come right off the top of your head, but others will be harder to come up with on the fly. Gathering the items you need will save you time. And while you can always go back later and populate your profile with info, giving thought first to how and what you want to do will keep you focused on your marketing message.

What You Need to Be on MySpace

Following are the basic items you should have on hand to create a MySpace account. Use this as your checklist. I'll go into greater detail later in this chapter about what you'll do with these things.

- An email account separate from your usual email account
- A main photo or graphic
- Other band photos
- Your viral, behind-the-scenes, or other promotional music videos
- Some basic thoughts about what you want your profile to look like, what backgrounds (if any) would be appropriate, and what color schemes you like
- A unique URL (web address) for your MySpace page
- A biography or short "about" write-up
- A list of band members and notable collaborators (such as producers, songwriters, vocalists, and other featured musicians)
- A compelling profile headline

73

- A selection of up to four songs for streaming, with a different accompanying graphic for each one

- Lyrics for songs

- Touring and gig dates and info

- Your main website URL

- Record label and management info

- A list of who you sound like

- A list of musical influences

- A list of genres that fit your musical style

- A list of keywords that Internet and MySpace searchers might use to find you

Picking an Email Account

On MySpace, your email address is your login name. The plus side to using your current personal email to sign up with MySpace is that friends who know that email will be able to search for you more easily. This is helpful for personal friends and family members who may have lost touch over time.

Some people, however, prefer to use a separate email account for their MySpace and other social networking activities. This is advantageous in a number of ways. You are very easy to locate if anyone can search for your commonly known email address. Using an unadvertised email makes you a bit harder to find by employers, students, military officers, and others you may not want to be privy to your MySpace activities. Using a separate email address also compartmentalizes everything so that MySpace marketing activities don't mingle with personal and business mail. Of course, never use an employer-provided email address to access MySpace or any other social site. For more details on using a unique email to protect your security, see Chapter 18, "Protecting Your Virtual and Physical Security."

Free email accounts can be obtained from a number of providers, including AOL, Yahoo!, MSN's Hotmail, and Google's Gmail, among others. If you have your own domain name, you can also create a special address just for social networking activities. Remember not to list your email address on your profile. It's better for fans to email you through the MySpace system.

Of course, if you want to let it all hang out and be easily found by everyone in your life, you can add multiple emails to your account. Then when someone searches for you by any of the emails you have specified, your profile will pop up. After signing up for your profile, go to your My Account link and add multiple emails under Contact Information.

Your MySpace.com Email Address

You may have heard that MySpace launched @myspace.com email addresses for users in 2009. You can create your own @myspace.com email address *after* your create your profile. If for some reason you feel you absolutely need to display an email address right on your profile for all to see, this is the best one to use. Fan emails to your @myspace.com address go directly to your MySpace account (see Figure 6.1).

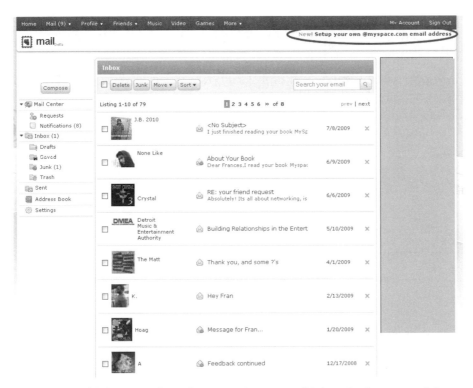

Figure 6.1   This is a snapshot of your MySpace email inbox. In the upper-right corner, MySpace prompts you to get your own @myspace.com email address.

Your Photos

The very first thing anyone on MySpace notices about you is your profile picture. This thumbnail pops up in searches, shows itself when you leave a comment, and peeks out from Friends lists (as in Figure 6.2). The kind of photo or graphic you choose to be your main profile pic is very important and should be considered carefully. It is your first impression with your audience, and it often determines whether someone will take a chance and click on your profile.

Here are some guidelines when choosing photos or graphics for your profile:

Music » Search Results

Nazia
Genre: Pop / Classical - Opera and Vocal /
Jazz
Location: , Washington DC
Last Update: Jan 26, 2007

Plays: 4,593

Views:
3,343
Fans: 419

Figure 6.2   This artist has a compelling photo that entices searchers to click on her profile.

- *Never* forego your main photo/graphic. Not having a photo is a marketing kiss of death (see Figure 6.3).

- Always be sure your pic is of good quality and clarity. Retouch as necessary to diminish dark shadows that obscure the photo or your face, sharpen blurriness, correct odd coloring (a person who looks unnaturally pink or yellow, for example).

Figure 6.3   If this is the image you're presenting to the world, you're in trouble. Always have a picture to represent you.

- Do not use blinking, flashing graphics or animated GIF images. They are annoying fan repellents that scream "amateur."

- Steer clear of cutesy pics that have nothing to do with your band. No thumbnails of your favorite cartoon character or some other jokey graphic.

- The best main photo is one that is compelling and ties into who you are as an artist. Ask yourself, would you click on this photo if you were seeing it for the first time?

- For solo artists, photos in which you can see your face are ideal. It doesn't have to be a happy-go-lucky pic; it can be edgy, moody, smirky, glam, or anything else you want that conveys the essence of you.

- Nothing says "click me" like a great photo of your gorgeous face, so don't hide it, especially if you're a female artist.

- Sexy photos are okay as long as they aren't outright porn. For more on the kinds of content and photos that are acceptable on MySpace, see the Terms of Use, consult

Chapter 19, "Managing MySpace," or view a snapshot of MySpace's photo rules in Figure 6.4.

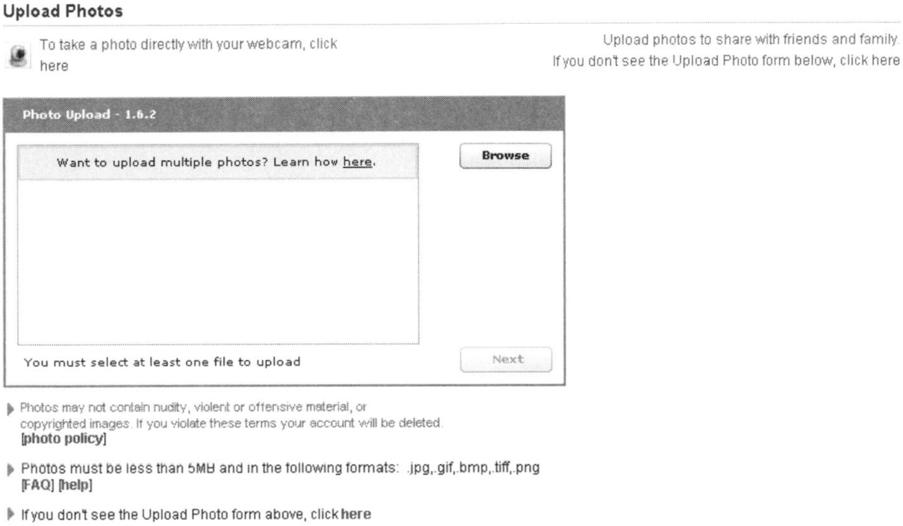

Upload Photos

To take a photo directly with your webcam, click here

Upload photos to share with friends and family. If you don't see the Upload Photo form below, click here

Photo Upload - 1.6.2

Want to upload multiple photos? Learn how here.

Browse

You must select at least one file to upload

Next

▸ Photos may not contain nudity, violent or offensive material, or copyrighted images. If you violate these terms your account will be deleted. [photo policy]

▸ Photos must be less than 5MB and in the following formats: .jpg, .gif, .bmp, .tiff, .png [FAQ] [help]

▸ If you don't see the Upload Photo form above, click here

Figure 6.4 The upload page for pics gives you a brief rundown of what you can and cannot use for pics.

- For music-related companies, a logo that is interesting works best. Just be sure that it's more than a bunch of teeny, tiny, unreadable text.

- Do some music searches in your favorite genres and see what compels you to click. Make a note of the boring and the repellent. This will give you an idea of what to use and what to stay away from.

In addition to the main photo that will represent you in the MySpace world, gather other pics of your band (or yourself if you're a soloist). You'll also have room to add short captions, as shown in Figure 6.5. Your MySpace account will hold hundreds of photos, so you've got plenty of room. Think of various band and soloist possibilities, live performance pics, photos of you in the studio, and of course, publicity stills.

Those of you who are starting out may not have any usable photos to speak of. Look for a photographer in your area by browsing through Internet classifieds, such as Craigslist.org or MySpace's classifieds sections, posting your own call for photographers, or contacting media arts programs at your local colleges. You may even be able to barter for photos—you get pics, and they get samples for their portfolio.

Some of you may want to go with a more established photo studio. Search the Internet on sites such as ModelMayhem.com for photographers in your area. Ask other bands whose

The Evolution V: Mr. India East
    Coast 2006 oh yeah!!

» **Post A Comment**
» **E-Mail to a Friend**
» **Report This Image**

    1 Comment(s)

Figure 6.5   This artist/model noted his latest accomplishment in his photo caption.

photos you like to recommend someone. Call around to local talent/modeling agencies and acting schools and find out whom they recommend. Beware of the agency who tries to get you to sign up with them and use their photographers. A reputable place won't take a cut; they will only give you a name or two of photographers whose work they like. Check references and ask to see samples of work. Still can't find someone? Inquire about student photographers at your local college's photography program.

Most photographers will retain their rights to their photographs, negatives, and digital files. Therefore, always ask for a copyright release and the image on disk. Make sure the copyright release implicitly states that you own the photos, negatives, and/or files and you have the exclusive right to reproduce them, put them on the web, and use them in any capacity you want. You may have to pay extra to buy the rights from the photographer, but the photos will be yours, and you won't be breaking any laws.

Your Profile URL and Website Address

You'll want to specify a unique address for your MySpace profile. It will be http://www.myspace.com/*insert one-of-a-kind name here*. Assuming you've already come up with a band name, you could simply insert that at the end. If you're a soloist, you could use your first and last name. A popular tactic to differentiate personal profiles from music profiles is to use the word "music" at the end. For example, Joe Performer's music MySpace page could be http://www.myspace.com/joeperformermusic. Here are a few more ways to craft a URL:

- Add the word "online" or "official" after your name to differentiate you from fake and fan profiles.

- Mirror your official website URL. For example, artist Pink's website is www.pinkspage.com, and her MySpace page is www.myspace.com/pinkspage.

- Should you find yourself competing with unofficial profiles for your band, you could also use "thereal" before your name.

- Of course, if your desired URL is already taken, you'll have to be imaginative and come up with a new one that still makes sense for your band.

Remember that the MySpace address you pick is yours forever and can't be changed, so make sure you can live with it before you commit.

When you sign up, you will also have an opportunity to add your main website address (www.yourdomainname.com) as a link within your profile. If you don't have a main website, don't worry. You can always plop that into your profile later when you get one.

Upcoming Shows and Appearances

Artists have a special place to add their touring and gig details (see Figure 6.6). Gather this info before you sign up so it will be a snap to add it all in. At the minimum, you'll need to list the show date and time, the name of the venue, the city/state, and the description (such as "CD release party"). It's not imperative, but if you've got more details, such as cost and a full address, so much the better.

Upcoming Shows			(view all)
Apr 3 2007	9:00P	Rose's Place	Jacksonville, Florida
Apr 6 2007	8:00P	Stucky's Bar and Grill	Braverman, Florida
Apr 15 2007	9:00P	MacInerney's	Clermont, Florida

Figure 6.6   Your gig list will look like this on a default music profile.

Band Members and Collaborators

You'll want to list the names of all your band members. A list of notable collaborators also is a great idea, especially for soloists. But you can list them if you're in a band, too. Is there a Bernie Taupin to your Elton John? Give props to those who help make your music what it is. This includes producers, songwriters, arrangers, DJs, side musicians, other vocalists, lyricists, and choreographers.

Pay special attention to names of note. Gather those names in a text file so you can just plug them in below your band members' names. There isn't a special field for collaborators, so you just have to put in a couple of paragraph returns after your list of band members and then note the title "Collaborators," as shown in Figure 6.7. See Chapter 8, "Customizing Your Page," for more information on customizing your profile using basic HTML.

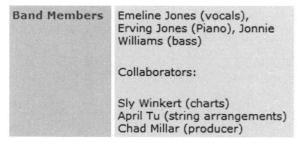

Figure 6.7   Be sure to note your band members and collaborators.

Your Posse

Your profile will also have room to note whether you're signed to a record label and the label name. You can say "unsigned" if you are. You may have a manager, a distributor, a publicist, a booking agent, or another member of your team who assists you in your career. List those who are relevant below your bio, especially the aforementioned ones. Your manager may prefer that all business queries be directed to her, and she may want you to note her email address just for that purpose (see Figure 6.8).

Please direct all booking and publicity queries to Vincent Management at 555-555-0000, or email VincentManagement@anyemail05.com

Figure 6.8   Listing your manager's phone number and email address is a suitable way to redirect business queries.

Profile Headline

Your headline is the short snippet or quote that appears next to your main photo on your profile. Many acts don't utilize this field, but they're missing out on another opportunity to market themselves. You don't have to quote Shakespeare or anything, but use that little slice of real estate to say something about yourself. Here are some headline ideas:

- A phrase you're known for.

- A quote from a positive review ("Angelic vocals and powerful songs – Littleton Ledger").

- A snippet from your lyrics.

- A mention of an award ("Voted Best New Jazz Artist by the *Sun Times*").

- "*[Album title]* now available on iTunes!"

- "*[Album title]* in stores 2-5-10" or "... in stores now."

- "CD release party in Miami May 1st!"

- "Touring Summer 2010."

- "The Official *[Your Name]* MySpace Profile."

- A boiled-down mission statement for your organization and company: "Supporting independent artist tours nationwide."

Just say no to desperate pleas for friend adds and album sales (as shown in Figure 6.9). No one likes someone who tries too hard.

Fran Vincent
Jazz / Blues / Folk Rock

"Pleeease be our friend!!! ADD ADD ADD!"

Jacksonville, Florida
United States

Profile Views: 23

Figure 6.9 A headline like this screams, "Lame!" Tout your new album release, gig, or lyrics or plug in a personal quip instead.

Genres, Influences, and Who You Sound Like

It's frustrating as an artist to feel as if you have to fit into a box. But this is marketing, and if you want electronic dance music fiends, classical music aficionados, or jazz hipsters to be able to find you, you'll have to figure out which categories you belong in.

You can choose up to three genres to help users locate your music. MySpace offers dozens of options, but it's always possible that you are so unique you won't find your particular niche. If that happens, you'll just have to think like a music consumer and determine which genres make the most sense. And you do have three options, so you can cross-reference.

Let's say you are a classical crossover vocalist who also sings jazz standards. This would be along the lines of Josh Groban, Linda Eder, Sarah Brightman, or Il Divo, all considered adult contemporary artists as well. There isn't a category for that or for classical crossover, so you might choose "Classical-Opera and Vocal, Pop, and Jazz" as your three categories instead.

Or if you're heavily into musical theatre favorites, perhaps "Classical-Opera and Vocal/Pop/Showtunes" would be more up your alley. Users search by categories when they're looking for new music in their favorite genres, and you want them to find you.

Before you sign up, brainstorm the types of genres that might fit you. To preview the list of available MySpace genres (accurate at the time of this writing), go to MySpace.com and click on Music; under the artist search bar, you'll see a link to Genres. Or, go to the MySpace Music section and click on Charts at the top of the page. In both places, you will find a menu of possible genres (see Figure 6.10).

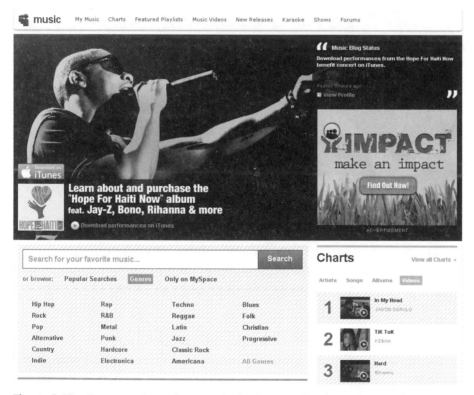

Figure 6.10 Get a preview of genres by looking under the artist search box in MySpace Music and clicking on Genres. You can also see a list of genres in the Charts section.

Likening Yourself to Others

Using the Influences and Sounds Like fields tends to generate a bit of debate among the MySpace music community (see Figures 6.11 and 6.12). Some people love listing their influences because they know it helps build an instant rapport with someone who loves the same artists they do. Those of you who dig Stevie Wonder and Al Green will instantly bond with an artist who is influenced by the same artists. You automatically have that in common, and you can see where the artist is coming from.

Influences	Diana Krall, Ella Fitzgerald, Dean Martin, Frank Sinatra, Raul Midon, Eva Cassidy, Julie London, Keely Smith

Figure 6.11   A list of influences in the default profile.

Influences	Queen, Harry Nilsson, Rufus Wainwright, Muse, Pulp, Bee Gees, Jobriath, Electric Light Orchestra, David Bowie, The Cardigans, Starflyer 59, Elton John, The Beatles, T-Rex, Suede, Prince, Mansun, Embrace, Blur, Oasis, The Verve, Sean Lennon, Marion, The Shore, The Charlatans, The Raspberries, Supergrass, Morrissey, AIR, Louis XIV, Spacehog, The Smiths, Manic Street Preachers, Kula Shaker, The Rolling Stones, Lou Reed, Joe Jackson, Jeff Buckley, Keane, Massive Attack, Blondie, Duran Duran, Adam Ant, Rialto, Ennio Morricone, The Who, Travis, Beck, Starsailor, The Dandy Warhols, Doves
Record Label	WWW.RCRDLBL.COM
Type of Label	Indie

Figure 6.12   California act Actress presents a comprehensive list of their influences.

There are artists who, for whatever reason, think telling people about their influences pigeonholes them. But remember that your influences don't necessarily sound anything like you. Alanis Morissette grew up idolizing Olivia Newton-John, and some sources say she credits ONJ for inspiring her to become a singer. However, Alanis doesn't sound anything like Olivia, and being influenced by her didn't make her a carbon copy. Fans understand this and see that your influences begin to paint a picture of what you like and whose talent is inspiring to you.

To list or not to list whom you sound like can be a contentious topic indeed. Many artists will indignantly declare, "I sound like myself!" (See Figure 6.13.) The very idea of someone likening them to anyone else is insulting. Well, maybe you don't sound like anyone else, and that's fine. But perhaps you are in a similar genre as other favorites who are better known than yourself (see Figures 6.14 and 6.15). It's okay to put that you sound like "a bluesier Sarah McLachlan" or "Michael Bublé with a country twist." Make it more creative if you're similar, but bring your own attributes to the mix.

Sounds Like	My sound is really it's own thing, but I will let you decide for yourself. A mixture of electronic, soul, pop, rock I would say. I learn and am influenced by everything.

Figure 6.13   Artist Chloe Lattanzi declares her sound her own thing.

When you explore profiles of major-label artists and unsigned artists alike, you'll notice that some ignore the Influences and Sounds Like fields, while others gamely fill them in. There's no set rule. You'll have to decide for yourself.

Sounds Like	Kristen Chenoweth, Linda Eder, Renee Fleming, Maria Callas

Figure 6.14   One would guess from this Sounds Like list that this artist is a classical or musical theatre–type vocalist. If you love these types of artists, you may be more apt to give this person a listen.

Sounds Like	etta james, big mama thornton, mildred bailey, big maybelle, koko taylor, janis joplin, billie holliday, dinah washington and patsy cline.
Record Label	www.deltagroove.com
Type of Label	Indie

Figure 6.15   Blues/rockabilly artist Candye Kane lists her Sounds Like as artists whose style is similar to her own, giving you an idea of her musical sensibilities.

The truth is, the more established an artist, the more likely they are to leave the Influences and Sounds Like categories blank or design them out of the layout all together. Consider keeping them while you're starting out. You can always get rid of them later when you've made a name for yourself.

If you're hesitant to list anything in the Influences or Sounds Like field, you can still use the fields for other information, as shown in Figure 6.16.

Influences	BUCKCHERRY NEWS: Sign up for Buckcherry's email list for tour info, ticket specials and latest news! Click here to sign up! www.indianlarry.com
Record Label	Eleven Seven Music / Atlantic Records
Type of Label	Indie

Figure 6.16   Buckcherry opted to list email signup info in their Influences field instead.

Search Keywords

You may be asking why you would want to list influences and similar artists. The answer is to help Internet search engines better categorize you through the use of keywords, which are words one is likely to use to search for your type of music or product.

Once you determine your Influences and Sounds Like artists, you'll want to list them elsewhere in your profile (such as in your bio), as well as in their designated fields. Internet search engines crawl through MySpace too, categorizing artists' and musicians' profiles like they do any other type of webpage. They notice repetition of phrases and words, and this helps increase your rankings in search results. This is true for webpages, profiles, and even online press releases. For instance, if you mention Pantera in your Influences and Sounds Like fields and once again in your bio, when users search for "Pantera" in their favorite search engine, you hopefully will be among the search results. By affiliating yourself with artists in a similar vein, you will be more likely to attract new fans who are searching by that keyword (in this case, "Pantera").

Keywords do not only have to be other artists' names. Think carefully about words you might use to describe your music. In addition to Influences and Sounds Like, think about genres and buzzwords for your music. What words might a searcher use to find you on the web? Are you into electronic dance music, or "EDM"? Are you following in the footsteps of techno founder "Derrick May"? Perhaps "screamo," "trip hop," or "booty music" is your thing. Are you collaborating with someone well known in his or her field?

Let's say you're a music organization or company. What keywords might someone type into a search engine to find companies like yours? Examples might be "booking agency," "tour support," "promote independent music," "music licensing consultant," or "entertainment law."

Think of what the key search phrases are that others might use to find an artist or company like yours and then pepper your profile with them. A good rule of thumb is three to four phrases, used two to three times. It must be a natural use; otherwise, your profile's copy will feel stilted and contrived. Too many uses, and you'll actually hurt your search engine rankings. The Influences, Sounds Like, Bio, and Band Members fields are all logical places for keyword mentions.

Your Bio and About Me Blurb

Now that we've covered a bit about keywords, let's move on to what is usually the biggest block of text in an artist profile...the bio.

Some bios are magazine-style write-ups and read like they were lifted out of the pages of *Rolling Stone.* Most artists' bios are more straightforward and to the point, like Fergie's (www.myspace.com/fergie). Still other artists don't have bios at all—they're so popular they don't need an introduction.

Writing about oneself (and doing it well) can seem like an impossible task. But you don't need to be a professional writer to say honestly who you are and what you're about. There's no one way to write a bio, no matter what all the websites on the topic say. There are professional writers who will do the job for you, usually for a fee of $200 or less. But if you're going it alone, take heed of these tips to build a better bio:

- Write about yourself in the third person. So instead of "I've just finished touring with the punk rock band Jonesy," use your name or the appropriate pronoun, such as "Betty Bassist recently finished touring with the punk rock band Jonesy." Treat it as if you were writing about someone else.

- The easiest way to start a bio is with where you're from and, if it has influenced your artistry, your ethnic heritage. If you're stuck, start this way.

- Steer clear of hyperbole, such as "the best artist ever," "the greatest jazz trumpeter of the twenty-first century," and "a better guitarist than Jimi Hendrix." All that hype is quite a load to back up, and few, if any, can do it.

- Clichés, such as "a diamond in the rough," "a musical force of nature," and other similar contrivances, are meaningless as well.

- Include quotes from yourself or band members about your music, your influences, how you came up, your struggle, and so on. This personalizes the bio.

- If you've won a lot of awards and recognition, resist the temptation to list them all. Pick four or five biggies and mention those.

- Talk about what makes you . . . well, you. What artists and life experiences influence your artistry?

- Discuss what kind of music you make, what themes you prefer to explore, and what your aesthetic sensibilities are.

- Keep your political preferences out of the bio. Remember that half your audience may well belong to the other party.

- Refrain from badmouthing other artists and rivals. It only makes you look petty.

- It's not necessary to list every place you ever went to school and every place you played. It *is* okay to note if you went to a prestigious high school or performing arts program and where you went to college. Only mention venues and places you've played that carry weight. Saying you've sung at the Met is a big deal.

- Namedrop carefully. Your bio is not the place to thank everyone you've ever worked with. But it is a place to recognize those influential collaborators who have contributed greatly to your sound, your career, and your latest album.

- Do discuss your latest project, album, tour, award, or achievement. Tell your audience what you're up to.

- Don't just use your word processor's spell check feature! *Read* your bio many times for spelling and grammar errors (and have others do the same). There's no excuse for sloppy errors.

- Don't pander to your audience. You do not have to write in colloquial urban slang or text message shortcuts just because that style of communication is popular with your target audience. Keep it professional.

- Have friends and relatives with fresh eyes read and critique your bio. Pick only those who aren't afraid to be honest with you.

- Always remember that your bio tells a brief story of you—what makes you the artist that you are, how your band came together, and where you're headed. Three to seven paragraphs should be plenty to bring readers into your world.

The more bios you read, the better you will be at writing yours. So start surfing MySpace and your favorite artists' official websites for inspiration.

Streaming Songs and Your Built-In Music Player

The most wonderful thing about MySpace artist profiles is that your visitors can listen to your music without having to download a bunch of external applications. Before you sign up, decide which of your songs you want to stream (up to 10), plus which graphics/pictures should accompany each. When a song plays, a photo/graphic appears in the player next to it. Ideally, each song should have a different photo, preferably of you or your band (as shown in Figure 6.17). The photo should be compelling, in focus, and interesting to look at, and it should help the listener identify with your song. See the "Your Photos" section earlier in this chapter for more tips on photos. Another option for those short on suitable photos or graphics is to use your album cover for all songs. You can even mock up an album cover just for this purpose.

After you've picked your songs, make sure they are converted to MP3 format. Do this with any CD ripper or other similar audio program. You probably already have a free program on your computer. Apple's iTunes player and RealNetworks' Rhapsody (see Figure 6.18) or RealPlayer will convert CDs to MP3s.

The best songs are those that are excellent not only in songwriting and musicianship, but also in sound and production quality. Choose clips that have been mixed and mastered, are free of audio anomalies, such as clicks and hisses, and have overall excellent sound quality. Avoid clips with muffled vocals. Also rethink putting extended songs that play automatically on your profile's streamer. Many listeners may find a 15-minute song or live cut that starts automatically and drones on and on to be a bit overbearing, and the download time can crash

Figure 6.17   The music player at www.myspace.com/naziamusic showcases a unique photo for each song.

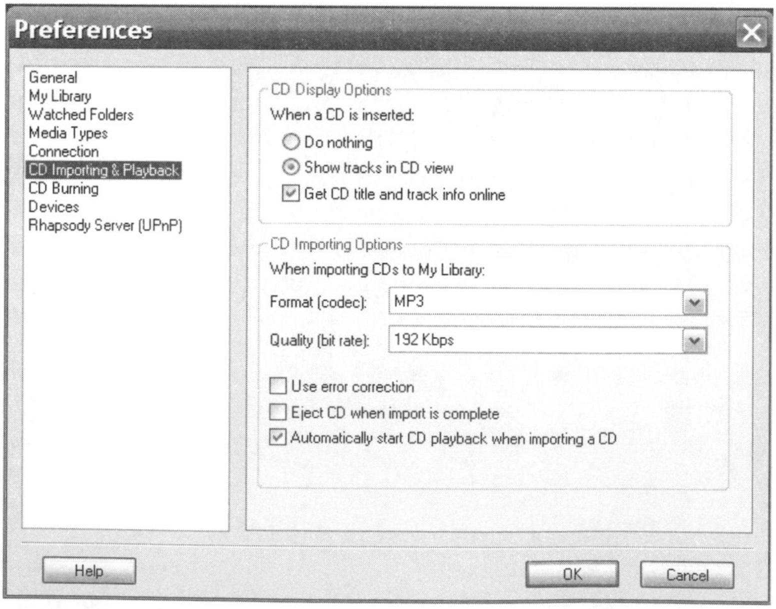

Figure 6.18   RealNetworks' Rhapsody Player 4.0 Preferences. Choose MP3 as your format for importing and converting CDs.

a browser. You can always cut it down to a more manageable size and encourage visitors to download it for a fee elsewhere on your page. Also, stay away from super-short snippets. That 20-second clip is not going to do it for most listeners—it's just not enough material. Instead, aim for standard song lengths, usually between two and five minutes. And, if you must do a snippet, 45 seconds to 1:15 is ideal.

You have the option of having the first song in the player load automatically, or the player can rotate through songs, loading a different one each time. Artists promoting a particular single or those with a song they feel is a great hook to bring in repeat listeners may prefer to designate the first song as the opener.

You're not bound to these 10 songs and settings forever. You can change your initial song/ graphics selections and settings at any time.

Remember that unless you have secured an on-demand streaming license (for listening only) or a digital download license (for downloading to desktop) from a music publisher or through the Harry Fox Agency, you are not supposed to upload cover songs. Doing so without proper compensation circumvents songwriters' and publishers' income stream and cheats them out of the right to make money from their works. Visit www.harryfox.com and look at digital licenses for information on how to secure the proper permissions to use another writer's songs.

Lyrics

Along with streaming audio, you can post lyrics for listeners to read. This is done from within the same module where you would upload your music. But just as you must have permission to use cover songs, so must you get permission (a print license) to post lyrics of cover songs. My best advice is to leave cover song lyrics off of your MySpace profile. There are plenty of infringers on the Internet who have probably posted them elsewhere.

But do consider putting lyrics to your original songs on MySpace. This is a situation in which lyrics are most important, because the listener may not be familiar with your music, writing, or themes. Reading lyrics often ties the listener to you in an emotional way and makes for a more profound experience.

To properly post lyrics, you must also include songwriter, copyright, and performing rights organization (PRO) information. An example of how this might be structured is:

[Song Title]

Written by [Songwriter(s) Names]

Copyright [year written] / [Publishing Company Name] / [PRO]

So it would look like this:

Happy Times

Written by Jenny Williams and Stan Fielding

Copyright 2007 / Williams-Fielding Music / ASCAP

This lets everyone know who owns the song, when it was written, and whom they can contact should they wish to license the composition or perform it publicly.

Your Style Scheme

You might think that coming up with a style scheme should be done first in one's plan. I like to put it at the end of the process because by now you will have already thought a lot about all the things you want to populate your profile, who your audience is, and what they will respond to. The look of your profile, the design and backgrounds, the colors you employ, the photos and music you post, and the bio you write must all be congruent with who you are as an artist. Here are some fantastic examples of profiles that jive with the artist and complement the marketing message of that singer or band:

- Matt Nathanson: www.myspace.com/mattnathanson. Melodic, acoustic pop/rock.

- Unearth: www.myspace.com/unearth. Dark, hard-driving metal.

- Taylor Swift: www.myspace.com/taylorswift. Young, colorful, pop country.

- Colbie Caillat: www.myspace.com/colbiecaillat. Fresh, laidback, acoustic singer-songwriter.

- Kari Jobe: www.myspace.com/karijobemusic. Inspirational, contemporary Christian.

These are just a few examples of profiles that fit perfectly with the artist and their target audience. Take a look at the friends each artist has accumulated. You'll notice that by and large, even the friends fit in with the theme of the profile. People don't want to be friends with artists whose music they find off-putting or uninteresting. At the time of this writing, the artists mentioned have tailored the look and tone of their profile perfectly to their music *and* the people they want to listen to it.

Your profile should also be tied in with your latest album, and you can take color cues and visuals from the album artwork. However, unless you totally change the kind of music you're making, the profile will still clearly convey who you are no matter which album you're promoting. Think of the other artists to whom your target market likely listens. How do those artists present themselves? Are their profiles dark and brooding? Fierce and scary-looking? Urban and edgy? Pink and flowery?

In Chapter 5, we explored how to identify your potential audience. Now is the time to look back at those conclusions and ask yourself what your music says and to whom it speaks. Think about which colors are suited to your music. What would be completely inappropriate for your profile? Start to have some general ideas of what you like and don't like. Again, the more profiles you look at, the more familiar you will become with the possibilities that exist.

Well, it's time to dive in! Next, we will sign up for our MySpace account....

7 Signing Up and MySpace Profile Basics

O nce you've got all your information in order and ready to go, signing up and uploading to the basic profile are a pretty easy affair. Should you get stuck, here is a
nuts-and-bolts guide to walk you through it. You'll have your very own profile up
and running in no time!

Let's get started on your artist account, also known as a *band* or *musician profile*. Mosey on
over to MySpace.com, and near the top of the page you'll see a blue navigation bar (Home |
Browse People | Find Friends | . . . and so on). On the far right side of this navigation bar is a
link to Sign Up. Click on this link to begin the process of creating your music profile. You will
be transported to an area where you can choose which kind of MySpace profile you want to
create (see Figure 7.1).

Step 1: Sign Up

As you can see in Figure 7.1, the Sign Up page first offers you the regular profile. Chances are
if you are reading this book, you will probably want the Musician profile, so be sure to look
on the bottom right of the page to choose the appropriate profile type. Otherwise, you'll end
up with an average, everyday profile with no music options. And as a musical artist, you
definitely do not want that to happen.

The first page in the artist signup area is unlike the other signup pages. You'll see the copyright
warning from MySpace (don't upload anything you don't own!), shown in Figure 7.2. Below
this you will enter info into a few initial fields, such as which email address you'll use for your
profile, a password, your band name (or your stage name if you're a soloist), your first choice
of genre, and your location (see Figure 7.3). You will also be asked to agree to the Privacy
Policy and Terms of Use. I recommend that everyone read and understand these agreements
before signing up. For additional information on these, see Chapter 19, "Managing MySpace."

Step 2: Provide Basic Info

The next page will ask you to specify your MySpace URL of choice and a few other details
(see Figure 7.4). This MySpace URL is the web address you can give out to people so they can
visit your MySpace page.

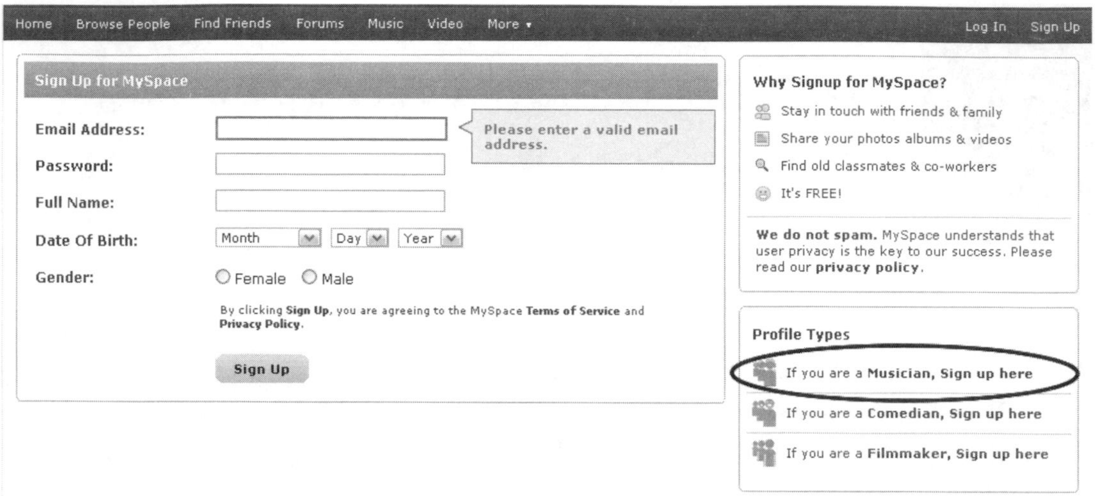

Figure 7.1   The Sign Up page allows you to create a regular account, as well as a Musician, Comedian, or Filmmaker profile.

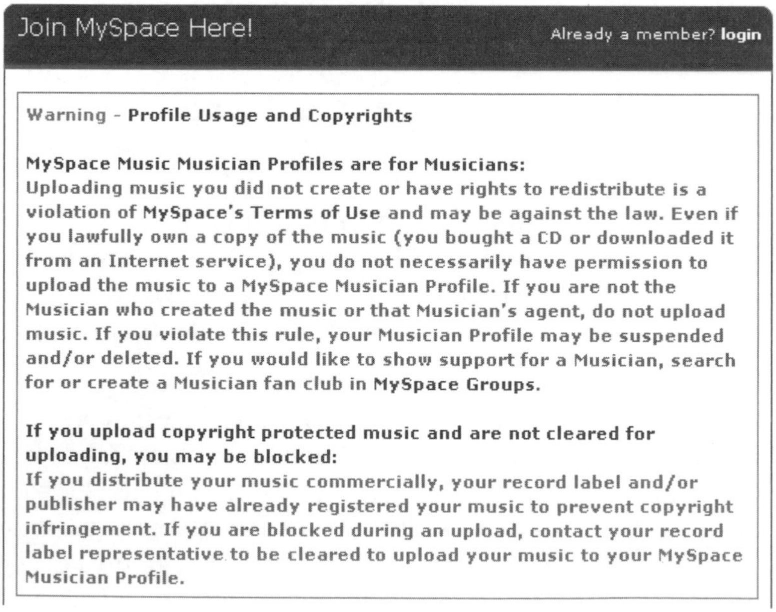

Figure 7.2   The copyright infringement notice is unique to the Musician profile signup. Be sure to read it and understand it before proceeding.

Pick up to two more genres to classify your music. You'll also enter the address of your main artist website (if you have one). The last two fields relate to your record label. If you are signed, list the name of the company. If not, simply put None. Under Label Type, you can

Figure 7.3   The first part of the signup process asks for a few initial account details.

Figure 7.4   Artists choose their label type, such as Indie, which lets visitors know their status. Should you be without a record label, choose Unsigned.

choose Major, Indie, or Unsigned. There's no shame in putting Unsigned. It lets labels know you are available.

Step 3: Add Profile Photos

Now it's time to upload those photos you've prepared, as shown in Figure 7.5. Make sure your photos are in GIF or JPG format and are no more than 5 MB each. Don't worry too much about the physical dimensions of the photos, because they'll be resized to fit properly into a standard web browser anyway.

Figure 7.5   Upload your photos by choosing them from your hard drive.

See the Browse button? Click here to find your first photo on your hard drive. Choose it and submit it for uploading. Continue this process one by one until you have chosen all the photos you want to upload at this time. You can always go back later and add more or delete some. You should upload at least one photo. Once your photos are uploaded, make sure you have chosen the one you want to be your default picture. This is the photo or graphic that appears to the outside world on your profile and in search results. It's that first impression, so choose wisely.

Additionally, you can create captions for each photo by filling in the Caption field. It's not necessary, but it's a nice, personal touch.

Step 4: Round Up Your Friends

The next stage gives you the option to paste in the email addresses of your real-life friends (or your band's mailing list), plus a short note to invite them to check out your profile (as shown in Figure 7.6). I recommended skipping this step for now. It's better if you invite people once your profile looks the way you want it to; at this stage, you still have a ways to go before you get all the information in there, get the layout customized, and so on. Once your profile is ready to reveal to the world, you can go back to your home control panel and invite people to view your page.

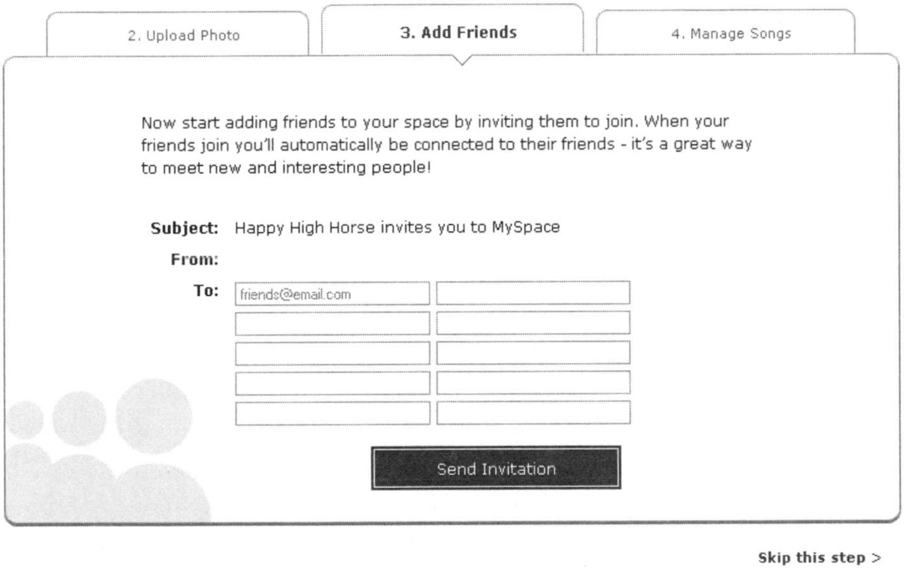

Figure 7.6   Although the system prompts you to invite your friends to view your profile, it's best to skip this step and invite friends later, when your profile is completely filled in.

Step 5: Add Your Songs

This section will give you the opportunity to upload up to 10 of your songs. After you click past inviting friends, you will be taken to a page to upload your music. Choose your profile's settings for your player by checking the appropriate boxes (as shown in Figure 7.7). Always allow users to add your music to *their* profiles. It's free advertising for you. (See Chapter 11, "Playlists and the Music Player," for more information.)

You will also have to choose how visitors will hear your music—the first song in your player will automatically start, or you can choose to randomize it. Choose to auto-start your first song to play when you are promoting a particular single. Otherwise, let the songs play randomly.

Edit Artist Profile » Manage Featured Songs   Promote your Shows on MySpace!

[Return To Home Page]

Edit, Delete, or Change Your Current Songs
You may upload a maximum of 6 songs.
You must own the copyright for the Music you upload. [MySpace Terms of Use]

Warning: Profile Usage and Copyrights

MySpace Music Artist Profiles are for Artists:

Uploading music you did not create or have rights to redistribute is a violation of MySpace's Terms of Use and may be against the law. Even if you lawfully own a copy of the music (you bought a CD or downloaded it from an Internet service), you do not necessarily have permission to upload the music to a MySpace Artist Profile. If you are not the Artist who created the music or that Artist's agent, do not upload music. If you violate this rule, your Artist Profile may be suspended and/or deleted. If you would like to show support for an Artist, search for or create an Artist fan club in MySpace Groups.

If you upload copyright protected music and are not cleared for uploading, you may be blocked:
If you distribute your music commercially, your record label and/or publisher may have already registered your music to prevent copyright infringement. If you are blocked during an upload, contact your record label representative to be cleared to upload your music to your MySpace Artist Profile.

Current Songs

Add a song to your profile!
No songs uploaded

Add a Song

These song settings apply to all songs uploaded to your Artist profile.

Song Settings
☑ Allow users to add songs to their profile
☑ Auto-play first song when my Artist profile is viewed.
☐ Randomize all the songs in my featured playlist when users visit my Artist profile.
[Update Settings]

Figure 7.7 Choose how your player will behave when visitors click on your profile.

Now, add your song's information (as shown in Figure 7.8). Enter the title, album name/year, and record label that released the song. There is a field to enter the lyrics as well. We discussed in the last chapter that you should only list lyrics for your original songs, plus author/publisher, copyright, and performing rights organization information. Lyrics are

Edit Song Details

Edit Song Information		
Song Title:		
Album&Title:		or Select from Existing ▾
Album Year:		
Record Label:		or Select from Existing ▾
Lyrics:		
	☐ Allow users to download this song [more info]	
	[Update] [Cancel]	

Figure 7.8 Add the info about your song and choose whether users should be able to download it for free.

optional, of course, but users often appreciate being able to read what you're singing so they can better understand the context and theme of your music.

Lastly, you can choose to allow people to download your song for free. (The details of this are shown in Figure 7.9.) I don't recommend doing this directly on your MySpace player. The free downloads on MySpace don't allow you to collect any information on the user. If you're going to give away your music for free, at least get the downloader's information so you can use it to market more of your music to that person later. To solve this issue, direct visitors over to your main webpage to get them to give you their names and email info to get that free download. Or use a service such as Backstage Share (http://go-backstage.com), where you can set up a promotion that requires users to input their email address and then directs them to a download link to get the song (see Figure 7.10). If you are already selling this song on iTunes or other download points, offer a different version, such as a remix, a live or acoustic version, or some other version that is different from what people can/have already purchased.

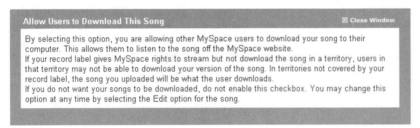

Figure 7.9 MySpace's details on downloading.

The only time a free download on MySpace is a good idea, in my opinion, is if you've uploaded an interview, a special message to fans, or perhaps a demo version of a song that you've already recorded, mastered, and released commercially. You can market it as a fun freebie to get people to your profile and then encourage them to pass on the word to their friends.

Once you've filled out the song info, you will upload your MP3 in the same fashion as you upload a photo (see Figure 7.11). Choose the MP3 file from your hard drive and submit it to the MySpace server for upload. The system will show you the progress (see Figure 7.12).

After your song has uploaded, it will take a little bit for the system to process it and convert it to MySpace's streaming format (see Figure 7.13). This could take up to 24 hours. In that time, be sure to not re-upload your file. Continue to click Add a Song until you have uploaded as many songs (up to 10) as you want fans to hear.

Figure 7.10   The Backstage Share service, here used by artist Prince "BlkMagic" Damons, allows you to create a free download promotion. Users must provide their email address in order to obtain the download, which helps you build your email marketing list.

Once the file has been processed and is ready for streaming, you will be able to go back and add an image that will appear in your music player when the song plays. In Figure 7.13, you can see that the Current Image link is not active because the song has not yet finished processing. However, after the song is ready, this link will be available to you, and you can upload an image to associate with the song, such as an album or single cover or an artist image. Always aim to upload a photo or graphic for every song in your player.

To access this Current Image link at a later time, simply go to your home control panel, click on Edit Profile and then the Manage Featured Songs tab, find your song to the right of the page, and go to the Upload an Image for This Song link. Follow the prompts and find your image on your hard drive. Your image should meet the requirements of the MySpace system, as noted in Figure 7.14.

The resulting music player will look like Figure 7.15.

You may upload a maximum of 6 songs.
You must own the copyright for the Music you upload. [MySpace Terms of Use]

If you don't see the Upload MP3 form below, click here

Figure 7.11   Uploading songs is a lot like uploading photos.

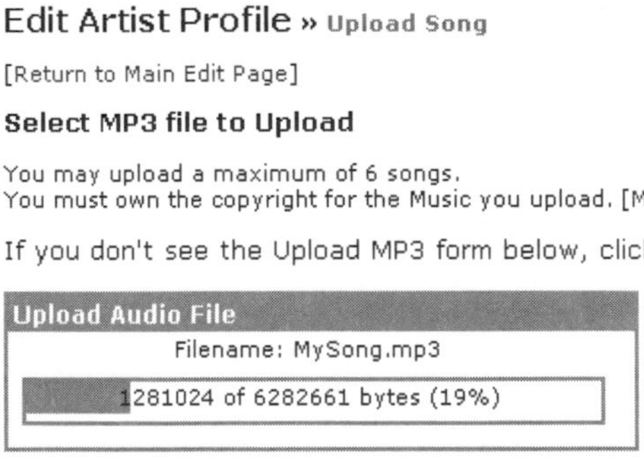

Edit Artist Profile » Upload Song

[Return to Main Edit Page]

Select MP3 file to Upload

You may upload a maximum of 6 songs.
You must own the copyright for the Music you upload. [MySpace Terms of Use]

If you don't see the Upload MP3 form below, click here

Figure 7.12   Your song's uploading progress will display in your browser.

Step 6: Populate the Profile

After this initial setup process, you will be directed to your account's control panel. From here, you will continue editing and populating your profile.

Click on Edit Profile above your default account picture. You'll notice that the Edit Profile link is among many other links next to and around your photo that will help you edit and manage your profile (see Figure 7.16).

Figure 7.13   While your song is processing, you will not be able to associate an image with the song.

Edit Artist Profile » Upload Song Photo

[Return to Main Edit Page]

Select image file for your song

Images may be a maximum of 5MB in GIF or JPG formats. [**help**]
Photos may not contain nudity, sexually explicit content, violent or offensive material, or copyrighted images.
Do not load images of other people without their permission. [**image policy**]
Uploading an image is optional, but once an image is uploaded, it can only be removed by replacing it with another.

If you don't see the Upload Image form below, click here

Skip

Figure 7.14   Always upload a photo to display with your song. Note the image parameters (current as of this writing) so you can prepare your graphics accordingly.

Figure 7.15   San Francisco–area pop artist Nicci Nix uses her EP cover image (NixMix) as the graphic for her song Best X Friend (www.myspace.com/niccinix).

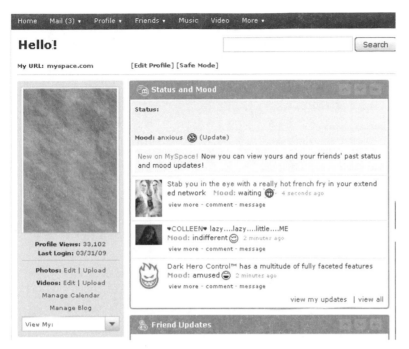

Figure 7.16 Get familiar with the editing/managing links near your thumbnail photo.

In the Edit Profile screen, you'll notice five tabs spanning the top. Click each tab to view the areas to edit.

■ **Upcoming Shows.** On this tab, you will enter all the information on your upcoming shows, including date, time, location, admission, and a brief description (see Figure 7.17).

■ **Musician Details.** You will get a lot of use out of this tab (see Figure 7.18). Musician Details houses the parts of your profile that have the most text. These fields are also where you will plug in code to customize your layout. Fields include Headline, Bio, Members, Influences, Sounds Like, Website, Record Label, and Label Type. You'll notice that Website, Record Label, and Label Type are already filled out because you entered these fields when you started the signup process. In Chapter 6, you crafted a headline and a bio, as well as info on your members, influences, and who you sound like. Now it's time to plug that information into the appropriate fields. When you first start filling in this Details section, you will not have any layout code already entered. However, please note that once you have plugged layout code into any of these fields (see Chapter 8), you may need to do all subsequent editing in Safe mode. The Safe Mode editing link is located right next to the Edit Profile link in your home control panel. For more on editing in Safe mode, please visit Chapter 8, "Customizing Your Page."

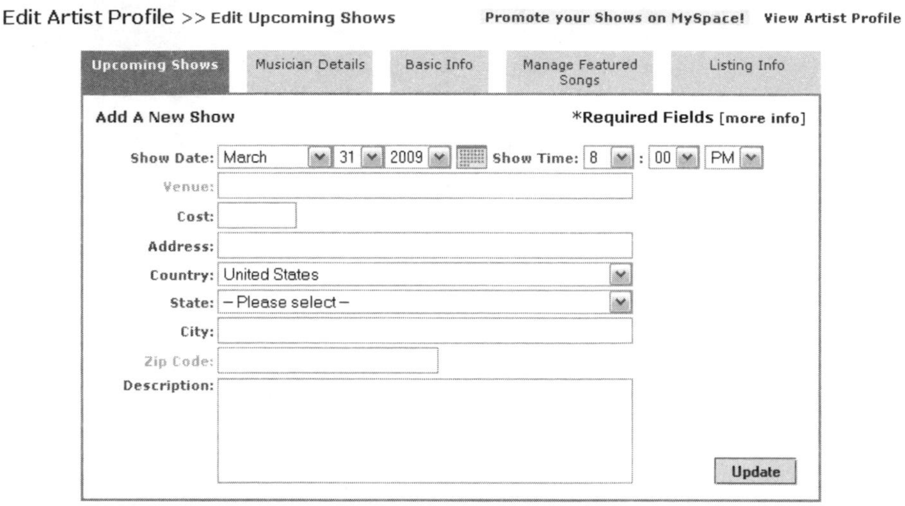

Edit Artist Profile >> Edit Upcoming Shows   Promote your Shows on MySpace!   View Artist Profile

| Upcoming Shows | Musician Details | Basic Info | Manage Featured Songs | Listing Info |

Add A New Show   *Required Fields [more info]

Show Date: March ▾ 31 ▾ 2009 ▾ ▦ Show Time: 8 ▾ : 00 ▾ PM ▾

Venue: [   ]

Cost: [   ]

Address: [   ]

Country: United States ▾

State: – Please select – ▾

City: [   ]

Zip Code: [   ]

Description: [   ]

[Update]

Figure 7.17   Entering your shows is simple and straightforward.

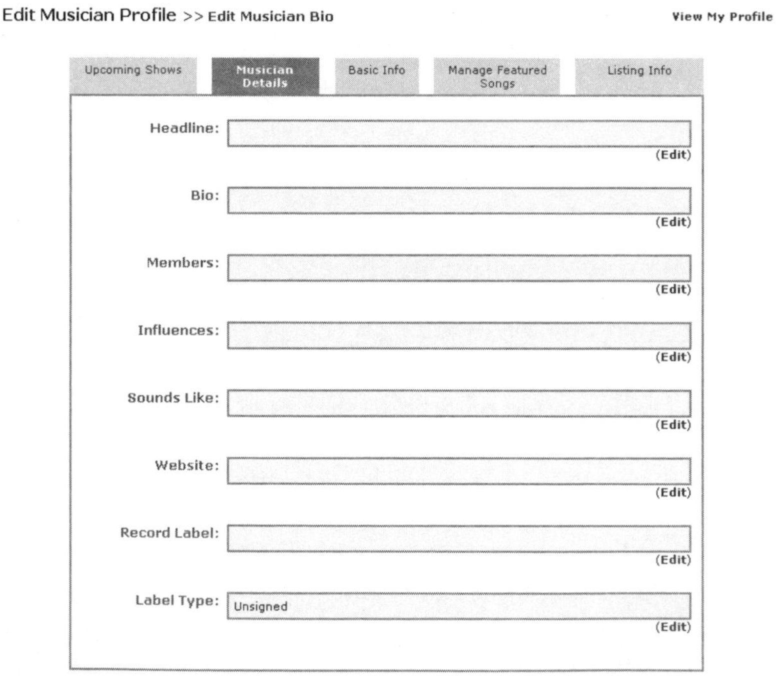

Edit Musician Profile >> Edit Musician Bio   View My Profile

| Upcoming Shows | Musician Details | Basic Info | Manage Featured Songs | Listing Info |

Headline: [   ]
                                                    (Edit)

Bio: [   ]
                                                    (Edit)

Members: [   ]
                                                    (Edit)

Influences: [   ]
                                                    (Edit)

Sounds Like: [   ]
                                                    (Edit)

Website: [   ]
                                                    (Edit)

Record Label: [   ]
                                                    (Edit)

Label Type: [Unsigned   ]
                                                    (Edit)

Figure 7.18   Your Musician Details section features several text fields.

■   **Basic Info.** Here is where you can change the name of your band and edit your location (see Figure 7.19). You can list your actual city and state or type in another location of your choice. For instance, you may not want to enter Sherman Oaks, California. Instead, you might choose to type in Southern Cali.

- **Manage Featured Songs.** Click on this section to add and delete songs from your profile's player (see Figure 7.20).

- **Listing Info.** Go here to tweak your genre selections (see Figure 7.21).

Edit Profile>>View Basic Info   Promote your Shows on MySpace!   View Artist Profile

Upcoming Shows	Musician Details	**Basic Info**	Manage Featured Songs	Listing Info

Musician Name: Fran Vincent   (HTML Not Allowed)

Country: United States

State/Region: Michigan   Or

City: Detroit

Zip Code: 48084

Submit

Figure 7.19   On the Basic Info tab, you can customize your location.

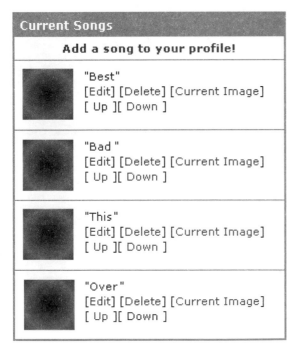

Current Songs

Add a song to your profile!

"Best"
[Edit] [Delete] [Current Image]
[Up][Down]

"Bad "
[Edit] [Delete] [Current Image]
[Up][Down]

"This "
[Edit] [Delete] [Current Image]
[Up][Down]

"Over "
[Edit] [Delete] [Current Image]
[Up][Down]

Figure 7.20   Your Manage Featured Songs section, which you used earlier to upload your music, will also show you what songs are in the queue.

You have just completed your initial profile! Take a preview of your profile and survey your good work. It might not be exciting to look at yet, but move on to Chapter 8, "Customizing Your Page," for info on how to make your profile unique.

Figure 7.21   The Listing Info lets you change your genre selections.

8 Customizing Your Page

Your profile has been created, and maybe you've even gone ahead and uploaded some music, written a bio, and uploaded a few photos. Still, it might look a bit boring. The default MySpace page, while clean-looking, is pretty dry (see Figure 8.1). No worries, though, because now you're going to learn how to customize your page and really make it your own!

Customizing a MySpace page, also called *pimping* it out or *tweaking* it, can go from the simple (embedding a few pictures and bolding some text), all the way to the very complicated (creating overlays that completely alter the MySpace layout and navigation until it's un-recognizable). All of these tweaks involve using some type of code, such as HTML. So, we'll start easy and work our way up.

Most of the codes you'll need can be found on the Internet, and you can just copy and paste the code into your profile. Some code is not very hard to manipulate, and you can write it up yourself. Still, there are other types of design alterations, such as div overlays, custom Cascading Style Sheets, and flash animation, that are very tricky and best handled by professionals or those proficient in various types of coding.

Before we dive in, let's revisit what we discussed in Chapters 5 and 6. If you haven't already done so, take a moment to jot down what you want your page to look like and what items you want it to include. What's most important to you and your fans? Revisit your Artist Summary and Target Market Summary. What is your brand as an artist? What are you trying to convey with your latest album? You might only need a very simple look, or your profile may require some heavy lifting by a graphic designer.

An initial look—including graphics and colors—is just the beginning. In this and subsequent chapters, we'll explore the various bells and whistles that can make your profile unique. These include widgets, slideshows, applications, videos, banners, and more. You don't have to have everything under the sun on your profile. But, you should give it some thought as to what is important to you right now. Then revise and add/delete from your profile as you go along. What you need now might be different six months from now. And if you're not sure what you want, spend some time looking at other musician profiles. How have other artists structured their profile? Write down what you like about a profile that catches your fancy. It

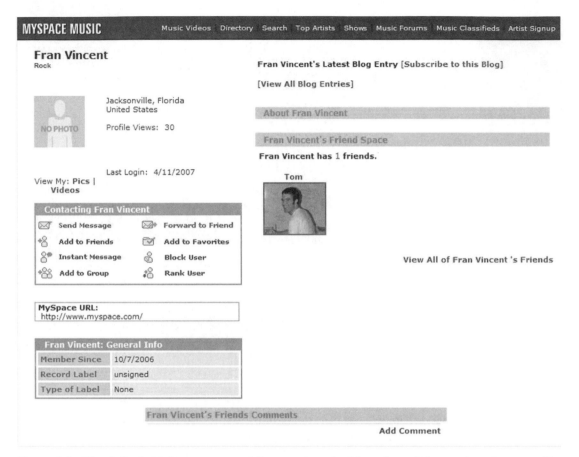

Figure 8.1   The default MySpace page, while very clean-looking, doesn't have a lot of personality.

might be a simple thing, such as the way the artist is displaying videos or even a color that you really like. Take screenshots of things you like. Now you will have a roadmap to work from.

Whether you decide to do it all yourself or go with a graphic designer, there are a few things to keep in mind while pimping your page. The first is that you must never cover up the banner ads that appear on the top of the MySpace pages (see Figure 8.2). That's how MySpace makes their money (since none of us is paying for the profiles we create). And as you can imagine, people get pretty ornery when you start messing with their bread and butter. Tampering with ads will get you kicked off the service.

Second, you should never delete or alter MySpace's functional links, such as the top-of-page navigation links that take you home, allow you to browse, or allow you to click through the MySpace Music section (see Figure 8.3). This also applies to the links at the bottom of the page (About, FAQ, and so on; see Figure 8.4). You will see layouts that have removed them, which often irritates fans who can't find the links they need. Leave the links alone and design around them. They're not that big of a design constriction.

Figure 8.2   The advertisement at the top of this graphic is a banner ad from a MySpace advertiser.

Figure 8.3   These are the top navigation links. They should remain intact.

Figure 8.4   These bottom links should not be covered up or removed.

Lastly, while this chapter will introduce you to the basics of customization, it can't cover every possible tweak that one can apply to a profile. That alone would take a whole book, and even then I don't think we'd get them all. Every day, programmers around the world are coming up with new toys we can use to spice up our profiles, from custom code and manipulations to Flash animation, sound, and video tools, little applications and games, and everything in between. So while you'll get a primer here, the purpose is not to turn you into a master programmer. I encourage you to browse the web for more bells and whistles that we haven't covered. Visit Appendix B, "MySpace Resources," for lots of sites you can try out, visit the discussion forum on MySpace (click on More > Forums > MySpace > Customizing), or do your own web searches on "myspace tweaks," "myspace layouts," and the like.

Finding the Friend ID

Before we get to all the tweaking, you have to know how to find your friend ID and that of others. There are some cool things you can do with your profile that require you to know what a friend ID is and where to locate it.

The friend ID is your special number that MySpace assigns you when you create an account. Everyone has one, whether he or she is a regular user, a band, a comedian, or a filmmaker. It's how the system identifies you. Here's how you find it:

1. Click on a profile. Start with your own for this exercise.

2. Look at the address bar at the top of your browser. Notice the URL will have the word "friendid=" and then a bunch of numbers after it. The numbers immediately after the equals sign and before any other characters represent your friend ID (see Figure 8.5). The friend ID is usually at the very end of the address, but sometimes it might be embedded in the middle somewhere.

3. Some profiles show the user's unique name at the end of the URL instead of the friend ID. If you cannot find the friend ID as described, click on other MySpace links in that person's profile, such as View Photos, Friends, or Comments, and you will see his friend ID in the URL displayed in your web browser.

http://profile.myspace.com/index.cfm?fuseaction=user.viewprofile&friendID=652875

Figure 8.5   In this example, this user's friend ID is 652875.

To make sure we're all on the same page, let's look for Tom's friend ID. He's your first friend, that lone guy sitting on your Friends list when you signed up, as shown in Figure 8.6. If you deleted him, go to www.myspace.com/tom. Click on Tom's profile and look in your web browser's address bar. Do you see his unique name or his friend ID? If you see his unique name instead of a number, try the technique in Step 3. You should see that his friend ID is 6221 (see Figure 8.7).

When a tweak calls for friend IDs, you'll know where to look!

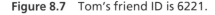

Figure 8.6   This is Tom, your very first friend.

Figure 8.7   Tom's friend ID is 6221.

A Few Basics

Let's start by adding a few basic items to your profile. We will do this using HTML, which stands for *HyperText Markup Language*. HTML is a type of computer language used to create web pages. This HTML code is like a set of directions to your web browser, which interprets and then displays a web page accordingly. Most HTML uses the < and > symbols, which are located above your comma and period keys, respectively, to enclose its directions to the web browser. Let's touch on some of the basic HTML tags you might want to use on your profile.

First, you can modify the text to make it stand out more, and you can add line spaces to break up copy. Go into your account's home control panel and, above your thumbnail picture, click on the Edit Profile link (see Figure 8.8). Then click on the Musician Details tab. Under the Bio field, click Edit. Let's experiment by typing the following text into your profile's Bio field:

> Welcome to my profile! This is my first MySpace profile. In just mere moments I am gonna rock this layout. I'll be adding photos, video, and revamping my layout completely.

Click the Preview button, and you'll see that your entry is just plain text (see Figure 8.9).

Now we're going to alter it, so click Edit. Add the following <P> and <BR> tags (which I've capitalized and bolded here so they'll be more visible) to your text:

> Welcome to my profile!**<P>** This is my first MySpace profile.**
** In just mere moments I am gonna rock this layout.**
** I'll be adding photos, video, and revamping my layout completely.

Hello, Fran Vincent!

My URL: myspace.com/franvincentmusic [Edit Profile] [Safe Mode]

What are you doing right

Mood: (none)

Figure 8.8 The Edit Profile link appears above your picture in your home control panel.

Edit Profile>> Edit Your Band's General Info   View My Profile

| Upcoming Shows | Musician Details | Basic Info | Manage Featured Songs | Listing Info |

Musician Bio:

Welcome to my profile! This is my first MySpace profile. In just mere moments I am gonna rock this layout. I'll be adding photos, video, and revamping my layout completely.

Cancel   Preview

Figure 8.9 Your plain-text entry doesn't have any special formatting.

Click Preview to see how your text looks now (see Figure 8.10). The paragraph tag (<P>) added a line space, which is like hitting Enter twice in a word processor. The
is a line break, which is the same as hitting Enter with the Shift key pressed in a word processing program. These tags do *not* require ending tags (</P> or</BR>). Although some editors and browsers add them in, they're not actually necessary.

Click Edit again and add the following tags (again, capitalized and bolded here) to your text. This time, I've added carriage returns so you can more easily see where the breaks and new tags are. You can also add these returns to your own code as you are editing if you like:

Edit Profile>>Edit Your Band's General Info   Promote your Shows on MySpace!   View Artist Profile

Figure 8.10   Now our text is broken up by paragraph and line breaks.

<H4>Welcome to my profile!**</H4><P>**

This is my first MySpace profile.**
**
In just mere moments **<B>** I am gonna rock this layout.**</B>
**

I'll be adding photos, video, **<I>**and**</I>** revamping my layout completely.

We just added a header format (<H4>) to the first sentence. You can apply header formats from <H1> to <H6>, with <H1> being the biggest text and <H6> being the smallest. We also bolded part of the third sentence and italicized the word "and" in the last sentence. Notice that these tags only modify the text they enclose. Therefore, you need beginning and ending tags. Put these types of tags *around* the text you want to modify. The ending tag has a slash (/) in it, indicating to the web browser that this is where you want the modification to stop.

Click Preview to see the changes (see Figure 8.11).

Edit Profile>>Edit Your Band's General Info   Promote your Shows on MySpace!   View Artist Profile

Figure 8.11   Our text is evolving to include variances in font style and size.

Now go back to Edit and add the following bolded tags. We're not finished yet!

<CENTER><H4>Welcome to my profile!</H4>**</CENTER>**<P>

<CENTER>
This is my first MySpace profile.
In just mere moments <B> I am gonna rock this layout.</B>
I'll be adding photos, video, <I>and</I> revamping my layout completely.
</CENTER>

Now we've added <CENTER>tags so our text will be centered. Again, only the text between opening and ending <CENTER>tags will be affected. Here, we decided to center the entire passage. We had to put two sets of <CENTER>tags, however. One goes around the text before the paragraph tag (<P>). The second set goes around the rest of the text because it is only broken up by line breaks. When you use <P>tags and add a whole line space, it's wise to treat that portion separately and give it its very own alignment tags. When you preview your new HTML tweaks, they should look like Figure 8.12.

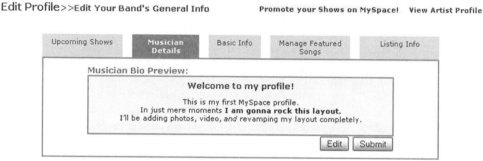

Figure 8.12   This time, we took our passage and centered it.

Edit the text again, and this time we will add a hyperlink to the MySpace home page. A hyperlink tag has beginning and ending tags also. You can create a link by using the following formula:

<A HREF="*insert Web address here*">Type the text you'd like to be highlighted and linked</A>

So now if we want to hyperlink the entire second sentence of our practice copy, it will look like this:

<CENTER><H4>Welcome to my profile!</H4></CENTER><P>

<CENTER>
**<A HREF="http://www.myspace.com">This is my first MySpace profile.</A>
**
In just mere moments**<B> I am gonna rock this layout.</B>
**
I'll be adding photos, video, **<I>and</I>** revamping my layout completely.
</CENTER>

Everything between <A HREF=" ....."> and</A> will appear as a clickable hyperlink (see Figure 8.13).

I hate to make things more complicated than they should be, but because MySpace doesn't always interpret standard HTML tags and code the same way regular web pages do, you sometimes have to alter the code to fit this environment so links will work correctly. The hyperlink code as is would work in most other web pages, but in MySpace, we sometimes have to omit the quotations marks and instead make it:

Figure 8.13 Now the second line is linked to the MySpace home page.

<A HREF=http://www.myspace.com>This is my first MySpace profile.</A>

If your link did not work correctly with quotation marks, try it without. The link should work correctly and will take you to the MySpace home page when clicked. Go ahead and try it!

You can see that although standard HTML will have you enclose URLs in quotation marks, MySpace doesn't always interpret the HTML properly unless you omit the quotation marks. When adding code to your MySpace profile, be willing to experiment, and if something doesn't come out the way it's supposed to, check your code first for errors. Make sure you have any ending tags if needed. And if your code is correct, play with it a little bit, omit the quotation marks, or move it to a different section of your profile to see whether it will work. There are times when you'll find that your code will not work at all. MySpace filters out certain tags and widgets it doesn't like, including various types of buttons and check boxes, so not every type of code tweak will be successful.

Additionally, you can try editing your profile in safe mode. This allows you to input and tweak existing HTML and text, but it won't load any customizations (see Figure 8.14). This is particularly helpful when you are working with lots of graphics, videos, large backgrounds, and special layouts that move sections around. Safe mode makes it easier for you to do your edits without having to wait for the web page to load all that custom stuff and refresh over and over again, which can cause your browser to crash. The Safe Mode link is located next to the Edit Profile link in a music profile, which you'll see back in Figure 8.8.

For regular account users, access safe mode by going to this link:

http://editprofile.myspace.com/index.cfm?fuseaction=profile.safemode

At this time of this writing, MySpace had, for some inexplicable reason, removed the safe mode editing link for regular profile users. You can still access your safe editing mode by using the preceding link, however.

Back to our editing exercise... You can submit your profile text edits now and then view your profile so you can see what it looks like on your page. Remember, if it's easier for you to see it

Bio:

> This is the official profile for the book MySpace for Musicians! You can also check out the web page at
> www.myspaceformusicians.com. Don't forget to send me a friend request and your questions/experiences with
> promoting yourself on MySpace. =) <p> <hr> <p> <H3>DISCLAIMER:</h3> I get a lot of questions on
> MySpace, so I have to clarify for you so there's no misunderstanding... I'm a Space <i>music marketer</I>,
> but I <b>do not</b> work for MySpace. I don't know Tom personally. I have no access to your account and
> cannot help you with customer service issues. Please contact MySpace customer service, the MySpace help FAQ
> or Tom for issues related to your account. <p> Whew, so now that we have that out of the way... Read on about
> the book! <hr> <p> <h3>Did you know A&R reps from music labels, publishers as well as film/TV music
> supervisors use MySpace to find new music?</h3> <p> MySpace is one of the most popular websites on the
> Internet today, with millions of pages of user-generated content. This makes MySpace an ideal tool for
> musicians interested in promoting their music to a ready-made audience. Acts have gone from the garage to a
> recording contract or film/TV/commercial licensing deals by using MySpace as their launching pad. <p>
> <strong>MySpace for Musicians: The Comprehensive Guide to Marketing Your Music Online</strong> is for
> every band, soloist, side musician, record label, publisher, music manager, and entertainment-affiliated
> company who wants to use MySpace to its fullest potential. It teaches musicians how to design a MySpace page
> optimized for music promotion and distribution and how to best use MySpace to effectively market music. It
> includes expert advice on how to market oneself to the MySpace community and how to best position and
> advertise MySpace pages in the real world. <p> <strong>MySpace for Musicians</strong> caters to musicians
> who are unfamiliar with the network, as well as musicians who already have a MySpace page but who want to
> learn how to make better use of it. This is the most comprehensive book on how musicians can maximize the
> most popular and successful band promotion site! <p> <center> <h4> MySpace for Musicians book available
> now!</h4>
 <img src=http://a256.ac-images.myspacecdn.com/
> /19/m_a9df76316a6f826f42c7a3f3d854f03f.gif>
 <a href=http://www.msplinks.com
> /MDFodHRwOi8vd3d3LmFtYXpvbi5jb20vTXlTcGFjZS1NdXNpY2lhbnMtRnJhbkhbbi1WaW5jZW50L 2RwLz
> /aWU9VVRGOCZzPWJvb2tzJnFpZD0xMTc3NTQ2OTY3JnNyPTEtMTI9Ym9tYTOZWxsYzYmVhdS0yMA==><h4>Get it
> from Amazon.com</h4></a> <p> You will also find MFM at your local Barnes and Noble, Borders, Guitar
> Center, and other book retailers nationwide.</center> <p> <hr> <p> <center> <I>Hey, psssstttt... Friends
> get up to date marketing and promotion tips, so...</I>
 <h3> DON'T BE A STRANGER! LET'S BE
> FRIENDS!</h3> </center> <p> <center> <a href=http://www.msplinks.com
> /MDFodHRwOi8vY29sbGVjdGC5teXNwYWNlLmN

Figure 8.14   This is what my profile looks like in safe edit mode. It's not pretty, but if you know how to look at the code and edit your text by hand, safe mode is a great alternative.

as it should be laid out, you can add manual line breaks to separate out your code when you type it up in your MySpace profile editor or in a text file. Either way, just hit the Enter button to bring your text to the next line, as you would if you were typing up any other document.

After the code has been saved in MySpace, the browser will probably run it all together anyway, so this way of editing shouldn't affect the functionality.

We've only started touching on what can be done with HTML. The next section will take a look at embedding images and videos. However, for further HTML study, there are a few great tutorials on the web that will really school you on all things HTML. You'll find an excellent one at www.w3schools.com/html/default.asp.

Try out some online HTML editors, too. You want one that will allow you to edit in real time, like a word processor. Two I use are www.zoodu.com/html-editor and www.pimp-my -profile.com/htmledit. They're almost identical in their interfaces (see Figure 8.15), but if one is swamped with traffic, you can always try the other. With editors like these, you can type in the text you want, format it, add some links and photos, play with the alignment, or add tables. Then the editor will generate the code for you so you can plug it into the appropriate section in your profile. Note that these HTML editors are not for creating MySpace layouts. They are only for editing content within a specific section of your profile.

Adding Photos, Images, and Other Graphics

To embed an image, you must first create it and upload it onto a server or image hosting site. When deciding what type of format and size your image should be, consider the constraints

HTML Editor

This WYSIWYG (What You See Is What You Get) editor is great if you don't know HTML. It lets you customize basic elements such as text, links and tables like if were using a word processor, so you can center and change size, color and fonts with ease. This is NOT for creating a layout, that is what the Profile Editor is for, this HTML editor is only for helping you customize the content you put on your profile.

To get the HTML code click the ᴴᵀᴹᴸ **image in the second row of buttons! Copy and paste the code that appears in the pop-up window.**

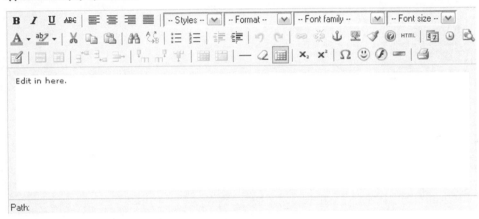

Figure 8.15   The HTML Editor at Zoodu.com lets you type in text, format it, and even add graphics, tables, and more.

of MySpace profiles. The sections and columns do not lend themselves to overly large pictures. Huge graphics throw your profile layout out of whack, making it necessary for visitors to scroll left to right to see everything. Therefore, a good rule of thumb is to keep your images to no more than 450 pixels wide and 550 pixels high. If you feel the urge to go larger, plug your graphics/photos into your profile and at least test it by viewing the profile on various-size screens and in multiple resolutions and types of web browsers. This way, you can see what your fans will see, and you can make adjustments as necessary.

Aside from dimension, images should also be in JPG or GIF format for web viewing. The file size is best kept to 200K or less, which is already pretty large. Even then, you don't want to load your profile with too many images. Bulky-sized graphics and/or too many pictures on a profile can cause a visitor's browser to crash. It can also cause you to max out your allotted bandwidth given by the image hosting site, resulting in an error showing up instead of your graphic.

As far as where to store photos, Photobucket.com, ImageShack.us, and Flickr.com are three of the most popular free media hosting sites with MySpacers. After you upload your graphic, the hosting site will give you the URL of the image (see Figure 8.16). You'll use this information to

click to add title

move | edit | share | delete

☐ herecomes...le-sm.jpg

URL Link   http://i9.photobucket.

Figure 8.16   An uploaded image on Photobucket.com shows the URL where the image is located.

construct an image source tag. The image source tag (<IMG SRC=...>) is one of those, like <P>and
and a few others, that stands alone. No ending tag is necessary.

So go ahead and upload a photo or graphic to your hosting site of choice. Then copy and paste the given URL into the HTML image tag, as indicated here:

<IMG SRC="http://*ENTER IMAGE URL HERE*">

This HTML command directs the web browser to display the image located at the indicated http address. Remember how MySpace is a little quirky with HTML? This is another one of those instances where you might have to remove the quotation marks to get the picture to load correctly. Take the image source tag you've created and paste it into the Bio (or another) section of your profile (see Figure 8.17). Preview and submit this new addition. View your profile, and you should see the image loaded into the page at the same place you inserted the HTML directions (see Figure 8.18).

If you want to center the image, then you add the <CENTER>tags around it, like this:

<CENTER><IMG SRC="http://*ENTER IMAGE URL HERE*">**</CENTER>**

Go ahead and try it with and without quotation marks. Your picture should now be centered in the Bio section!

Edit Profile>> **Edit Your Band's General Info**   View My Profile

Figure 8.17   Place the image source tag in the Bio field.

Figure 8.18   The profile loads the image because the image source tag directs it to do so.

You can also link your photo to an outside website, such as your official website. Remember how we created hyperlinks? Instead of surrounding text with the hyperlink tags, we will surround the new image tags. Your code will look like this:

```
<A HREF="http://ENTER WEBSITE URL HERE">
<IMG SRC="http://IMAGE URL HERE"></A>
```

Again, you may need to take out the quotation marks so it will work correctly in MySpace. Feel free to add some text or other images/media before or after by using <P>to insert some space. This keeps everything from running together on your layout.

Special Photo Treatments

Slideshows are very popular on MySpace. They allow people to showcase a lot of pictures, but they only take up a small amount of real estate on the profile. MySpace has a built-in slideshow feature that takes the pictures you have loaded into your account and converts them into a little presentation (see Figure 8.19). You can customize the show by adding captions and altering the dimensions of the slideshow, the colors of the borders, and even the kind of slideshow, such as a regular linear presentation or one where photos randomly "fly" in. When you're finished tweaking, you copy and paste the provided code into your profile at the point you want the slideshow to appear. To try it out, go to Add/Edit Photos from your home control panel. You'll see a link to the slideshow utility.

There are some other really cool slideshow utilities available on the web. My favorite sites for creating slideshows are Photobucket.com, Slide.com, and RockYou.com. All three have lots of options for customizing your show, including interesting transitions. RockYou, for instance, lets you make a show that uses stars to transition from photo to photo (see Figure 8.20). Slide has one that looks like white-bordered photographs being scattered on a table (see Figure 8.21). And Photobucket boasts a cool skin that looks like a retro television set, complete with staticky picture (see Figure 8.22). All three sites are free, and you simply load your photos and choose what kind of slideshow you want. Like the MySpace slideshow utility, these sites give you code to plug into your profile wherever you want it to appear (see Figure 8.23).

For information on uploading photos and graphics directly to your MySpace account, see Chapter 12, "Photos and Videos."

Adding Video to Your Profile

You have the ability to upload videos into your MySpace account, or you may choose an outside website to host your videos. Of course, you could even do both just to have all your bases covered and get the most exposure possible! But that's another discussion altogether. See Chapter 12 for more on how and why to use video.

There are various websites out there that provide server space for video clips, which are then converted into embeddable content. YouTube.com is probably the most well-known video

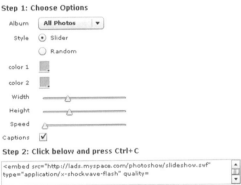

Figure 8.19   The MySpace slideshow page lets you create shows from pictures you have uploaded to the MySpace servers.

site out there. It's simple to use and has a community of its own that is active in viewing and commenting on user videos. It also has special musician and comedian accounts, and you can place your YouTube videos anywhere, including on MySpace, in email, in blogs—pretty much any web-based environment. You'll find many other video hosting options in Appendix B as well.

Whichever hosting site you choose, the process of inserting videos into your profile is a fairly simple one involving pasting and tweaking code. MySpace, and any other site that hosts user videos, will provide the embed code needed to plug a video anywhere into your layout.

To get the embed code for a MySpace-hosted video, first go to Video > My Videos in your home control panel. Now, click on the thumbnail picture of your video (see Figure 8.24). You'll be taken to a screen that will not only allow you to view the video, but will also provide details about that clip, including the needed code. Scroll down and see two types of

Figure 8.20   RockYou.com can make a 3D cube slideshow like this one.

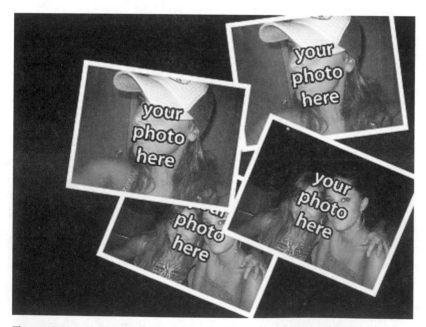

Figure 8.21   Slide.com has a realistic "photos on the table" slideshow.

Figure 8.22 This fun Photobucket.com slideshow emulates a retro television set, replete with a little white noise.

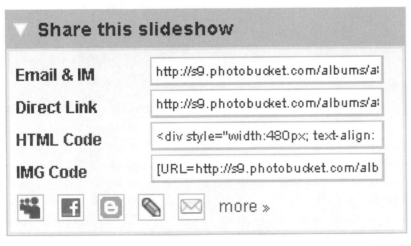

Figure 8.23 Like other slideshow providers, Photobucket.com provides different types of URL links to your slideshow.

Figure 8.24   Your uploaded videos appear in your MySpace account under Add/Change Videos. Click on the video you want to embed.

code—Embed Code and Video URL. The Video URL is simply the address where your video is being stored, and this address can be emailed to friends who may want to click to see your clip. However, in order to embed the video, we need the Embed Code (see Figure 8.25).

Figure 8.25   Copy the Embed Code onto your computer's clipboard.

Click once on the Embed Code box, and you will see the code is now highlighted. To copy the code, right-click with your mouse and choose Copy, or on your keyboard, use the shortcut Ctrl+C. Then, as you did for pictures and slideshows, insert this code into the spot on your profile where you want your video to appear.

The process for uploading videos into a YouTube.com (or other video hosting) account is similar to that in MySpace. YouTube and other sites will also ask you to title, describe, tag, and categorize your clip. And, like MySpace, other video hosting sites will also give you video embed code that may look something like this:

```
<object width="425" height="350"><param name="movie" value="http://
www.youtube.com/v/a5ujuBgk0Q01"></param><param name="wmode"
value="transparent"></param><embed src="http://www.youtube.com/v/
a5ujuBgk0Q01" type="application/x-shockwave-flash" wmode="transparent"
width="425" height="350"></embed></object>
```

Again, paste this code into your profile at the point where you want the video to appear.

Revamping Your Profile Layout

Although adding media and a few text formats are important things to know, it's over-hauling your profile's look that you're probably most interested in! You may be wondering how you are going to add an awesome background and different colors to your page. This section will show you how you can completely revamp your profile.

In Chapter 6 and at the beginning of this chapter, I suggested you start thinking about what you want your profile to look like so that it jives with who you are and the music you make. Hopefully, you wrote some ideas down, because now you'll need them to shake up your MySpace default page.

I can't stress the importance of looking at a lot of other profiles to get a feel for what's possible. This will also give you a feel for what you do and don't like. Take note of what strikes you as attractive and what looks positively ugly. Which profiles inspire you? What kinds of features do you covet? Which ones make you question the sanity of the profile owner? You may notice fairly quickly that there are many really cluttered pages on MySpace. Some of them work, but most are just such a mess that you want to navigate away from them as quickly as possible—as with the one in Figure 8.26, with a background so busy you can't read the too-light text. Flashing and busy graphics, glittery text, dark type on dark back-grounds, white type on light backgrounds, so many photos and videos your browser is in-capable of loading them all, lots of blinky logos in every corner...the eyestrain is enough to give a person a migraine.

My recommendation is to go ahead and try out lots of toys and tweaks, but test, test, test. Spend the time looking at your profile as a fan would. Try it out on Internet Explorer, Mozilla Firefox, and Mac Safari. Get your friends and family to visit it and rate it honestly. If it takes forever for you to load your page, it's going to bog down everyone else, too.

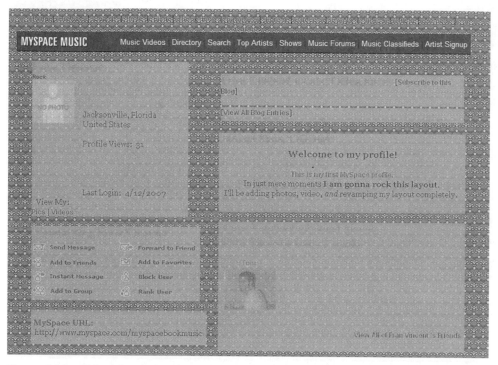

Figure 8.26 This ugly profile has a busy background, but the rest of the profile is rendered transparent, and the font colors are too light to stand out.

Having trouble reading your text? Change your background or your text color so there is enough contrast to make reading easy. Go for higher contrast. Keep the number of text colors and font styles and sizes to a minimum. Watch for overly busy backgrounds and obnoxious, animated artwork. Your profile can have some really cool features, but it must be usable.

Since this book is dedicated to musicians and focuses on the artist profile, we won't be spending much time on the profile customization features available to regular MySpace users. At the time this book was written, these features were not available for users with musician accounts. However, if you have a regular account (say you are in an affiliated entertainment industry business), you can access these special customization features by going to Profile > Customize Profile while logged in (see Figure 8.27). You'll be asked to upgrade to Profile 2.0 in order to access these features (see Figure 8.28). When you do, you can access the customization panel. You'll also notice that your MySpace profile layout has changed quite a bit (see Figure 8.29). If you don't like it, you have 90 days to go back to the original MySpace setup (a.k.a. Profile 1.0).

Using Style Sheets

Most of the customized MySpace profiles out there are created using Cascading Style Sheets. CSS, as it's commonly referred to, is a type of programming language that defines how

Home
Mail (1)
Profile
Friends
Music
Hello, F
My Profile
Edit Profile
Customize Profile
My Apps
My Blog
My Comments
My Favorites
My Photos
My Playlists
My Videos
View My:
Profile | Pics | Videos
Comments | Friends |
Groups
My URL: myspace.com/franv

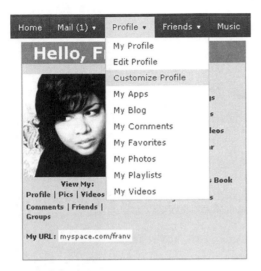

Figure 8.27 Regular users can access these profile features from their home control panel.

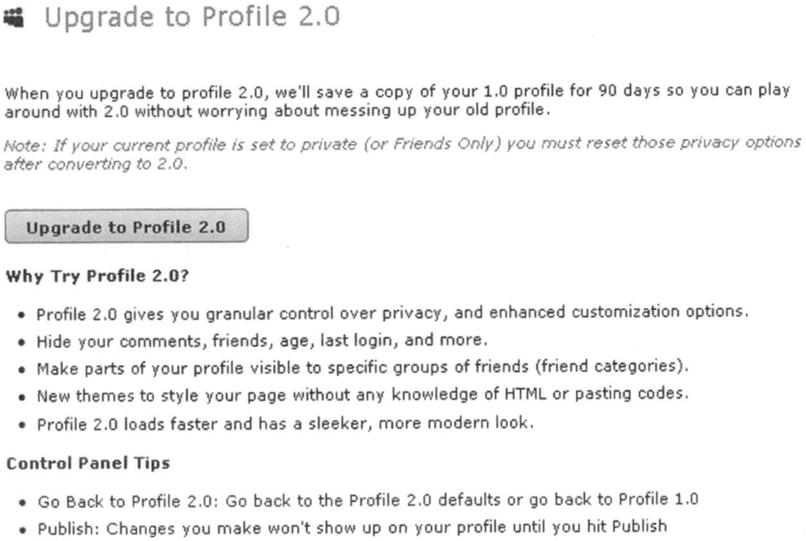
Upgrade to Profile 2.0
When you upgrade to profile 2.0, we'll save a copy of your 1.0 profile for 90 days so you can play around with 2.0 without worrying about messing up your old profile.
Note: If your current profile is set to private (or Friends Only) you must reset those privacy options after converting to 2.0.
Upgrade to Profile 2.0
Why Try Profile 2.0?
Profile 2.0 gives you granular control over privacy, and enhanced customization options.
Hide your comments, friends, age, last login, and more.
Make parts of your profile visible to specific groups of friends (friend categories).
New themes to style your page without any knowledge of HTML or pasting codes.
Profile 2.0 loads faster and has a sleeker, more modern look.
Control Panel Tips
Go Back to Profile 2.0: Go back to the Profile 2.0 defaults or go back to Profile 1.0
Publish: Changes you make won't show up on your profile until you hit Publish

Figure 8.28 MySpace asks you to upgrade to Profile 2.0 to access the panel that allows you to add themes and move around your MySpace sections.

various HTML elements should be formatted. For example, if you want all of the headers in your profile to be kelly green and an 18-point font size, then you can specify that once in your style sheet, instead of going through and changing each and every header to this specification. CSS cuts down the work and streamlines the code.

We won't dive into the ins and outs of this style sheet language. I'll leave that to programmers. Instead, you'll learn how to find ready-made style sheets and how to use editors to

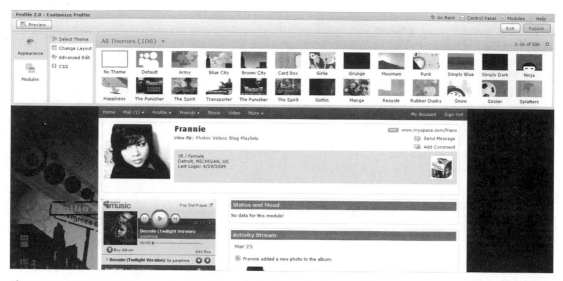

Figure 8.29   This is the new Profile 2.0 panel where all the magic happens. You can see it changes the way your profile is laid out. As of the time of this writing, this option is not available to those with musician accounts.

create your own. For those who really want to learn how to do it manually, try out www.w3schools.com/css/default.asp for an excellent tutorial.

Pre-Made Layouts

The web abounds with ready-made layouts for MySpace profiles. Some of them are great, and some are hideous. The first thing you should do is start shopping for layouts. They're free, so you can download as many as you want and try them all on for size. Peruse Appendix B for a list of sites that offer layouts and codes. Or, do your own web search for "myspace layouts."

A word of caution about layout sites: Most are heavily laden with annoying banner ads, sponsored links, pop-ups, and other types of advertisements. Unfortunately, some may also be carrying adware or spyware. Before you go layout shopping, make sure your virus scan is in working order. Delete your cookies (in the Tools > Internet Options screen for Internet Explorer users) and run a malware scan with a free software product, such as Ad-Aware (www.lavasoft.com).

When you find a profile layout that you like, copy and paste the provided code into a text file and save it on your hard drive so you can go back to it later. To try it out in your profile, paste the provided layout code into the bottom of your Bio field (for bands) or your About Me field (for regular users). Save changes and reload your profile to see how it looks. Not quite right for your image? That's okay; keep shopping!

Should you find something that has the color scheme you like, but perhaps you're not loving the main or table backgrounds, save it in a text file anyway. You can tweak it to suit your needs by removing the offending background or replacing it with one of your choosing (such as a picture of yourself). Here's how to tackle this.

Search through the code (or use the Find function in your text program) to locate the "background-image" phrase. It should be fairly near the beginning of the code:

background-image:url('http://*LOCATION OF BACKGROUND IMAGE*');

We're going to replace whatever is in the pre-made layout with a background picture of you. The *maximum* size of your background should usually be no more than 800 pixels by 700 pixels (see Figure 8.30), though it may be necessary to experiment. Different screen sizes and resolutions will affect how your background looks, so be sure to test it out.

Figure 8.30   Artist India.Arie has an 800×700-pixel background on her profile. Notice that her image only appears on the far left side, and the rest of the background was left white.

Load this background into your favorite photo hosting site. Take the provided URL and paste it into the code in place of the URL that's already there. Now, take the entire layout style sheet with your new background and paste this code into the Bio section of your profile. Load it up and see how it looks!

Suppose you don't want a background image at all. Search for the same code and just remove all the text between the parentheses:

background-image:url();

If you decide later that you want to add a background image back in, simply put the URL of your new background location between the parentheses.

You may see a couple of instances of "background-image" in the code. The one toward the top is likely the main background image. Another occurrence of "background-image" is likely to be a table background. You can remove/replace backgrounds that appear in the section boxes (tables) in your profile by following the same procedure.

Recall the ugly profile with the busy background in Figure 8.26? Once we take out the background, it starts to look a lot cleaner (see Figure 8.31).

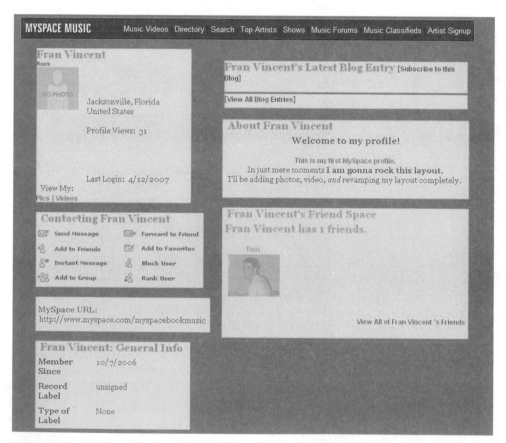

Figure 8.31   Without the horrible background, this profile is starting to look better.

Layout Editors/Generators

Pre-made layouts might not be your thing, so try creating your very own profile layout from scratch by using an online layout editor/generator. Two I like are located at pimp-my-profile. com/generators/myspace.php and http://tinyurl.com/yeb729z. (I created a tinyurl for this

Zuuga.com editor because they have recently stopped linking to it from their home page, but it is still available if you know how to get to it!)

The one at pimp-my-profile.com (see Figure 8.32) is very comprehensive, though you can't see your layout as you build. The generator at www.zuuga.com (see Figure 8.33), however, does less, but its WYSIWYG interface lets you see what your layout will look like as you build it, which is great for beginners.

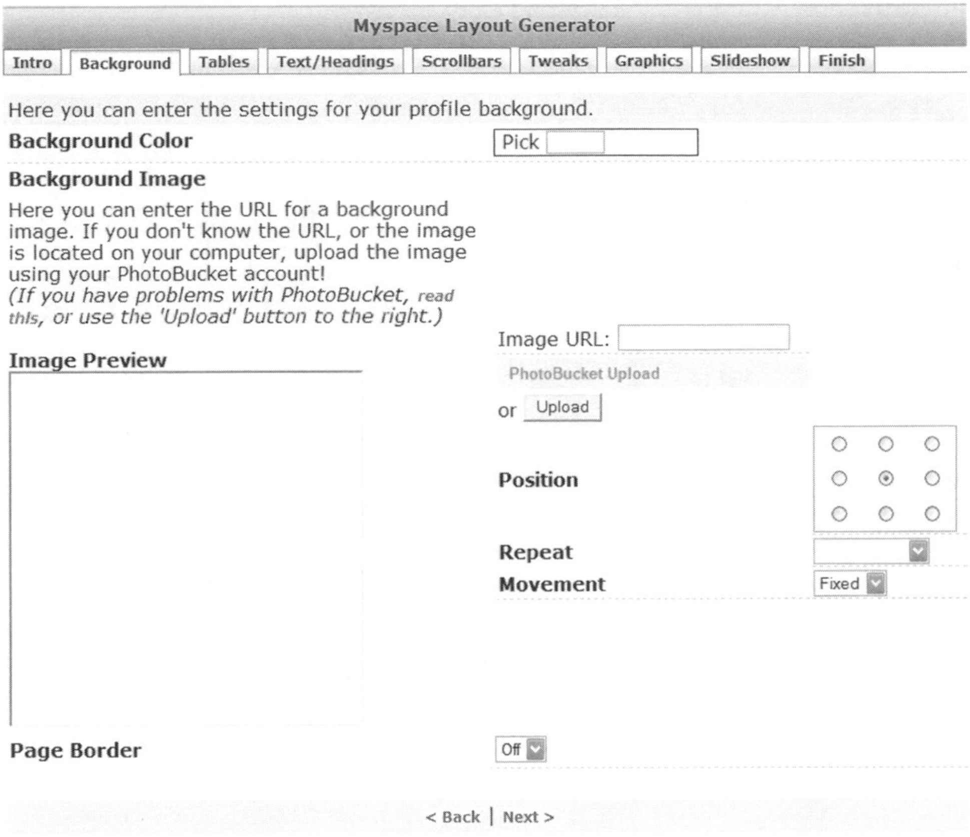

Figure 8.32   This pimp-my-profile.com layout editor has a lot of options to make your profile shine.

When using code from a layout site or a layout editor/generator, you are likely to get advertisement code that is embedded into the end of your layout code. This is the stuff you see on others' MySpace profiles touting where they got their layout from, usually appearing as text in their bio or as a little banner in the corner of the profile. You can still give credit where credit is due by discreetly placing a little mention as to where you got your layout where *you* want and where it looks the best on your site. Something like "Layout from www.xyzlayouts.com" should suffice. You've already learned how to create a hyperlink and place it in your profile. If you want to remove advertisement code from a layout you want to use, look to the bottom of the code block and delete everything after the </STYLE> tag (bolded below):

color:rgb(255,255,255)!important;   font-size:11px!important;}   .navbar:hover {font-family:verdana!important; font-weight:normal!important; text-decoration:none!important; font-style:normal!important; color:rgb(255,255,255)!important; font-size:11px! important;}</STYLE>
<a href='http://www.blahblahlayouts.com'>Get a ba-zillion myspace layouts from our supercool site!</a>
 <a href="http://www.blahblahlayouts.com/pi.asp?=tn-85441" target="_blank"><img   src="http://blahblahlayouts.com/art/9/layouts/use.gif"   alt= "Get your layout now!" border="0"/> </a>

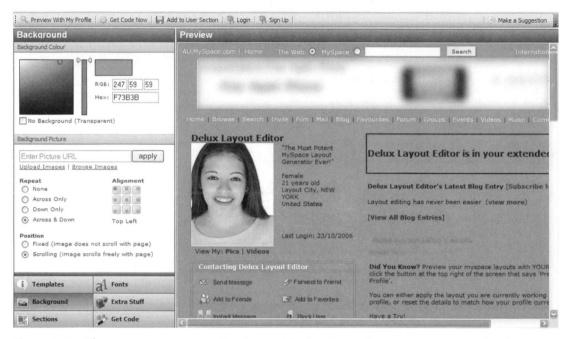

Figure 8.33   The www.zuuga.com editor is great for beginners because you can see the changes as you make them.

Layout editors are excellent tools to help you get your profile looking spiffy, particularly if you don't have any CSS experience. So, if you have the time and the creative initiative, then develop your own layout!

Overlays and Flash

Overlays, also called *div layouts* or *div overlays*, are a much more intricate way to alter your profile. They sometimes include Flash animation, too. The code in the overlay completely covers up the way MySpace profiles are currently structured and lets you make your profile look like just about anything you want. Figures 8.34 and 8.35 are just two amazing examples of what div overlays can do.

Figure 8.34 This profile promoting the compilation *CD Wow Hits 2009* (www.myspace.com/wowhits) hardly looks like a MySpace profile at all. It incorporates a lot of varied elements, all focused on the CD's tracks and artists.

Working with overlays is not for the beginner. However, it is an option that's available to you. First try out one of the many free overlays available online. Search for "myspace div," "free divs," "myspace overlays," and the like. If you decide you want to create your own, I've provided links to several div overlay generators in Appendix B. You can also look to a professional designer to create a custom div layout or Flash animation for you.

Figure 8.35   Joss Stone's profile is so different that it's barely recognizable as a MySpace page.

You can also turn your profile into a wonder of Flash animation. A particular favorite of mine is a site called LoveMyFlash.com. They have lots of free Flash layouts to choose from. This can be a fun way to perk up your profile! Aside from the templates offered at free Flash sites, many designers can create custom Flash profiles and headers for you.

More MySpace Tweaks

There are so many more ways to alter your profile that it'll make your head spin. In this section, we'll touch on a few that musicians might need to maximize their pages.

Adding Interest Tables

Regular MySpace accounts have a section called Interests, where users can list general interests, movies, music they like, and so forth (see Figure 8.36). Although bands do not have a place to list interests, they do have an area called General Info, where you'll find details about band members, the official website, and the record label (see Figure 8.37).

Fifi's Interests	
General	Watching TV and surfing
Music	Green Day, Sublime, Front 242
Movies	Blue Crush, The Godfather

Figure 8.36 This is a sample of an Interests table from a regular MySpace account.

Fran Vincent: General Info	
Member Since	10/7/2006
Band Website	[insertwebsitehere].com
Band Members	Ellen Mets (guitar/vocals) Jeff Honcho (drums)
Influences	Staind, 3 Doors Down, Evanescence, Aerosmith
Sounds Like	Hole, Seether, Veruca Salt
Record Label	unsigned
Type of Label	None

Figure 8.37 Bands have General Info tables, which behave the same way as Interests tables.

For layout tweaking purposes, both of these areas are referred to as Interests tables, and you are not limited to the fields MySpace gives you. You can add more fields of your choosing. The code to accomplish this looks like:

```
</td>
</tr>
<tr>
<td valign="top" align="left" width="100" bgcolor="b1d0f0">
<span" class="lightbluetext8">INSERT TABLE TITLE</span></td>
<td style="WORD-WRAP: break-word" width="175" bgcolor="d5e8fb">
INSERT TEXT OR MEDIA HERE
```

So let's put it into practice. For this example, we'll add Collaborators to your band's General Info section after Band Members. Here's how it's done.

Go into Edit Profile mode > Band Details > Members. Paste the following code at the bottom of the Members field, below any text you want to appear in the Band Members section (see Figure 8.38).

```
</td>
</tr>
<tr>
<td valign="top" align="left" width="100" bgcolor="b1d0f0">
<span class="lightbluetext8"> Collaborators </span></td>
<td style="WORD-WRAP: break-word" width="175" bgcolor="d5e8fb">
```

Sly Winkert (charts)
April Tu (string arrangements)
Chad Millar (producer)

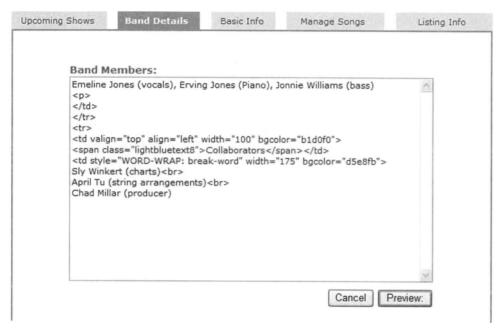

Figure 8.38 Create a new field in your Band Details table by adding the appropriate code after your bio.

When you hit Preview, the resulting page will look odd, but don't worry, because it's not a true representation of what it will look like in your actual profile (see Figure 8.39). Click Submit and then reload your profile to see the changes. You'll notice that the new Collaborators field

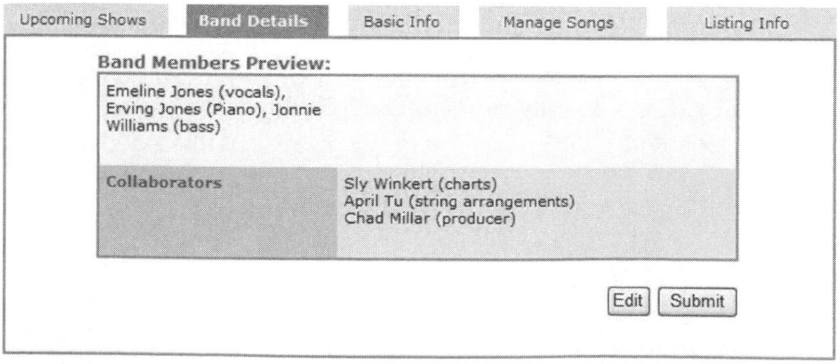

Figure 8.39 The Collaborators field appears in the preview. It won't look quite like this in the actual profile, however.

appears below the Band Members field and has taken on the formatting and style of whatever layout code you've previously entered into the Bio section (see Figure 8.40). Use the afore-mentioned code to add as many fields as you like. You can even add small images instead of text by using <img src> tags, if you prefer.

Fran Vincent: General Info	
Member Since	3/24/2006
Band Members	Emeline Jones (vocals), Erving Jones (Piano), Jonnie Williams (bass)
Collaborators	Sly Winkert (charts) April Tu (string arrangements) Chad Millar (producer)
Influences	Diana Krall, Ella Fitzgerald, Dean Martin, Frank Sinatra, Raul Midon, Eva Cassidy, Julie London, Keely Smith
Sounds Like	Kristen Chenoweth, Linda Eder, Renee Fleming, Maria Callas
Type of Label	None

Figure 8.40   Now Collaborators appears below Band Members in the General Info table.

Adding Content Tables or Sections

The sections that appear throughout regular and band profiles are also referred to as *content tables*. The About (or Bio) section is an example of a default content table in a music profile. In a regular profile, About Me and Who I'd Like to Meet are default content tables. Again, you are not restricted to these default sections. You can create more and call them whatever you want! Here's the code to do it:

```
</td>
</tr>
</table>
</td>
</tr>
</table>
<br />
<table bordercolor="ffcc99" cellspacing="0" cellpadding="0" width="435"
bgcolor="ffcc99" border="0">
<tr>
```

```
<td class="text" valign="center" align="left" width="300" bgcolor="ffcc99"
height="17"  style="word-wrap:break-word">   <span  class="-
whitetext12">INSERT SECTION TITLE HERE
</span></td>
</tr>
<tr>
<td>
<table  bordercolor="000000"  cellspacing="3"  cellpadding="3"  width="435"
align="center" bgcolor="ffffff" border="0"
<td valign="top" align="center" width="435" bgcolor="ffffff" style="word-wrap:
break-word">
INSERT TEXT OR MEDIA HERE
```

Similar to constructing another interest table, the content table code will be placed in the field *after* which you want the new section to appear. In a music profile, there's really only one main section—that's About, also called Bio. For our example, we'll add a section for Media to our band page. Paste this code at the end of your Bio section (see Figure 8.41):

```
</td>
</tr>
</table>
</td>
</tr>
</table>
<br />
<table bordercolor="ffcc99" cellspacing="0" cellpadding="0" width="435"
bgcolor="ffcc99" border="0"
<tr>
<td class="text" valign="center" align="left" width="300" bgcolor="ffcc99" height="17"
style="word-wrap:break-word">   <span class="whitetext12">
Media</span></td>
</tr>
<tr>
<td>
<table bordercolor="000000" cellspacing="3" cellpadding="3" width="435" align="-
center" bgcolor="ffffff" border="0">
<td valign="top align="center" width="435" bgcolor="ffffff" style="word-wrap:break--
word">
Excerpts from interviews, positive reviews, etc. would appear here.
```

This new Media table now appears on your profile (see Figure 8.42). You can put whatever you want in this section, from text to images, videos, or Flash animation. You may have

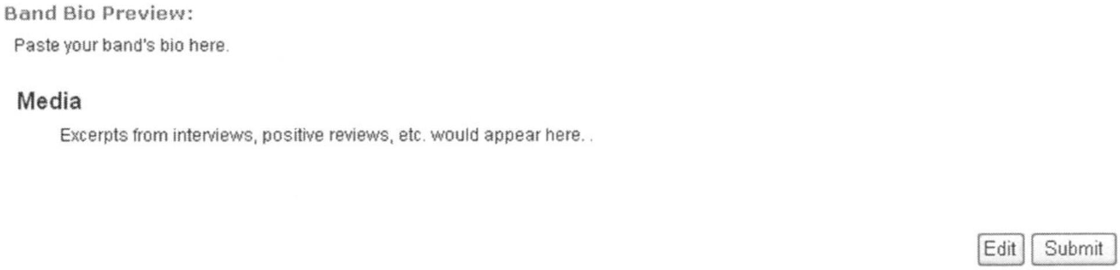

Band Bio Preview:
Paste your band's bio here.
Media
Excerpts from interviews, positive reviews, etc. would appear here. .
Edit
Submit

Figure 8.41 The preview of the new Media content table appears here.

About Fran Vincent
Paste your band's bio here.
Media
Excerpts from interviews, positive reviews, etc. would appear here. .

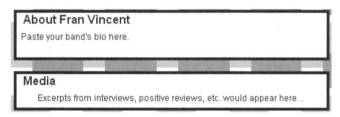

Figure 8.42 Now you have a new field in your profile. It will take the formatting of whatever layout codes you have input.

noticed that the code for both interest and content tables contains "bordercolors" and "bgcolors." The values inputted here tell the tables to take the colors of the default MySpace profile. However, any premade or custom layout codes loaded into your profile will override these default values.

Customizing Contact Tables

Your contact table (or *contact box,* as it is sometimes called) is that small section containing links to Send Message, Add to Friends, and Forward to Friend, among others. You're not stuck with the default. You can actually create your very own contact table or use a premade one.

To make your own contact table, you obviously have to be pretty good with graphics programs. So, assuming that you are, your contact table should be about 300 pixels wide and 155 pixels tall. A default contact table appears in Figure 8.43. You'll have to keep the same position of these links in your new contact table. The fun part is that you can call these links whatever you want. The system will maintain the links in the same location. All you have to do is create the artwork. Figure 8.44 is a contact table I created. As you can see, I played with the wording. You can add a background image or color to your contact table design if desired.

If you don't have graphic software to create a contact table, you can go to a site that will help you create it. I find that the contact table generator at freecodesource.com does a nice job. (The

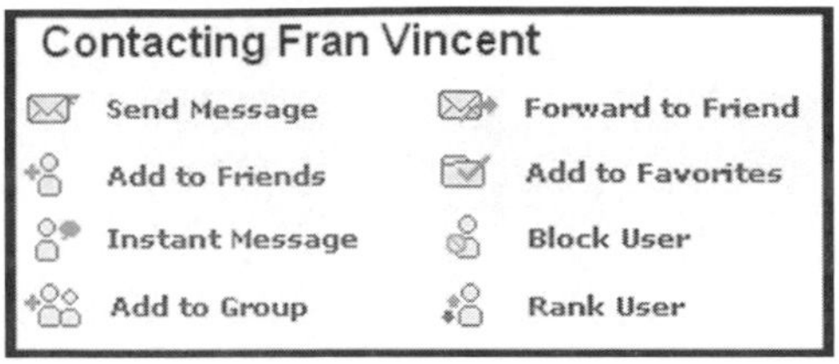

Figure 8.43 The default contact table always contains these same links. Your new contact table must do the same.

Figure 8.44 This is a custom contact table. Note that the links are in the same place, but they are labeled in a more fun way.

shortcut URL to take you right to the contact table page is tinyurl.com/da6mph.) You'll see in Figure 8.45 that the site lets you switch up the fonts, change the contact table text, and load a background image. It then gives you the code to plug into the Bio section of your profile.

Even if you create your contact table on your own graphic software at home, as I did, you can still use this very same link at freecodesource.com to get the code to load your contact table. When you are finished designing your contact table, save it as a JPEG or a GIF image and load it up to your photo hosting site of choice. Copy the URL. Go to the freecodesource.com link, and, where it asks for a background image, provide the URL of your newly designed contact table. Delete the text from the fields Send Message, Forward to Friend, and so on (see Figure 8.46). Click the Generate button and copy the provided code. Paste this code into your Bio section, below your Bio text but before any other code.

You may also notice that some profiles don't have contact tables at all, but instead these links appear toward the top of the profile. These are special customizations, and you should seek the help of a designer if this is the route you want to go.

Profile Banners

Adding banners to your profile can help you use underutilized space and advertise new albums, merchandise, ringtones, tours, song downloads, and more. This section will show you a few different types of banners and how to use them.

Figure 8.45   The contact table generator at freecodesource.com does a good job of helping you create your very own contact table.

Top Banners

Bands seem to love to add their own snazzy banners above or below the MySpace banner advertisement that appears atop every page. These are referred to as *top banners*. Browse through major-label artists' profiles, and you'll see many top banners. First you have to create a banner, and then you can pop it into your profile. Use this code to do it:

<style type="text/css">
body{background-position:top center;margin-top: *ENTER HEIGHT OF BANNER IN PIXELS HERE;*}
div.topbanner {top: 0;left: 49%;margin-left: -225px;
width: 100%;height: *ENTER HEIGHT OF BANNER IN PIXELS HERE*px;position: absolute;}
</style>
<div class="topbanner"><a href="INSERT LINK TO YOUR OFFICIAL WEB SITE"><IMG SRC="*INSERT URL OF YOUR BANNER IMAGE*" border="0">
</A></div>

Figure 8.46   You can use a contact table generator to get the code for a contact table you created yourself. Just be sure to delete all the text from the generator's text fields.

The first time you are asked to enter the height of the banner in pixels, insert a number only, without *px* after it. The second time the code calls for it, enter the same number with *px* right after it (for example, 150px). The margin-left: value is used to position your banner left to right. The lower the value, the farther left the banner will be. In the example, we used -225px, which placed our banner for Ariel's Closet in the center of the profile (see Figure 8.47). You will have to play with the value to get your banner example where you want it. Place the code into the very bottom of your Bio field. Load it up and see how it looks. Play with the margin-left: values as needed.

Figure 8.47   The top banner for Ariel's Closet is placed above the MySpace advertisement and doesn't interfere with it in any way.

Extended Network Banners

Musician profiles don't have extended network banners, but regular profiles do. If you're using a regular profile, consider replacing the extended network text with a banner. This extended network section appears on every regular profile, and most consider it wasted space (see Figure 8.48). Don't let it just sit there. Make a banner announcing a new product or service, or do an image banner that fits into the look of your layout.

You can create your own banner with your graphics program, or you can use a banner generator online. To create your own banner, keep the width between 435 and 475 pixels and the height between 60 and 75 pixels. Use the following code:

```
<style type="text/css">
table table table td {vertical-align:top!important;}
span.blacktext12 {visibility:visible!important;
background-color:transparent;
background-image:url("ENTER THE URL OF YOUR BANNER IMAGE");
background-repeat:no-repeat; background-position:center center;
letter-spacing:-0.5px; width:ENTER BANNER WIDTHpx;
height:ENTER BANNER HEIGHTpx;
display:block !important; } </style><br>
```

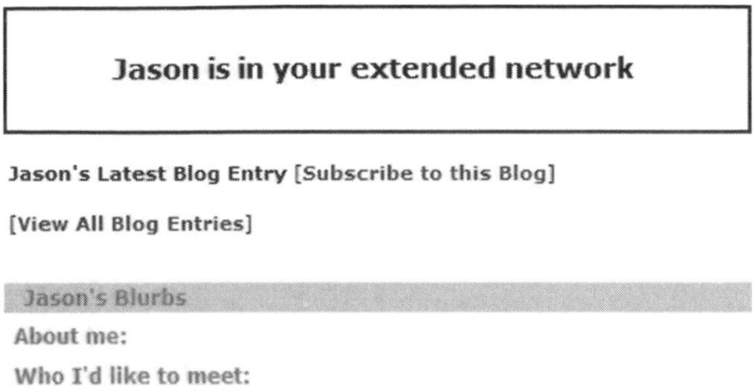

Jason is in your extended network

Jason's Latest Blog Entry [Subscribe to this Blog]

[View All Blog Entries]

Jason's Blurbs

About me:

Who I'd like to meet:

Figure 8.48   The extended network banner is another MySpace constant, but it can be covered up with a more useful banner.

Change the values as indicated and paste this code into the end of your About Me section.

You can also make extended network banners with the help of online generators. Try www.mywackospace.com/extended-banner-editor to design yours (see Figure 8.49). After you've made your unique banner, the site will generate the code you need to place it in your profile.

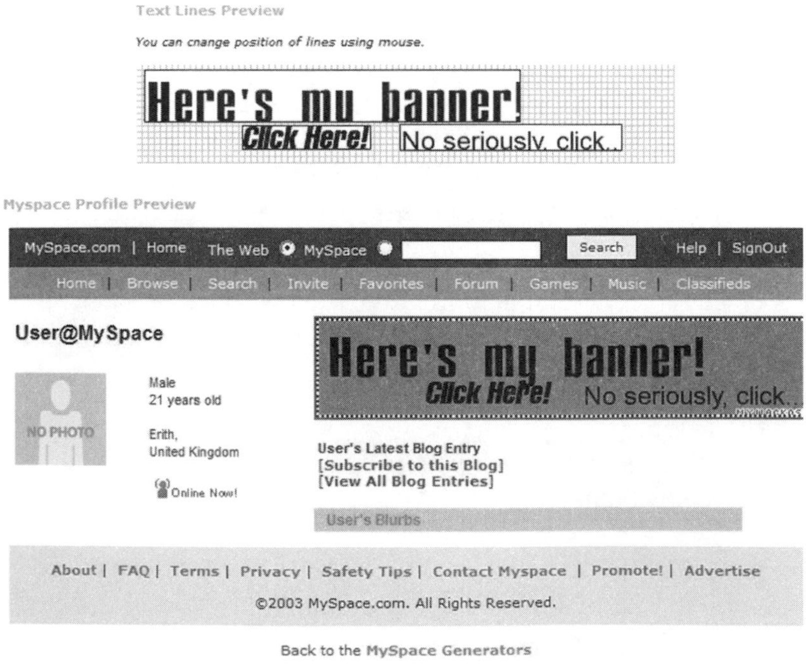

Figure 8.49   The extended network banner generator at MyWackoSpace.com shows you just what your banner will look by using a sample profile.

Other Banners

You can pop banners anywhere in your profile. In fact, you'll notice that some musician profiles utilize a series of banners before the main profile (see Figure 8.50). And some even have smaller banners peppered throughout the profile (Figure 8.51). Advertise merchandise or link to your official website or even download sites that carry your music.

Figure 8.50   Artist Ludacris has two banners below his top banner and above the main profile.

We previously discussed in this chapter how to add interest tables and sections. At that time, I showed you how to add text headers to these new sections. If you want to make your new sections jazzier, try creating a graphic banner to use as a header instead (as shown in Figure 8.51). Instead of putting text in the spot where you are to enter a title, create an img src tag in its place.

MyBannerMaker.com is flexible generator that makes banners of all different sizes (see Figure 8.52). You can use these banners anywhere in your profile.

In Chapter 12, I'll show you how to add a text box to your profile so users can grab your video code and embed your video into their profile. You can do the same thing with banners. Want fans to display your banners on their site? Give them the code by using the text-box tweak discussed in Chapter 12, in the "More Video Tips" section (see Figure 8.53).

More MySpace Toys

Is your new layout all finished? Before you get comfortable, check out this list of other things you could do to your profile. For links, check out the appendixes or run your own web searches for code.

- **Move stuff.** Don't like where your music player sits? Visit Pimpwebpage.com/band.php for codes to move around the music player and other elements of your profile.

- **Online Now icons.** Ditch the default Online Now icon and try one that says "Rockin' Out!" instead. ProfileGoodies.com has a bunch to choose from.

Figure 8.51   Singer/songwriter Ingrid Michaelson has various banners and flyers dotting her profile. In this case, her banners promote tees and sheet music. You may also notice the little banner "More" that acts as a header for this newly created section.

- **Image filters.** These filters change the way your profile's images behave. For instance, you can make an image blur or flip when a mouse pointer hovers over it. Try Nackvision. com/myspace/filter/index.php.

- **Hide last login.** Trying to evade stalkers? Get some "hide last login" code to mask your MySpace activities. Go to Myspacemaster.net/myspace-codes-hide-last-login.

- **Add an email signup list.** Plug an email form into your profile or create a link to your main mailing list signup on your official website. Get yours from ReverbNation.com,

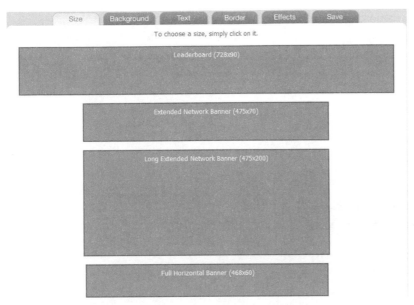

Figure 8.52   MyBannerMaker.com makes banners of many different sizes. You can use these almost anywhere on your profile.

Fanbridge.com, or a variety of other email marketing sites, such as ConstantContact. com or VerticalResponse.com

- **Sell your music downloads.** Plug in icons to where people can buy your music, such as iTunes, Amazon.com, CDBaby, and so on.

- **Wireless alerts and voicemail.** Let fans leave messages for you or sign up for your text message alerts. Visit Saynow.com and Mozes.com.

- **Other online properties.** Create icons to direct fans to your Facebook fan page, Twitter page, blog, and other important profiles, or simply download ready-made ones from iconspedia.com.

- **Podcast.** Link to your podcast and let fans stream or download your very own radio show.

- **Sell merch.** Direct fans to where they can buy your tees, caps, and hoodies. CafePress. com is a good place to start.

- **Offer ringtones and mobile content.** Get fans to purchase your ringtones, mobile videos, and wallpapers. Oodles of mobile marketing sites are popping up all over the Net.

- **Add another MP3 player.** This is really cool for regular account users. Flash-based MP3 players are all over the web in various styles. Some look like iPods and others like '80s boom boxes. Surf over to MyFlashFetish.com.

Figure 8.53   Artist Ingrid Michaelson showcases a banner for her European tour, as well as a smaller banner touting her new album complete with links to buy. Fans can then grab the code and post it to their MySpace pages, in bulletins, in emails and comments, or on their own websites.

So many tweaks, but only so many hours in the day. Looks like you've got a lot of work ahead of you! Don't take a break just yet. Head over to Chapter 9 and learn how to add friends and customize your friend space.

9 You Gotta Have Friends

People often wonder how a website started by two guys looking to keep their buddies in the know about the L.A. club scene could balloon into a community of hundreds of millions in just a few short years. The answer is friends. What started as a select few grew as their immediate pals invited their friends, who invited more friends, and so forth. This grassroots type of marketing is what makes MySpace and other social communities so attractive. People go where their friends are. And they make that community thrive by persuading more of their real-life friends to join, as well as making new online contacts. As a musician, you will be doing the same.

This chapter is all about friends—what a Friends list is, how to add and deny friends, how to customize and manage your Friends list, and how to block abusive friends. In this chapter, we will discuss how to:

- Make a list of people you know, including friends, family, coworkers, classmates, and industry contacts
- Use MySpace to search for friends by email address
- Add your favorite bands, comedians, and celebrities
- Add other musicians in the same genre as you, as well as complementary genres
- Add the friends of the aforementioned musicians
- Employ the use of a friend adder (optional)
- Have a plan to add friends regularly
- Work your MySpace URL into all your materials
- Brainstorm ways to attract people to your MySpace profile

The Friends List

In the MySpace world, everyone has a Friends list. It is a compilation of people who have requested that you add them to your list and those who have approved your friend request.

The list appears as a collection of thumbnail pictures just above the comments section of your profile page. Some may be actual friends that you know, while others may be strangers you only know in the Internet world. Adding and requesting friends is how you build a following in this online community.

Building a strong Friends list is important because this list becomes your marketing audience. You can post bulletins, which are like broadcast emails, to everyone on your list at once. And you and your friends can leave comments for each other on your profiles. You can encourage the friends on your list to add your music to their profile, tell others about you, and more. Plus, being on a Friends list is like being a part of an exclusive club. Always remind yourself that building a strong following through your Friends list is an important goal of every MySpace marketer.

Your Friend Space and Tom

In your profile control panel, you'll see a section at the bottom right called *Friend Space* (see Figure 9.1). This is where thumbnail pictures of your friends and fans will appear. The options in the Friend Space section allow you to control various functions of your Friends list, including deciding who appears on your profile, deleting and organizing friends, and viewing their birthdays. It also shows how many friends you have accumulated. Users visiting your page will see your Friends list as well. Your profile will only display so many friend thumbnails at once, but visitors can click on View All to see more.

Friend Space (1)

Your Friend Space shows friends you've added on MySpace. Tom is your first friend.

Find friends, including classmates, you know who are already on MySpace!

Tom

Tom Anderson

View: All

Figure 9.1   Your Friend Space allows you to control aspects of your Friends list and shows pictures of all of your friends, including Tom, your first MySpace pal.

If you've just opened up a musician account, you'll notice that a mysterious stranger has popped onto your Friends list. Hmmm . . . you don't remember adding him? This is Tom, and he is everyone's very first MySpace friend. Tom is one of the site's founders and appears automatically in every new account that is created. You'll also have an email from him, welcoming you to the community. From time to time, Tom will post bulletins and notices to keep the community informed about new MySpace developments, system glitches, and the like—as well as the occasional hilarious video or joke!

Finding Friends

Now that you've met Tom, it's time to fill in your Friends list!

Start with the People You Already Know

You'll want to make sure that before you invite anyone to your profile, you've got your music and other content already uploaded, and you have done some housekeeping so your page properly represents you and your music. Assuming you've done this, let's keep going!

The very first step in building your Friends list for your new MySpace profile is to gather email addresses of your current real-life friends, family, acquaintances, and fans. MySpace offers a tool to import addresses from your AOL, Gmail, Yahoo!, and other accounts. In your home control panel, look for the Friends link in the blue navigation bar. Click here, and from the resulting drop-down menu, choose Find Friends, as pictured in Figure 9.2.

Figure 9.2   The Find Friends link is located under Friends >Find Friends in the blue navigation bar. A link to Find Friends is also seen in your Friend Space.

Now that you are on the Find Friends page, you can upload your address books and search for friends already on MySpace or invite those who aren't yet members (see Figures 9.3 and 9.4).

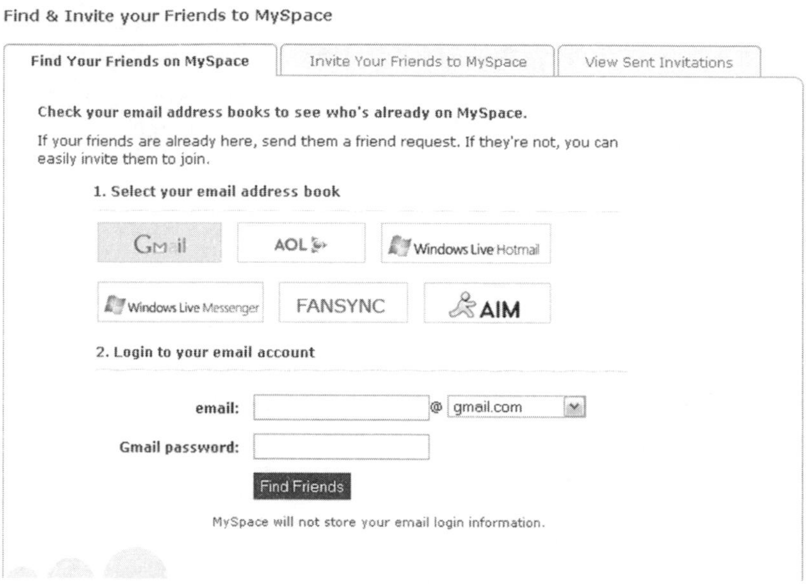

Find & Invite your Friends to MySpace

Find Your Friends on MySpace	Invite Your Friends to MySpace	View Sent Invitations

Check your email address books to see who's already on MySpace.

If your friends are already here, send them a friend request. If they're not, you can easily invite them to join.

1. Select your email address book

Gmail   AOL   Windows Live Hotmail

Windows Live Messenger   FANSYNC   AIM

2. Login to your email account

email: [   ] @ [gmail.com ▾]

Gmail password: [   ]

[Find Friends]

MySpace will not store your email login information.

Figure 9.3   Enter your login information for the shown accounts, and MySpace will download your address book and send each person on your list an invitation to visit your profile and be your friend. The newly added feature, FANSYNC, lets you upload your large database of fan emails (500 to 25,000) directly into your account, and MySpace will find everyone on the list who is already a MySpace member and invite those who aren't.

Find & Invite your Friends to MySpace

Find Your Friends on MySpace	Invite Your Friends to MySpace	View Sent Invitations

Invite your friends to become your MySpace friends

Your friend will automatically be added to your friends list when they join!

Enter email addresses:

Subject: MySpace for Musicians invites you to MySpace

From: retro_marketing@

To: [   ]
(Separate multiple
emails with comma)

☑ Show my full name in this invitation: **MySpace for Musicians**

[Send Invitation]

———————— OR ————————

⁂ Send a Custom Invitation Link

Send friends your custom invitation link by copy and pasting it into your own email application. When your friend joins, you will automatically be connected:

[http://www.myspace.com/reloc.cfm?]

Figure 9.4   Copy and paste email addresses of friends, fans, and others you know, inviting them to your page.

Send your invite to everyone you know. Enter emails you've gathered at gigs and from fans who have provided their email address to you through your website email list or by purchasing online merchandise or music from you.

If someone already has a MySpace account using that email address, the system will find that person. And if your email buddy doesn't have a profile, MySpace will invite that person to join. Once the person joins, he or she will be automatically added as your friend. It's a nifty little process that saves a ton of time in searching for people one by one.

If you want to check and see whether someone in particular is on MySpace without sending them an official invite yet, go to Friends > Find Friends on the medium blue navigation bar toward the top of the page and search for them. This can be particularly helpful if you don't have someone's email address. For instance, look for venue and artist managers, booking agents, music reviewers, and radio DJs whom you have met along the way—all are good candidates for your Friends list.

Sending Friend Requests

When you search by email address or name, the results page will show the person's thumbnail picture (if the person has a MySpace account) and some options for what to do next. You can add them as a friend or send a message right from the search results (see Figure 9.5).

 Nazia
Dallas, TEXAS
www.myspace.com/naziamusic

 Add to friends
Send message

Figure 9.5   A successful search will return results that look like this. Add them as a friend by clicking the link on the right.

You can send a friend request to any user you encounter on MySpace by first going to their profile. Once you're on that person's profile, there will be contact box (sometimes called a *contact table*), usually located below the person's picture. This contact section appears on every profile and contains all the functions related to contacting the user or saving his or her information for later reference. Some users have created custom layouts that remove the contact table and display the contact links elsewhere on the page, usually toward the top of the profile in a linear fashion.

To send the person a friend request, click on Add to Friends (see Figure 9.6). Note that the contact box seen in Figure 9.6 is the standard-style box provided by MySpace. However, users can create customized contact boxes that may say something similar, such as Add Me or Be Friends. The words may be different, but the function is the same.

The system will ask you to confirm that you want to add this person as your friend. Click Add to Friends to proceed. MySpace will notify the user that you have requested to be added as a friend. The MySpacer will then have the option to accept or deny your request.

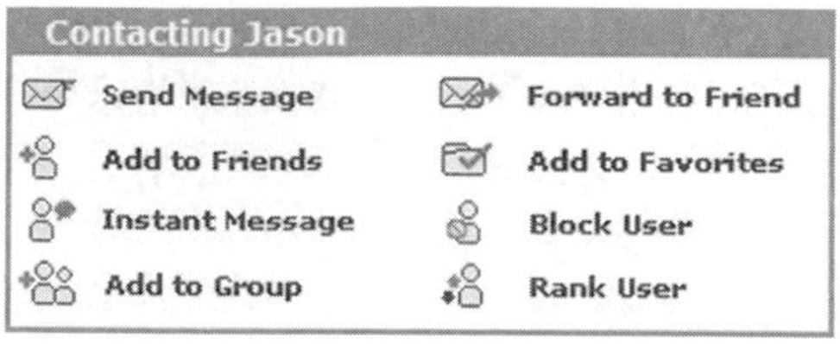

Figure 9.6 Send a friend request by clicking Add to Friends in the contact box.

Some users have an additional privacy setting that requires requesters to know either their last name or their email address. The system will prompt you for that information if it is required. As a musician, make sure that *you* have not set your profile to only accept friend requests from fans who know your email address or last name. Of course, few fans are going to know your email address and the last name of the band member who is maintaining the profile. It's a silly move I've seen by artists, a particular pet peeve of mine. If your goal is to build a fan base, you don't want to create obstacles for your fans. Let them add you freely!

While adding friends, you may notice that some users block bands from sending them friend requests entirely. If that is the case, the system will inform you of this. You can either move on to friendlier pastures or send the person an email introducing yourself. There are fellow MySpace bands who also block other bands from adding them. Personally, I think this is a mistake. Musicians have their favorite bands just like any other fan, and bands *should* be networking with one another and creating alliances.

MySpace is still the best place to discover indie music and keep up on chart-topping artists. But, not everyone on MySpace is interested in music. Don't take rejection personally.... There are millions of other people on the service who might be future fans!

Expanding Your List

Now that you've sent friend requests to people you know in the real world, it's time to venture out and make new friends. By this point you hopefully have built up a respectable-sized Friends list filled with people you know and fans who already know you. But if you don't know many people and you are a new band with few contacts, you needn't worry. We'll explore ways to build up that Friends list to rock-star proportions!

Start with the Entertainers You Know and Love

The ugly truth is that people like to join band profiles that already have a lot of friends. They click on a profile, and if it says, "Rock Band has 5 friends," the impression is that this profile and the music aren't all that interesting. Yet you have to get people to join in order to have a lot of friends that will attract others in the first place. It's sort of like a teenage party—no one wants to go if they don't think there'll be a lot of people there. It may be unfair and reek of a high school popularity contest, but when you are new to MySpace, you have to work at building up your Friends list quickly.

The fastest way to do this—after starting with people you already know, of course—is to seek out bands, comedians, and filmmakers whose work you like. Most entertainers will add anyone who asks. So go after them first! Almost all of the major label artists and entertainers you know and love will be on MySpace (see Figure 9.7).

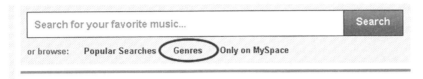

Figure 9.7   On the MySpace Music home page, you'll find the Genres list below the artist search bar (as of this writing). Look for bands that are similar or complementary to yours.

Your Friends Are My Friends

Pay close attention to artists in the same or a complementary genre as your music. For example, if you're an R&B singer, add R&B, gospel, hip-hop, and soul artists, too. Their audience is your audience. Once you are their friend, send friend requests to people on their lists as well. Do not, however, approach this in an assembly-line fashion. It is important to actually look at each person's profile, paying close attention to anything that would indicate he or she won't add anyone who doesn't have the courtesy to offer a polite hello. There are many people on MySpace who do not appreciate getting friend requests from strangers who don't bother to send them an introductory email (see Figure 9.8). They see these requests as an insincere intrusion, meant only to rack up thumbnails on a list. Instead of offending someone's sensibilities and raising their ire, respect their wishes and send them a brief but sincere email saying you saw them on so-and-so's profile and you thought they might like your music, too. Or, send them a message to accompany your friend request. You may get ignored, but then again maybe you will earn a new fan.

> I love to make new friends, however now that I've gotten the hang of this thing, I no longer just approve friend requests from strangers. So, please EMAIL ME FIRST to say Hi and tell me about yourself before asking me to add you to my friend list. Unless I already know you or your make some kind of effort to say hello, there is no chance you will be added.

Figure 9.8   Picky potential friends won't tolerate a friend request from a stranger, so pay attention and remember to say hello first!

So start browsing the music and comedian directories for your favorites as well as compatible-genre artists and send them friend requests. Make a concentrated effort in the beginning to add friends quickly, followed by a consistent ongoing plan to contact new people every week. Then watch your Friends list grow into a happening party that everyone will want to attend!

Let MySpace Suggest Your Friends

Pay attention to the spot in your home control that says People You May Know (located on the right-hand side of the panel as of this writing). MySpace suggests people it thinks you may already know or would like to know based on mutual friends, interests, and geographic area. I've found tons of great contacts this way, as MySpace has suggested local music companies, venues, journalists, and more. A list of People You May Know also comes up after you've sent a friend request, which is very handy when you're trying to build a Friends list and need help expanding it.

Friend Bots, the Incredible Adding Machines

For the serious music marketer with little time to spare, the use of a friend bot can be a great way to add lots of friends in a short amount of time. A friend bot is a software program you install on your computer that automates adding friends, sending messages, leaving comments, and posting bulletins. You can go to any MySpace page and tell the program to add everyone on that page, and it will do so. It can also automatically email a prewritten message to everyone who accepts your friend request. Some bots even allow you to post comments to many friends at once, saving time and hassle. Another perk is that some of them will keep backups of your Friends list so that if your account is ever compromised or deleted and you need to start all over, you know who was on your list, and you can add the same people back in.

Friend bots are often referred to as *friend adders*. Very few, if any, are free, so it is a small investment to make toward marketing and promotions. Because they tend to come and go, I'll refrain from listing any here. Instead, do a web search for "MySpace friend adder" to see what's available. While a friend adder can be a time-saver, it does take away the personal touch and doesn't allow you to make a unique pitch to each and every potential fan.

It's important to note that, per the terms of use, MySpace does not allow the use of bots to add friends or send mass messages or comments because of spamming concerns. Using a friend adder program is a violation of the MySpace rules, and your account will be deleted if you are discovered. In recent years, MySpace seems to be cracking down on developers who offer adders to the public. You want to make sure that if you use an adder program or some other bot program, you do not add, send, or comment to more than 150 to 250 friends in one day. Some people may tell you that up to 400 per day is acceptable, but the truth is anything more than 100 will start to draw attention to you. Anything more than 150 or maybe 200, and you may be flagged as a spammer, and your account may be frozen, suspended, or deleted. If you decide to use an adder program, be aware of the risk, back up your Friends list and all your MySpace profile content, and proceed at your own peril!

All Aboard the Friend Train!

Some people add the masses to their Friends list by using a friend train. It's also called a *MySpace train* or a *whore train*. (We won't even go into why it's called that last one!) When you "ride" a friend train, you post the friend train code into a bulletin and send it out to your friends, asking them to add everyone on the train. You will now show up on the train, and people will post similar bulletins asking everyone to add you. I personally don't recommend taking this approach. First, MySpace seems to be employing more filters to disallow the kind of code needed for a friend train bulletin post. Second, although you can inflate your friend numbers, it doesn't necessarily mean you're actually targeting people who might be interested in your music and who will attend a show or make a purchase. I also think it's just plain tacky for a band to do this. However, if you're bent on giving it a go, do a web search on "myspace train," "friend train," or "whore train," and you'll find many to choose from.

Add Me Groups

There's a discussion group for everything! There are even groups whose sole purpose is to get everyone to add the members to your Friends list. Like friend trains, you're not getting any kind of targeted audience, but your Friends list numbers will grow. For some, this is a beginning tactic just to have *some* friends so their list doesn't look so empty and won't scare away would-be fans. To find Add Me groups, go to the More link in the medium-blue navigation bar and then pick Groups. On the resulting page is a groups search box. Type "add me," and voila! You'll see many groups that are dedicated to adding friends. Follow the group's instructions, which are usually just posting a message that says "Add me!"

Add Me Links

Another way to encourage friend adds is to post an Add to Friends link on your profile below your bio text. You can also post this type of link in any comments you make to others or embed it into emails you send out to non-friends. It's just another way to put your add link out there so it's readily available for users to find.

In Chapter 8, we took a look at how to create links and how to locate a friend ID. And in Chapter 10, "Comments, Anyone?" we will look at posting comments in more depth. You can consult this how-to information for more instruction on embedding the link in a profile or comment. Basically, this is the HTML you'll need:

1.   First, create an <img src> tag for the Add to Friends icon. We will use the same graphic that appears in the contact table of your profile. Currently, the Add to Friends artwork is located at http://x.myspace.com/images/profile/friend_1.gif. Windows users find this by right-clicking on the graphic and then clicking Properties.

2.   The tag will therefore look like <img src=http://x.myspace.com/images/profile/friend_1.gif>

3.   Now, take this link and add your friend ID where the Xs are: http://collect.myspace.com/index.cfm?fuseaction=invite.addfriend_verify&friendID=XXXX. Your ID number maybe longer than four numbers. (For helping in finding your ID, see Chapter 8 under "Finding the Friend ID" section.)

4. Enclose the <img src> tag with a hyperlink tag using the preceding formula and with your friend ID in place of the Xs. We'll also center it. Now the tag will look like this:

    ```
    <center>
    <a href="http://collect.myspace.com/index.cfm?fuseaction=invite.addfriend_verify&
    friendID=XXXX> <img src=http://x.myspace.com/images/profile/friend_1.gif></a>
    </center>
    ```

5. Note that the code does *not* include any quotation marks (" ") around the URLs. This works best for the MySpace environment. If you have any coding problems, try the URLs with quotation marks. Remember, MySpace can be finicky sometimes, so you might have to experiment.

6. Embed the code into your profile or a comment. Users will then see the Add to Friends icon (see Figure 9.9), and when they click it, they will be able to ask you if you'd like to be that user's friend!

Figure 9.9   Your Add to Friends icon embedded in your profile copy will look something like this.

Fans Spread the Word

One of the best ways to develop qualified leads is to come up with a program where your current fans can easily evangelize you to their friends. Put up a banner on your profile along with the code that fans can copy and paste into their own profiles. (See Chapter 8 for instructions on how to do this.) Invite fans through bulletins and comments to add your music to their profile playlists and to direct their friends to your page. Personally email your best fans (those who comment or email you) and invite them to help you spread the word. You can also create giveaways for fans that bring the most new friends to your page and reward them with buttons, stickers, posters, CDs, or other merch.

Partner with Other Artists

Another great way to develop a fan base is to cross-promote with another artist whose fans might like your music and vice versa. This tactic would only work with an artist on a similar level as you. Diddy is not going to plug your band on his MySpace. But find another up-and-coming artist in the same career stage as you with a growing fan base and introduce yourself.

If that person digs your music too, propose that you will put a banner on your profile promoting that person if he will do the same for you. This lends credibility to both of you because fans are more likely to take music recommendations of a band they like. And at some point you may even explore the idea of working together on some other level, such as writing, recording, or even performing together.

Webpage Icons

Remember to put MySpace icons and other invitations to become friends on MySpace right onto your official home page, blog, email signature, and other web profiles.

It's Not You, It's Me

One's Friends list is a dynamic entity. It changes all the time. People come and go. They lose interest or become overwhelmed with their burdensome lists and start to clean house. Often, bands they don't follow regularly are the first to get the ax. When you have tons of friends, you may see the number of them fluctuate here and there. But with so many on the list, you probably won't notice who has left.

Then, there are those who from the beginning have blocked all friend requests from bands and musical artists in their Account Settings. Usually, this is because they don't want to be inundated by requests from bands they don't know. As mentioned before, you can opt to send them a pleasant email introducing yourself, asking them to check out your music and add you if they like. However, if they're not interested, don't take it personally—just move on. You have more than 200 million other people from whom to choose!

Approving and Denying Friends

Requesting friends is a natural and expected part of being in the MySpace community. You are sure to get requests from people who happen upon your page while browsing the music area, see you in another's Friends list, or hear about your music from others. You will also likely get requests from people who are interested in selling you products and services, including porn and live webcams. Although you are in the business of promoting your music, you don't have to approve every request that comes your way. Use your discretion.

When someone asks you to be their friend, you will see a notification in your profile control panel's Alert section (see Figure 9.10). Click on the notice to go to your Requests page in your Mail Center.

You will see a picture of the person requesting your friendship, as well as their handle, and buttons to Approve, Deny, or Mark as Spam; the option to add them to your Activity Stream; and a link to Send a Message (see Figure 9.11). You may even have a brief message from the person that was sent along with the friend request.

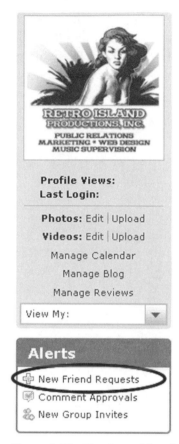

Figure 9.10   You have friends! MySpace lets you know when others want to be your friend.

This is the same screen others see when you send them a friend request. Most of the time you will be approving requests, but when you get one that looks fishy, as if it's for a product or service with which you don't want to be associated, hit the Deny button. The requester does not receive notice that you denied the request. The system is discreet in that regard. The request to you simply disappears from the person's console. Often, that is that. Sometimes the persistent ones will keep sending you friend requests and emails. You have the option of blocking them from ever contacting you again, which is explored at the end of this chapter, under the "Deleting and Blocking" section. You should be wary of anything that looks like it might be a webcam/porn site, as many of these profiles contain hacker codes that could damage your computer or hijack your MySpace account.

It is easy to approve or deny several requests at once by checking off the users in your Friend Request Manager and then hitting the Approve Selected or Deny Selected button at the bottom of the console.

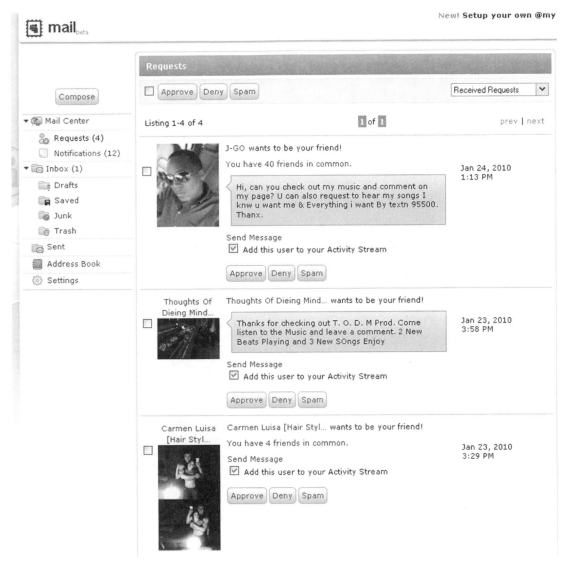

Figure 9.11   Your Requests page keeps track of everyone wanting to be in your inner circle.

The Top of the Heap

Once upon a time, MySpace allowed you to designate your Top 8 friends who would appear on your profile's first page. It is considered a coveted spot to be in the Top Friends area of someone's profile. MySpace has since expanded options to allow up to the Top 40 friends to be displayed on the main page of your profile. How many people and whom you choose to display on your profile's My Friend Space is entirely up to you. Those who don't appear there are accessible when users click on View All at the bottom of your Top Friends list on your profile. People may also choose to view your friends who are online now, and your recently added friends ("new").

By default, friends generally appear in the order they were added. To reorganize your top friends, click on the link Change My Top Friends in your control panel's My Friend Space section (see Figure 9.12). Make sure the Customize button is clicked. Then, choose the number of top friends you want to display from the drop-down menu on the page that appears. You'll see all your friends' thumbnail pics displayed. Browse through your pages or use the search option to find and place friends in the order you want them to appear in your Top Friends list. The Top Friends spots are highlighted in red. Once you're satisfied, click the Save Top Friends button, and your new Top Friends list will be complete!

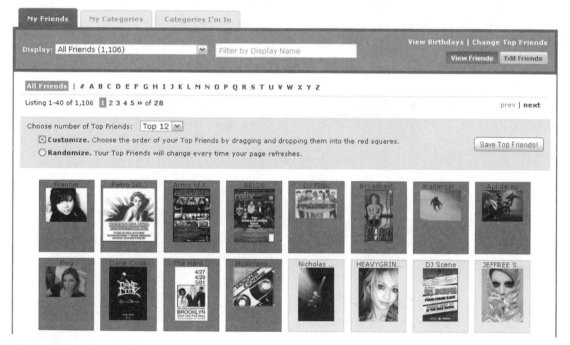

Figure 9.12   Change your Top Friends list as often as you like. Even use the list to reward loyal fans.

Another option is to "randomize" your Top Friends list. Follow the same procedure, except instead of choosing friends to fill your top spots, simply choose the button that says Randomize, and the system will choose new friends for your list each time your profile is loaded.

Categories

When you click on Change My Top Friends, you'll see there is another tab on that page that says My Categories. This area allows you to create groups of friends (see Figure 9.13). For

Figure 9.13   Create categories of friends.

instance, you might create a group that says "Music Press" and put all the profiles of music magazines on your Friends list in that group. You can use categories to sort your friends for your organizational benefit. But, if you keep your groups to 60 or fewer friends each, you can actually email that group all at once by typing the group name into the To field of a MySpace message. If you add more than 60 friends to that group, you can't email them all at once (as of this writing). This is one of those times where a friend adder program is handy, as it can handle a friend category with more than 60 members. You can keep a list of friend groups on file, and when you are ready to email them, load the list into the adder program, type one email to your group into your program, and it will send to everyone in your group list all at once. Just keep the number you email in one day to fewer than 150 and remember that you use a friend adder at your own risk.

Happy Birthday

Another convenient item is the birthday list. Also in your Friend Space in your home control panel is a link to View Upcoming Birthdays. You may wonder why you care about your fans' birthdays. You should, because you can view upcoming birthdays each week (see Figure 9.14) and post a comment to each friend's profile wishing him or her a happy day. Just another way to build a relationship with your fan base and encourage goodwill!

Friend Updates and the Activity Stream

The first friend update section you are likely to encounter is the Status and Mood section. Here you can enter your status (such as "up late working") and mood (such as "cranky" or

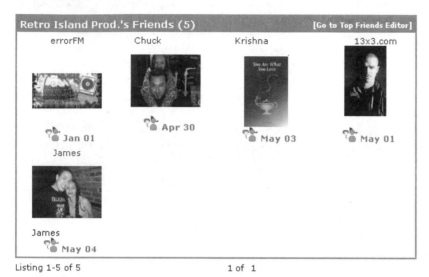

Figure 9.14   Remember your fans' birthdays. Leave them a thoughtful or fun comment during their birthday week!

"artistic"). You see the statuses/moods of friends, and when you enter yours, your fans will also see what you're up to! A great trick to minimize the number of status updates you have to enter across all your social networks is to download an app that allows you to enter a status once. The best way to do this is to first open a Twitter account, then in MySpace search for "twitter" in the apps section (see Chapter 13) and install an app that will update your MySpace status automatically when you update your Twitter status. There are apps on Facebook that will do the same thing for your FB status. Allowing Twitter to update your status on all compatible accounts will save you time and energy. Keep your status updated regularly so your fans don't think your activity is getting stale and boring.

The other friend update section is the Activity Stream, which also appears in your home control panel (see Figure 9.15). Here you see changes your friends have made to their profile. You can control what people see about you, as well as whose updates appear in your stream. In your Stream section in your home control panel, click on View All: Activities. Here in your Activity Stream page, you can browse all updates from friends and change whose updates you subscribe to, as well as what information about yourself you allow those who have subscribed to your stream to see. Click on Privacy Settings and check off all the things you want to make public (see Figure 9.16). As a band, you will probably want to keep most things public, since you want people to see your updates and you want to keep yourself in the minds of your fans.

Stream

view all: status & mood   activities

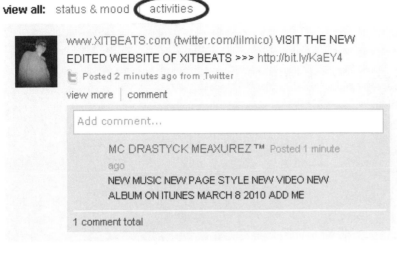

UN1QE **In ohio almost at ny**

Mood: yeeeah

Posted 6 minutes ago from Mobile

view more | comment

Midwest Music Mafia **is now friends with** Xiao Dong Wei (aka
Madame XD)

Xiao Dong Wei (aka Madame XD)

Band

7135 friends - Add to Friends

Figure 9.15   Your Activity Stream shows updates from your friends. You can unsubscribe
from receiving updates from select friends by going to View All: Activities.

Customizing Your Friends List

Your Friends list doesn't have to look like everyone else's Friends list. There are a few ways to
make yours unique.

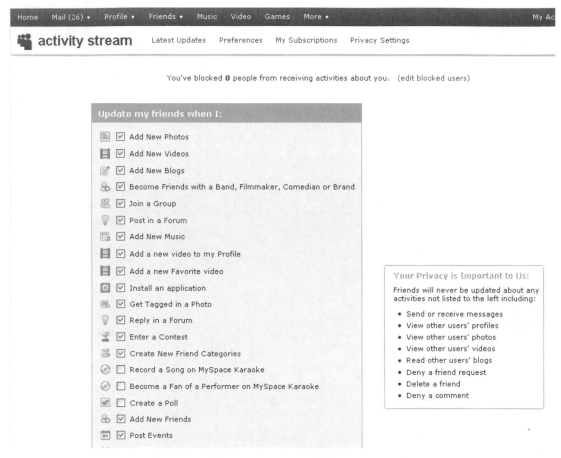

Figure 9.16   In your Activity Stream Privacy Settings, tell the system what you want your friends and fans to see when you make changes to your profile or account.

The Possibilities

While MySpace gives you the option to change how many and which friends appear on the first page of your profile, it doesn't allow you to customize that list further. The Internet is full of websites that will generate code to change the look of your Friends list. Some options include creating a Top Friends list of more than 40 friends; tweaking the number of friends that appear in a row or column; changing the word "friends" to "fans" (or any other word); altering the names of friends from their actual profile alias to a name of your choice; choosing which of your friends' pictures you want to show on your profile; making two friends lists; and reversing the order, scrolling, and hiding friends.

How and Where to Find Code

There are many ways to customize your Friends list by manipulating the code. Let's take a look at the possibilities.

Tweaking Your Top Friends List

You don't need to know any kind of HTML or other programming language to generate custom code for your profile. Plenty of resourceful people have already done the work for you. What you need is a code or script generator (sometimes called a *gen*) that will ask you to input your friends' information and then will create the code for you. My favorite Friends list code generator is Top 16+ Code Generator / Editor for MySpace Profiles (www.locohost.net/myspace_top16); see Figure 9.17. It is easy to use with a very simple interface. Even though the title is Top 16, it will actually generate lists up to 80 friends strong to turn your default Top Friends list (see Figure 9.18) into a new, custom list (see Figure 9.19). Paste the newly generated code (see Figure 9.20) into your profile as directed by the generator to see the results.

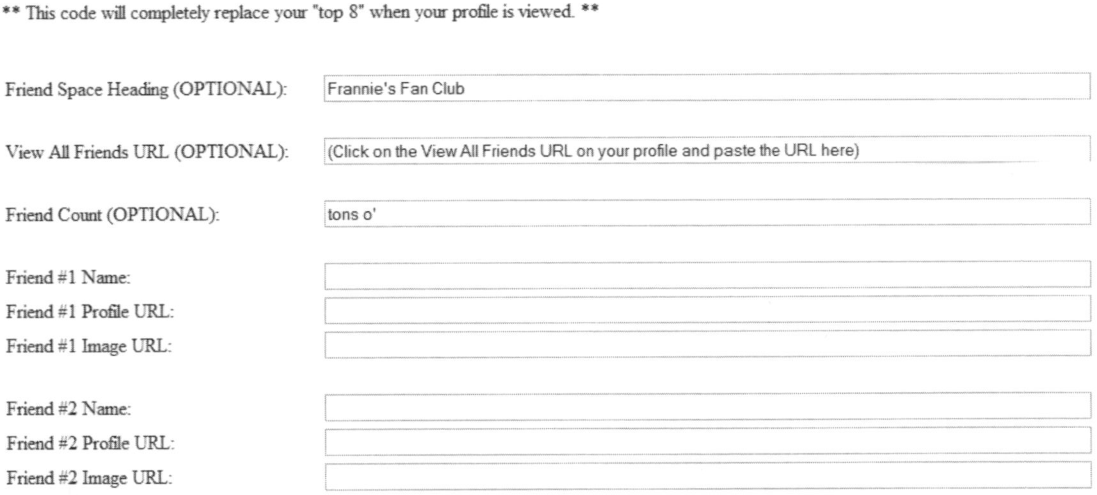

** This code will completely replace your "top 8" when your profile is viewed. **

Friend Space Heading (OPTIONAL): Frannie's Fan Club

View All Friends URL (OPTIONAL): (Click on the View All Friends URL on your profile and paste the URL here)

Friend Count (OPTIONAL): tons o'

Friend #1 Name:
Friend #1 Profile URL:
Friend #1 Image URL:

Friend #2 Name:
Friend #2 Profile URL:
Friend #2 Image URL:

Figure 9.17   The code generator at www.locohost.net/myspace_top16.

Another generator that does a variety of things to your Friends list can be found at www.htmate.com/friendgen. If the recommended code generators don't suit you, do a web search for "MySpace friend list codes," and you will be amazed at the dozens and dozens of results.

A code generator will usually include instructions on where to paste the code while you're in Edit Profile mode. However, these code generators are made for regular MySpace accounts, and musicians' profiles are set up a little differently. You may not be sure where to paste the code, but here are few tips:

1. First, paste the code into the end of the Bio section, save changes, and view your profile to see whether the changes took.

2. If the code doesn't execute correctly, make sure you don't have any broken HTML tags in that section. Broken, missing, or incorrect tags, which are noted by < >, would

Figure 9.18   A default MySpace Top Friends list.

include opening tags but no closing tags (for example, <center> but no </center>) and vice versa, as well as misspelled tags. Note that <img src>, <br>, <p>, and <hr> do not require closing tags. These are used by themselves.

3.   Check the rest of the profile's fields to be sure there are no other tag problems.

4.   Other code in a field can sometimes cause conflicts. Remove all previous code in the field and paste in only the Top Friends code. Save and check for correct execution.

5.   Still doesn't work? Try pasting the code into another field.

6.   If it still does not work, create a new field or section in which you can paste code. (See Chapter 8 for details.)

MySpace can be buggy, and customizing profiles is often hit or miss. Being flexible, patient, and willing to try new things will yield the best results in your customization efforts.

More Friends List Tweaks   Try some of these other Friends list code gens:

■   Hide your friends: tinyurl.com/ybzw6p4 (from MySpaceGens.com)

■   Reverse your friends (place them on the other side of your profile—they're usually the left side): tinyurl.com/d9xc5w (from MyWickedSpace.com)

■   Scroll your friends: tinyurl.com/c2edeg (from Profile-Tweak.com)

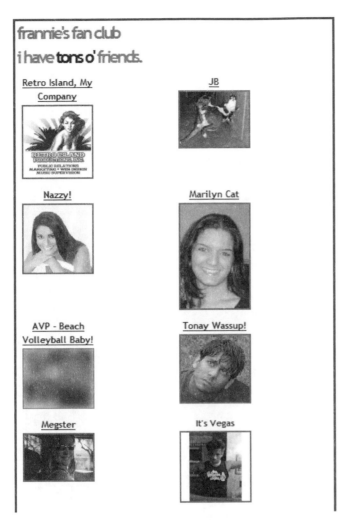

Figure 9.19   The new MySpace Top Friends list, altered by custom code. Notice that the layout, aliases of friends, and pictures have changed, as well as the headers for the Friends list.

Deleting and Blocking

Now that your Friends list is getting bigger, you'll need to spend some time managing it. Here are a couple of things to keep in mind.

Most bands will not make a habit of deleting friends, but there may be times when you need to do so. Stalker types, hate mailers, inappropriate comment writers, and people who leave long profile and blog comments promoting themselves are possible candidates for deletion. Deleting friends is easy. In your profile's control panel, choose the Change My Top Friends link in your Friend Space section. Now click the Delete Friends button on the right, check off offenders, and remove friends from your list.

INSTRUCTIONS:
1. CLICK ANYWHERE INSIDE THE BOX, THEN USE CTRL+A TO SELECT ALL.
2. COPY AND PASTE THIS CODE INTO THE <u>BOTTOM</u> OF YOUR "I'd Like To Meet" BOX:

```
<START CUSTOM FRIEND SPACE />

<style type="text/css">
FriendSpaceCode {Created-At: url(http://www.locohost.net/myspace_top16)}
td.text td.text table table table, td.text td.text table br, .rid br, td.text td.text
table .orangetext15,
td.text td.text .redlink, td.text td.text span.btext {display:none;}
td.text td.text table td, td.text td.text table {height:0;padding:0;border:0;}
td.text td.text table {background-color:transparent!important}
td.text td.text table td {font-size:0}
td.text td.text {height:0}
a.fs{position:absolute; right:0; top:0; z-index:9; height:18px; width:155px; background-image:url
(http://www.locohost.net/myspace_top16/top16.jpg); background-repeat:no-repeat; background-
position:bottom right;}
note {'change "8" to suit your needs if your comment text seems smaller or larger than usual'}
td.text td.text table b, td.text td.text table table td {font-size:8pt}
note {'comment padding fix'}
td.text td.text table table td {padding:3;}
td.text td.text table table br {display:inline;}
</style>
```

Figure 9.20   The new code for a Friends list to be pasted into one of the user's profile fields while in Edit Profile mode.

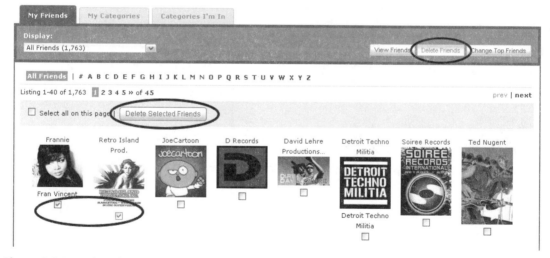

Figure 9.21   Delete friends by checking them off and clicking the Delete Selected Friends button.

For those users who really are becoming too weird for you to handle, blocking is an appropriate measure. Blocking a MySpace user not only removes that person from your Friends list, but also bars him or her from ever contacting you again through the blocked profile. Go to the offending MySpacer's profile, and in the contact box, click Block User. Manually delete any comments the user has left for you on your profile. If a user threatens you, MySpace recommends you call law enforcement immediately.

Now that your Friends list is in place and growing, it's time we talked about commenting.

10 Comments, Anyone?

O ne of the most integral parts of being a MySpacer is leaving comments for your friends and fans. As you browse around the place, clicking on various people and perusing their comments, you'll notice that the Comments section is used as a community bulletin board of sorts. Friends old and new remark on the happenings of the weekend, make inside jokes, and of course tell their favorite bands how much they love their music. Artists leave comments for fans, announcing gigs and thanking people for adding them to their list.

The Comments section, as public as it seems, is really a sort of walled garden. You can see it, but you can't access it . . . unless you are a friend, as Figure 10.1 shows. By now you have realized the importance of building a strong Friends list, and hopefully you have begun to assemble your own. It's time to start cementing relationships with your friends and making them a part of your community through commenting.

Error: You must be someone's friend to make comments about them.

Figure 10.1 Only friends can leave comments.

This chapter will explore the basics of commenting, embedding media into your comments, and using marketing tips to maximize your commenting efforts.

The Basics

There are four main types of comments—profile comments, which are left on a MySpacer's profile home page; image (or picture) comments, which are made in response to a posted picture or graphic in the View Pics section; video comments, displayed in the video section of MySpace; and blog comments, which are responses to entries in a user's blog. This section provides a rundown of the various types of comments, where to find them, how to leave them for others, and how to approve/deny/delete those left for you.

The Profile Comment

The starting point for all comments is the profile. Users who employ custom layout codes may move their friends' comments, rename or reorganize the way the Comments section looks, or hide it all together. However, when a profile is in default mode and unchanged by any formatting scripts, profile comments appear below your Friend Space (see Figure 10.2), where all the little thumbnail pictures of one's friends are gathered. On profiles where the owner has hidden his friends, you may still see the comments displayed.

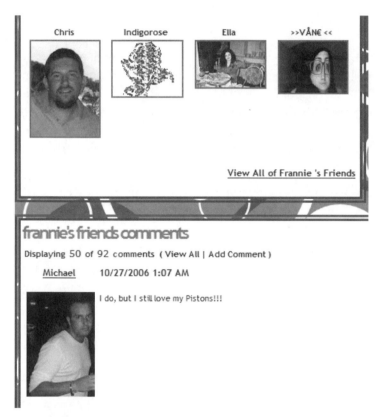

Figure 10.2 Profile comments appear just below your collection of friends in your Friends Comments section, which contains various links and information related to comments.

This section is aptly named *[Your alias]*'s Friends Comments. At present, only a limited number of comments are displayed directly on your profile. Eventually, you'll accumulate so many that they'll spill over into subsequent pages.

You'll also notice in this area that MySpace keeps a running count of how many comments you have and how many are displayed, and it provides links to View All. Clicking on this link will do several things. First, it lets visitors see all of your comments. Second, clicking on this link within *your own profile*, while you are logged in, allows you to delete comments left for you by others (see Figure 10.3). This is handy when you want to delete a comment that you

Figure 10.3 Clicking View All on your own profile allows you to delete comments from friends.

deem inappropriate or too long or one that contains a graphic that has distorted the look of your profile layout. In addition, clicking this link on a *friend's profile* allows you to delete comments you left for that person. This is convenient if you accidentally hit the Submit button twice and left the same comment over and over again! You are also able to leave comments on your own profile, which can be used to make an announcement or to respond to another's comment left for you.

Leaving Text Comments

Now you'll learn how to leave basic text comments for friends, starting with the profile comment. The process is nearly identical for image and blog comments.

At the top of the Friends Comments section is the Add Comment link. On some custom layouts, the link appears at the very bottom of the Comments section and can be easy to miss on pages with many comments. Figures 10.4 and 10.5 show you both types of Add Comment links. Be sure to scroll all the way down to the end if you don't see the link at the top!

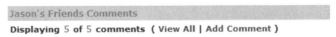

Figure 10.4 The default MySpace Friends Comments section.

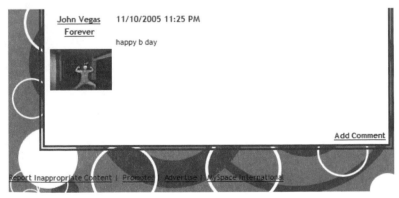

Figure 10.5 In this custom layout, the Add Comment link appears at the bottom of a MySpacer's Comments section.

When you want to leave a profile comment for a friend, you click on Add Comment. A page will come up that will allow you to type in your comment, as shown in Figure 10.6.

Retro Island Productions - Profile

Figure 10.6   Type your comment into the text box.

When you are finished, click Post a Comment. The system will give you an opportunity to review your comment once more and edit it if necessary (see Figure 10.7). When you are satisfied, click Post a Comment again.

Confirm Comment

Here is the display of your comment. Click the button below to confirm.

I love your new profile!

Post A Comment   Edit   Cancel

Figure 10.7   Confirm or edit your comment.

Depending on your friend's account settings (see Figure 10.8), your comment either will post immediately on the profile or will be sent to your friend for approval (see Figure 10.9). Figure 10.10 shows the notice you'll receive indicating that approval is required.

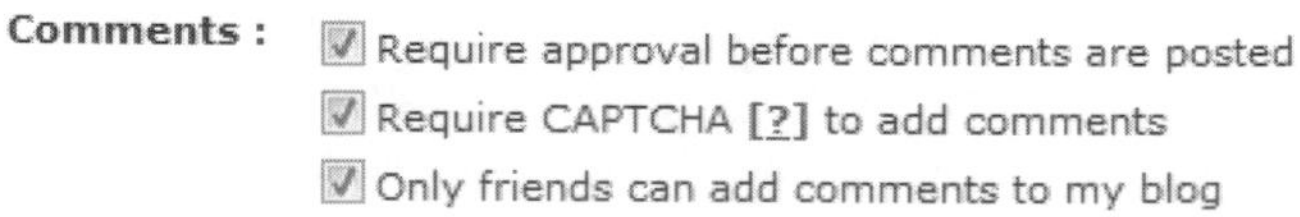

Comments :   ☑ Require approval before comments are posted
☑ Require CAPTCHA [**?**] to add comments
☑ Only friends can add comments to my blog

Figure 10.8   MySpacers who opt for it can approve all comments before they are posted to their profile.

Your comment will appear in the Comment Approvals section in your friend's home control panel, as shown in Figure 10.9, with buttons allowing your friend to approve or deny it (see Figure 10.11). If your friend chooses to approve your comment, it will post to his or her profile, as shown in Figure 10.12. If it is denied, the message will not be returned to you, nor

Figure 10.9   Notification of a pending comment appears in the Alerts section under Comment Approvals.

Awaiting Approval

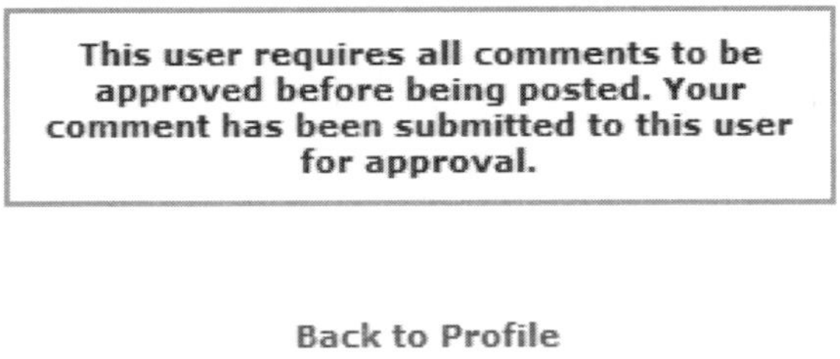

Figure 10.10   If your friend requires comment approval, you will see this message.

Figure 10.11   The user will see the comment request displayed like this, with options to approve or deny.

will you be notified—your comment will simply not be posted to your friend's profile. If, for whatever reason, you look at your comments to be approved but do not act, you can still access your unapproved comments under Notifications (see Figure 10.13).

Of course, you will go through the same process when someone leaves you a comment!

Displaying 25 **of** 459 **comments (View All | Add Comment)**

Frannie   Mar 23 2009 12:59 PM

Hey Chrystal! How was your weekend?

Figure 10.12   The approved comment will appear on the profile.

**Mail Center
Inbox**

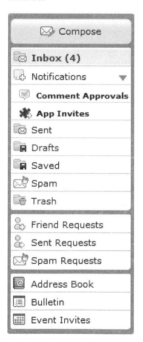

Figure 10.13   Your pending comments can also be found under Notifications.

The Image and Video Comment

MySpacers are given space to upload a number of pictures to their accounts. Images are accessible via the View My Pics link of one's profile, located near the top of the profile, as indicated in Figure 10.14. Friends can click on these links and peruse your pics and graphics (see Figure 10.15) and even make remarks, called *picture* (or *image*) *comments*.

While you can embed graphics and photos hosted on a non-MySpace server directly onto your profile's layout, only photos uploaded onto the MySpace server can be commented upon. You'll see that each photo has a set of options below it, as well as an empty box where

frannie

View My: PICS | Videos

Figure 10.14   Friends can comment on photos loaded into the View My Pics section.

Figure 10.15   Uploaded photos will appear on your profile like this.

you can enter a comment. Type in your text, hit Submit, and your photo comment will be posted below the photo, as shown in Figure 10.16.

Me and little brother John circa 1979

| Post a Comment | E-Mail to a Friend | Report This Image |

< Previous | **Next** >

Listing 1 - 2 of 2

From	Comment
Michael	**February 14, 2006 12:47 AM** Look how cute & innocent John USE to be.
	Delete

Figure 10.16   A finished image/picture comment.

Unlike profile comments, image comments left for you do not require approval (as of this writing). However, you will see a New Photo Comments! alert in your home control panel (see Figure 10.17). Click on the links to your new photo comments, and if you don't like what you see, you can delete them. You can also delete your image comments left for others by visiting the picture you commented on, finding your post, and clicking Delete My Comment.

Figure 10.17   The New Photo Comments! notification tells when someone has made a comment on your picture.

Leaving comments about videos works in much the same way as photo comments. Simply go to the video section of MySpace or to a friend's personal video section and add your text comment. Note that like image/photo comments, video comments post immediately and do not require approval. You may also go back and delete your own comment if you wish.

The Blog Comment

Every MySpacer has the ability to post *blogs* (short for *Web logs*), which are online entries that can be used like a journal or a bulletin board that appears on your profile. The user can then choose to allow the entire MySpace public to comment on his entries, or he can limit it to all of his friends or a preferred list of users. Blogs are located near the top of the profile, as shown in Figure 10.18. (For more details on how to use blogs, see Chapter 15, "Blogging in the MySpace World.")

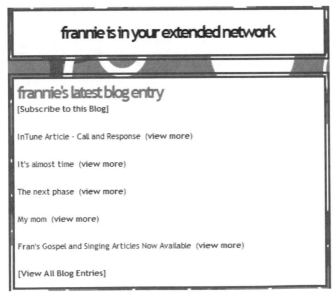

Figure 10.18   The Blog section of a profile.

To leave a blog comment, click on the blog entry and scroll to the bottom. If the user is allowing others to leave their thoughts, you will see a text box where you can add your comment (see Figure 10.19).

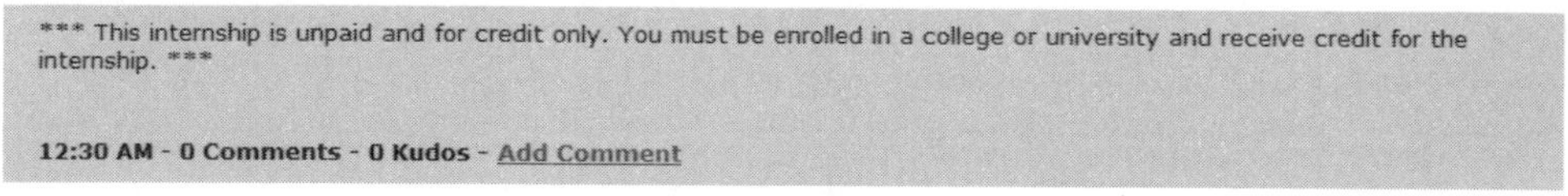

*** This internship is unpaid and for credit only. You must be enrolled in a college or university and receive credit for the internship. ***

12:30 AM - 0 Comments - 0 Kudos - <u>Add Comment</u>

Figure 10.19   This user allows comments to be left in response to his blog entry.... Note the text box at the bottom.

Type in your comment, hit Submit, and it will be posted on the blog (see Figure 10.20). You can also comment on your own blog, which is especially helpful when responding to other's comments. You may even give "kudos" if you like, which are like a thumbs up.

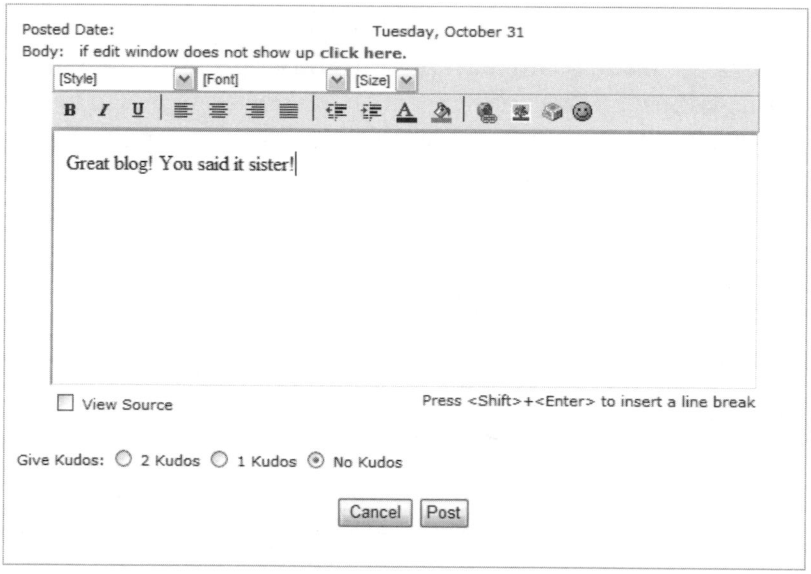

Figure 10.20   A posted blog comment looks like this.

The biggest difference between blog comments and profile or image comments is that blog comments do not allow you a final chance to edit your remarks, nor do they allow you to delete your comments later. So be absolutely sure of what you want to say before you hit Submit!

And, like image comments, blog comments post immediately. Only the blog owner may go back and delete your comment later.

Leaving HTML Comments

Unlike plain text, HTML code allows you to leave comments containing images, videos, hyperlinks, and more. Not only can you make your comments for friends more fun, but with embedded graphics and links, you can also use comments to build your brand among fans.

In Chapter 8, you learned about basic HTML and how to use it when customizing your MySpace profile. The HTML needed for adding links, photos, and video to comments is identical.

This section will focus on embedding images, hyperlinks, and media in comments. Please see Chapter 8 for further information on HTML tags and using images and video within MySpace.

Embedding Images

Leaving image-embedded comments is an excellent way to catch the eye of visitors. Photos and graphics can be used to generate even more interest in you as an artist or as a way to advertise gigs and special events.

Keep images less than 200KB, no wider than the average Comment section column (about 250 to 400 pixels), and no longer than 550 pixels. Users who are left comments with large embedded images—even if those images are short in width but long in length, leaving the profile layout intact—are apt to delete them without posting. No one wants to feel like an advertisement is sucking up all their comment real estate.

While Chapter 8 gave you the basics of how and where to upload content, as well as the HTML code, here are the necessary steps for including an image in a comment:

1. Create/edit an image and save it as a JPG or GIF in a manageable size.

2. Upload the image to an outside server (such as Photobucket, Flickr, or your personal web host).

3. Locate the URL of your image.

4. Insert the URL into an <img src> tag (see Figure 10.21).

5. Place code and any introductory text into the comment box.

```
Post A Comment About Frannie

Body:    <img
         src="http://i9.photobucket.com/albums/
         a81/franv/Myspace%
         20artwork/justsayinghi300.jpg">

                    Post a Comment
```

Figure 10.21 The <img src> HTML tag as it appears in the comment box.

6.   When you are finished, click Post a Comment, review, edit if necessary, and click
      Confirm (see Figure 10.22). Your approved comment will appear on the profile,
      as shown in Figure 10.23.

Figure 10.22   Confirm that your image appears properly by reviewing the Confirm Comment
screen.

Figure 10.23   The comment with embedded image as it appears on a profile.

Hyperlinks

Our next task is to create a hyperlink in a comment. This is a great way to direct people to your home website or music download shop. Leaving a comment with a clickable URL is the same as embedding a hyperlink in a profile. See Chapter 8 for details on creating hyperlinks.

If we were leaving a simple text message that included a website address that was not clickable, it would look like what you see in Figure 10.24.

Post A Comment About Frannie
Body:
Hey thanks for the add! Visit our Web site at www.retroisland.com for more info on how to market your music!
Post a Comment

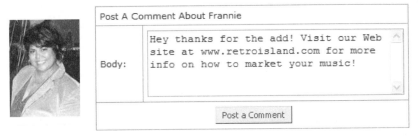

Figure 10.24 Our comment entered in plain text only.

In plain text, the URL to the website would not be activated (see Figure 10.25). As marketers, however, we want to make it very easy for our fans to access our website, so we want to create a hyperlink that a visitor can click and be transported to our website. When we add HTML tags, our comment will now be inputted as you see in Figure 10.26.

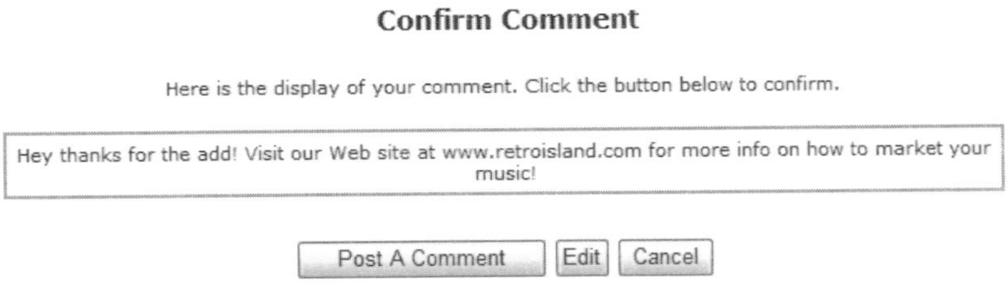

Confirm Comment
Here is the display of your comment. Click the button below to confirm.
Hey thanks for the add! Visit our Web site at www.retroisland.com for more info on how to market your music!
Post A Comment
Edit
Cancel

Figure 10.25 The website will not appear as a link because no HTML tags were included.

Post A Comment About Frannie
Body:
Hey thanks for the add! Visit our Web site at <a href="http://www.retroisland.com">www.retroisland.com</a> for more info on how to market your music!
Post a Comment

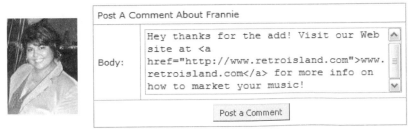

Figure 10.26 Our comment is now formatted to create a hyperlink for www.retroisland.com.

You can surround any text with hyperlink tags. Let's say we want to link the name of the website. It would look like this:

Hey thanks for the add! Visit our Web site at
<a href="http://www.retroisland.com">www.retroisland.com</a>
for more info on how to market your music!

Take a look at Figure 10.27 to see how your comment will look in the MySpace environment with HTML encoding, and the final result as it appears on a profile in Figure 10.28.

Confirm Comment

Here is the display of your comment. Click the button below to confirm.

Hey thanks for the add! Visit our Web site at **www.retroisland.com** for more info on how to market your music!

[Post A Comment] [Edit] [Cancel]

Figure 10.27   Now we can see that the website address has been turned into a link (in bold). Users who click on it will be taken to the site.

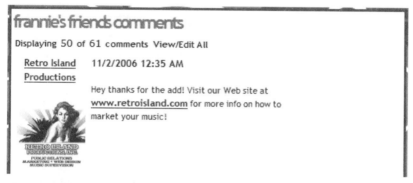

Figure 10.28   The final comment appears in a profile like this.

You can hyperlink graphics as well as text. The hyperlink tags remain the same, but instead of enclosing them around text, you will enclose them around HTML image tags.

Figure 10.29 shows a sample of what the HTML of a linked image would look like.

Be sure to double-check all of your tags to ensure that you have included </a> at the end of every item you want to hyperlink! The final comment pulls the image from the server where it's stored and links it to the retroisland.com website. The border around the image indicates that it is hyperlinked. See what it looks like in Figure 10.30.

Embedding Video

Friends often love leaving humorous videos in comments for each other. As a music marketer, however, you must be very judicious when using video on another's page. Post no

Figure 10.29   The hyperlinked image as it appears in HTML.

Figure 10.30   The final comment featuring a hyperlinked image.

more than one video in a comment and always aim to use video code that does not automatically start playing when the page is loaded. Consider using video clips of your live shows, recording-studio B-roll, interview footage, and even promotional music videos. Whichever you choose, be sure your clip not only has good visual quality, but also has excellent audio quality. This is especially important when you are using live show footage, which can sometimes look dark and grainy and sound distorted. Also be sure that your videos do not contain any pornographic content. Most hosting sites, including MySpace, will delete your accounts if you upload porn.

Whether you upload your videos onto MySpace or use another provider, such as YouTube.com, you'll need to copy (Ctrl+C) the video code to paste into the comment, as shown in Figure 10.31.

Figure 10.31   MySpace video code is pasted into a comment box.

Go to a friend's profile where you wish to leave a comment containing your video and click on Add Comment. When the comment box comes up, paste this copied code into the box by right-clicking with your mouse and choosing Paste or by pressing the Ctrl+V keyboard shortcut.

You can leave the comment like this or add some introductory text, as shown in Figure 10.32. To add text before the video, put your cursor before the tag (which starts with <a href=...>) and type in your text. After you have finished your introduction, type the tag<p> on the next line to add some space between your text and the embedded video.

Figure 10.32   Add introductory text to your comment.

The resulting comment will look like Figure 10.33.

Chapter 12, "Photos and Videos," contains more details on video.

More Comment Settings

Some MySpacers do not allow HTML comments to be left in their profiles (see Figure 10.34). If you paste HTML code into a comment box where it is restricted, the code will not be processed. Instead, it will be displayed as plain text, tags and all. The user's account will warn you ahead of time that HTML comments are not allowed for this profile. In this case, leave plain text comments only.

You can also set your account to notify your cell phone when you receive a profile, image, and/or blog comment. Access your Mobile Alert Settings through My Account: Settings to modify these options.

Figure 10.33   A comment with introductory text and a video clip.

Note: This user disables HTML comments.
Any HTML codes in your comment will be removed.

Post A Comment About	
Body:	
	Post a Comment

Figure 10.34   This user does not allow HTML comments.

Customizing Comments

There are three main ways to customize commenting—mass commenting, scrolling comments, and the use of profile comment boxes. Some MySpacers like to hide their comments, but as a music marketer you won't want to do that. User interaction is vital in growing a fan base. Comments should remain visible.

Mass Commenting

In Chapter 9, we talked about friend adder programs that automate the process of finding and adding friends by using bots. These types of programs sometimes incorporate mass commenting and mass bulletins. Because many of the comments you will be leaving will be the same for all your friends, a mass commenter that will automate the arduous task of leaving many comments can really help you maximize your marketing efforts. The cost normally runs between $30 and $70, depending on the features of the program. The time it saves is well worth it, though you run the risk of losing your account if MySpace discovers it.

Remember that the MySpace powers-that-be do not like bots and adder programs, so be frugal in the number of comments you leave in a 24-hour period. More than 50 to 100 will begin to attract attention, and you have a higher likelihood of being flagged as a spammer by the MySpace system. You always run that risk when using bots. If you decide to be a marketing daredevil, be sure to always save copies of any custom code you used to alter your profile, and use the bot program to back up your Friends list on a regular basis. If MySpace freezes or deletes your account, at least you'll have all of your profile info and a comprehensive Friends list handy should you need to start over.

Comment Boxes and Scrolling Friends

Earlier in the chapter, we learned that leaving a comment starts by clicking the Add Comment link on a friend's profile. Some users prefer to remove this extra step and plug in code to create a profile comment box. This box appears right on your profile, near your Comments section, and consists of a text box and a submit button. Visitors will no longer have to find the Add Comment link, click it, and then leave a comment. Should you see this feature on a friend's page, you'll know what to do.

Integrated profile comment boxes, as shown in Figure 10.35, are an added convenience that MySpacers love. Plus, they serve as visual encouragement for fans and friends to leave comments for you. Let's discuss how you can incorporate a comment box into your music profile.

The code to create a comment box can often be bundled with the ability to scroll through comments and friends at the same time. It basically takes the Friends list and Comments sections of your profile and partitions them off so they become a scrollable section all their own. This is helpful when you want to show off a ton of top friends and lots of comments, but you don't want to force visitors to scroll endlessly to the bottom of your profile. People tend to lose interest that way, so this set of code packages friends and comments into a tidy, manageable segment.

My favorite comment box/scrolling friends code generator, shown in Figure 10.36, can be found at www.myspace.nuclearcentury.com/commentbox.php. I like it because it's super easy to generate, and even the least web-savvy person can use it. It's pretty basic and will give you a comment box and scrolling friends/comments (see Figure 10.37).

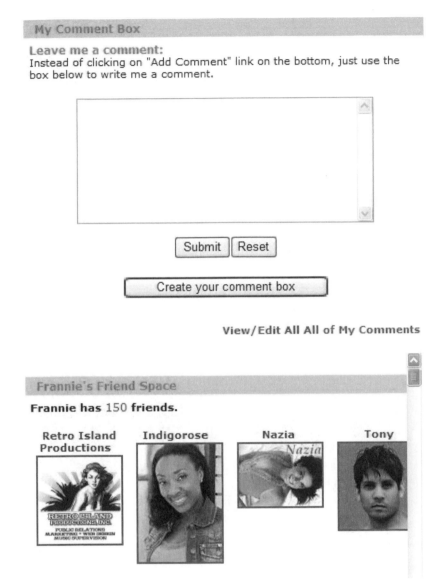

Figure 10.35   An example of an integrated comment box with scrolling friends/comments.

Want to get fancy? Try customizing your comment box with colors, various fonts, custom button text, and backgrounds. A simple-to-use generator is located at www.htmate2.com/commentbox. I like this one because it generates color codes for you, shows you fonts to choose from (see Figure 10.38), and allows you to preview your comment box first, so you can tweak it if it doesn't look exactly how you want. However, this comment box doesn't have a scrolling feature bundled with it. Try using a picture of your band or a logo as the comment box background—just make sure that it is enough of a contrasting color that a

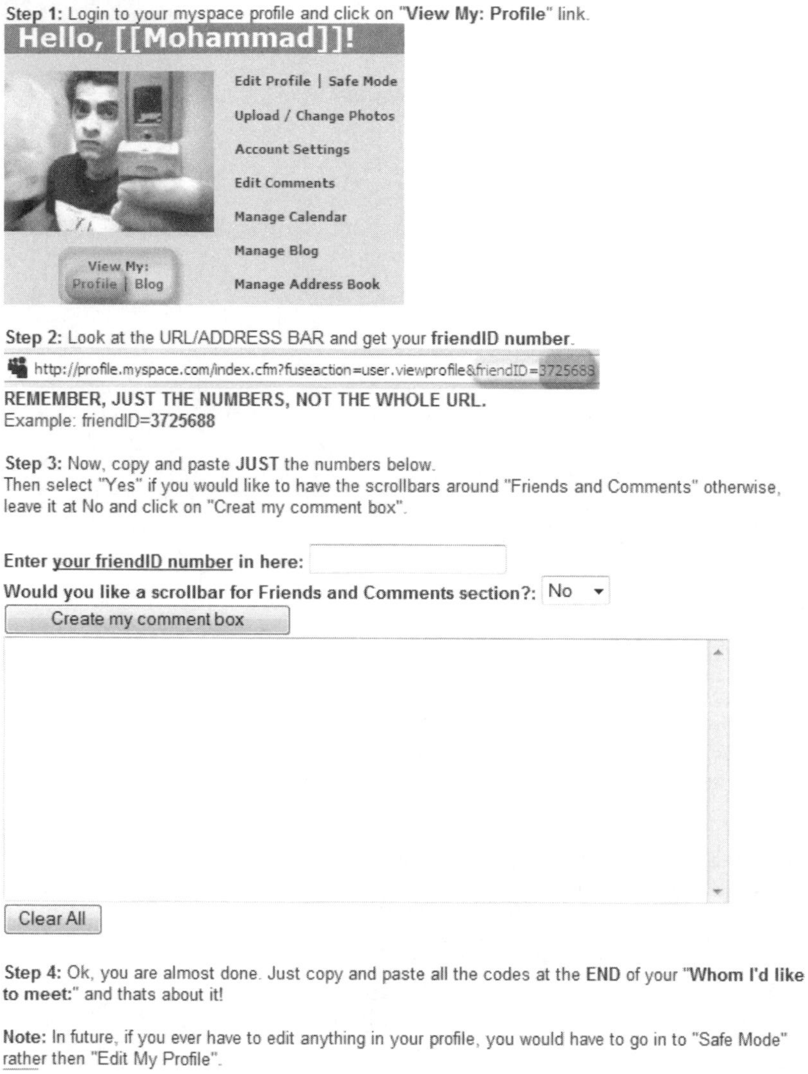

Step 1: Login to your myspace profile and click on "**View My: Profile**" link.

Hello, [[Mohammad]]!

Edit Profile | Safe Mode

Upload / Change Photos

Account Settings

Edit Comments

Manage Calendar

Manage Blog

View My:
Profile | Blog   Manage Address Book

Step 2: Look at the URL/ADDRESS BAR and get your **friendID number**.

http://profile.myspace.com/index.cfm?fuseaction=user.viewprofile&friendID=3725688

REMEMBER, JUST THE NUMBERS, NOT THE WHOLE URL.
Example: friendID=3725688

Step 3: Now, copy and paste JUST the numbers below.
Then select "Yes" if you would like to have the scrollbars around "Friends and Comments" otherwise, leave it at No and click on "Creat my comment box".

Enter **your friendID number** in here: [   ]

Would you like a scrollbar for Friends and Comments section?: No ▾

[Create my comment box]

[   ]

[Clear All]

Step 4: Ok, you are almost done. Just copy and paste all the codes at the END of your "**Whom I'd like to meet:**" and thats about it!

Note: In future, if you ever have to edit anything in your profile, you would have to go in to "Safe Mode" rather then "Edit My Profile".

Figure 10.36   The comment box generator at Nuclear Century.

person can see the text they are typing into the comment box. Or, simply integrate colors that fit with your band's image. Figure 10.39 shows an example of a customized comment box.

A web search for "myspace comment box" will kick out many other possible generators for you to use.

In the musician profile, these comment codes should be placed at the end of the Bio section. Once you have put comment box code into your profile, you may need to do all future profile edits in safe mode. Also, be aware that some codes do not play well together. You may be

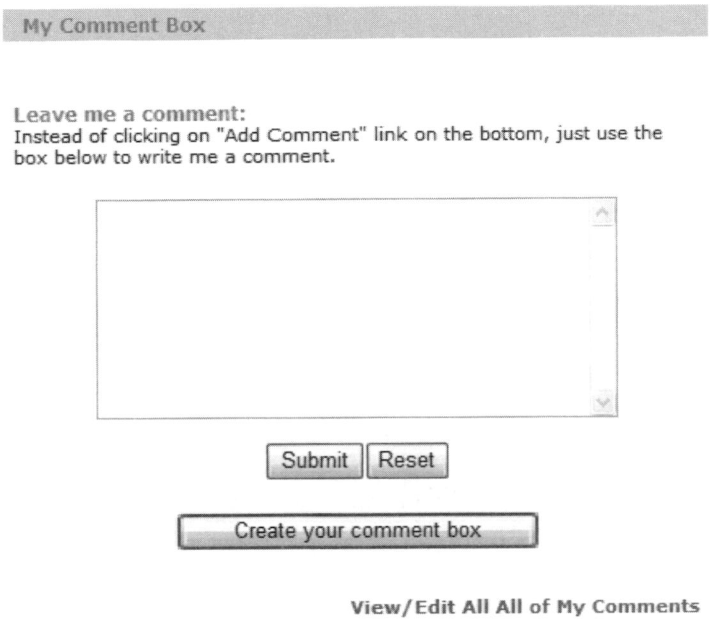

My Comment Box

Leave me a comment:
Instead of clicking on "Add Comment" link on the bottom, just use the box below to write me a comment.

Submit Reset

Create your comment box

View/Edit All All of My Comments

Figure 10.37 The comment box as it appears on a default music profile.

Textarea Background Color Click here to choose Color

Words In Box by Default

Address URL to Background Image

Button background Color Click here to choose Color

Button text Color Click here to choose Color

Color of text in the box Click here to choose Color

Choose a Font:

- Arial
- Courier New
- Comic Sans MS
- Georgia
- Verdana
- Lucida Console
- Times New Roman
- Helvetica
- **Impact**
- Trebuchet MS
- Small Fonts
- Monotype Corsiva
- Garamond
- Tahoma

Figure 10.38 The custom-designed comment box generator at htmate2.com, with options to change fonts and colors.

Figure 10.39   An elaborate comment box on a default profile.

able to have a comment box, but the custom Top Friends list may stop working. It's buggy, so if you're plugging in code without professional help, there may be times when features won't behave as they should, and you will have to decide which feature is most important to you to keep. You can also try moving various codes to other sections of the musician profile, such as Influences or Band Members, and see whether that allows all your codes to play nicely together.

Comment Spam

Why must a few evildoers ruin a good thing? Yes, even comments sometimes contain spam. It was inevitable, I suppose, considering that spammers are *everywhere* these days. Comment spam happens when someone bombards your comments with the same message over and over again. Often it's offers for meds or cell phones, photos of hot chicks, or some pyramid-scheme business opportunity. And sometimes it's an overzealous musician who thinks leaving 20 identical comments for the same person saying "Listen to my music" is actually going to attract new fans to his profile. (Hint: It doesn't.) This type of bombardment is aptly named *comment bombs*. These bombs are sometimes sent by bad people, but some are sent by users who have no idea it's happening because their account was commandeered by a virus or a hacker. It's gotten so bad that some of these comments are programmed so they stay at the very top of your comments list, and you cannot delete them by normal methods.

First, never allow comment spam to remain on your profile. It is an absolute turnoff to all the legitimate fans who visit your page. Delete the offending comment spam by going into safe mode editing and deleting the comments from there.

Second, always enable comment approval in My Account > Spam. This way, no comments will get posted to your page without you seeing and approving them first. Third, require CAPTCHA from anyone leaving you a comment—this is where the user must enter the alphanumeric code MySpace presents to them, thereby verifying they are a real person and not a program (see Figure 10.40). Fourth, delete anyone on your Friends list who is spamming you. And lastly, change your password every month or two (or more often if you suspect someone might have compromised your account) by going into My Account. Hackers can spam your friends when they gain access to your account, so changing your password often will keep them guessing.

Confirm Comment

Here is the display of your comment. Click the button below to confirm.

Hey I can leave myself a comment!

Security Measure: The image with the crazy letters is called a Captcha and it's used to figure out if you're a person or a computer. Filling out the Captcha helps us to stop spammers and phishers on MySpace.

Please enter the text from the image above:
The letters are not case-sensitive.
Do not type spaces between the numbers and letters.

Post A Comment   Edit   Cancel

Figure 10.40   Some users require you to enter a CAPTCHA code, which limits the possibility that a spam program is leaving a comment.

Making Comments Work for You

Using comments to your advantage is the best way to build a relationship with your fans and attract new ones. Of course, you don't want to abuse your relationship by bombarding friends with too many remarks, lest you be regarded as a weird stalker musician. Plan on leaving no more than one comment a week, unless something super newsworthy happens. Can't think of what kind of messages to leave or what you might say? Here are some great reasons to leave comments for your friends and fans:

■   **When you add, or are added as, a new friend.** Leave a comment thanking your new friend for the add or just saying hello. Invite your friend to check out your profile, listen to your songs, and leave a comment telling you which is his or her favorite. You may even create a graphic to embed in the comment.

- **When someone leaves a comment for you first.** It's polite to return the favor and say, "Thanks for stopping by." Plus, it gives you one more opportunity to build a relationship and possibly attract new friends.

- **When it's holiday time.** This is when software for mass commenting comes in handy. Again, it's one more opportunity for exposure. Why not say "Happy Thanksgiving!" to everyone on your list?

- **When you change your profile layout or main website or you add new content.** Let friends and their visitors know that you have an awesome new profile or website and you have just added T-shirts for sale!

- **When you upload new music.** Ask friends to listen to your new songs and comment on which ones they like best. Ask them to add their favorite to their profile.

- **When you want to announce gigs, tour dates, personal appearances, and CD listening/release parties.** Have you just posted gigs for the next two months? Or maybe a summer tour? In-store appearances and TV and radio interviews are also ideal opportunities to leave comments. You can create a graphic or post a simple, "Hey, we're playing at a bunch of places the next couple months. Check out the schedule and see whether we'll be in your area!"

- **When you want to announce a special giveaway or contest.** Tell everyone you're giving away a CD to the person who refers the most friends to you this month.

- **When you need support.** Vying for the top spot in a battle of the bands? Perhaps you need people to vote for you for best artist. Mass commenting is a great way to ask everyone to support you in your time of need.

- **When you have news.** Did the local paper or a CD reviewer give you a great write-up? Or maybe you're one of the top artists on MySpace or another music site. Brag a little with, "Hey, we were just voted the best new band. Check out our profile for all the details." Press coverage, awards, changes in band lineup, CD sales milestones, and the like are all newsworthy tidbits.

- **When you post new photos or videos.** People love checking out photos and video clips.

- **When your music is available for sale on a new site.** If your music is now available on iTunes or any other download service, your friends will want to know!

- **When you want to recruit street team members.** Advertise that you're looking for people who love your music to help you promote your CD and gigs in their area.

■ **To wish fans happy birthday.** Your birthday notifications will tell you who on your Friends list has a birthday that week (see Figure 10.41). This is located in your home control panel, and a link exists in your Friend Space as of this writing. People love when artists leave them a personal happy birthday. Awww, it's endearing, no?

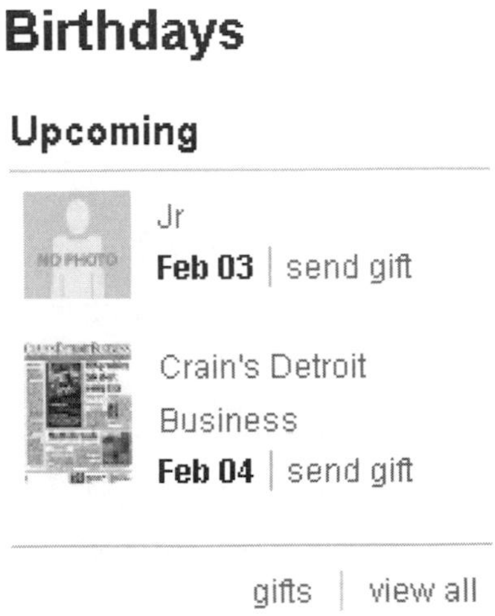

Birthdays

Upcoming

 Jr
Feb 03 | send gift

 Crain's Detroit Business
Feb 04 | send gift

gifts | view all

Figure 10.41 Click on your birthday notifications for a list of your friends/fans with birthdays this week. Then leave them a happy bday comment!

Now that we've covered almost all there is to know to get you started with commenting, it's time to move on to the next step . . . profile songs.

11 Playlists and the Music Player

Regular users can add music to their profiles from their favorite MySpace musicians, giving the artist exposure to new listeners. But to take advantage of this free promotion, you, the artist, must first ensure that your music player is set to allow adds. This chapter will explore how to use your music player to market your music and encourage promotional buzz.

There are two basic ways users listen to music on MySpace—through the music player that appears on a musician's profile and through playlists that users create and share with others on their profile. Let's take a look at the differences and how they can be used to market music.

The Artist's Music Player

The music player that appears on your artist profile can hold up to 10 songs as of this writing. (You may notice that some major-label artists and a few indie artists are able to upload more than 10 songs to their artist profile player. This is because those labels have special agreements with MySpace. The rest of us are limited to 10 presently.)

Users can click on any song in the player to listen to your music. Depending on your settings, listeners may also have the option to download your songs for free, read your lyrics, or set your player to repeat or randomize your songs. Review Chapter 7 for a more in-depth refresher on how to upload music to your player. (See the section "Step 5: Add Your Songs.")

In addition to the features mentioned above, your artist music player offers a few other nice bells and whistles to enhance the user experience. When you upload an image along with your song, that image appears next to the song each time it plays, creating a visual association with that song. In Figure 11.1, artist Allie Moss associates her song with the cover of her EP.

Listeners who want to keep listening to your music but wish to surf away from your page can click Pop Out Player on your music player (see Figure 11.2). This puts the player in its own web browser window (see Figure 11.3) so that listeners aren't tethered to the artist's page anymore. The pop-out player also shows the artist's recent status updates.

Figure 11.1 Artist Allie Moss has uploaded accompanying artwork for her songs (www.myspace.com/alliemossmusic).

Figure 11.2 The Pop Out Player link on the artist's music player. Notice also the Random, Repeat, and Volume controls just below the Pop Out Player link.

Your music player displays the number of times each song has been played, plus the number of total player views that day and all time (see Figure 11.4). This helps you and other profile visitors keep track of spikes or slowdowns and the overall popularity of your songs.

Figure 11.3   A snapshot of my desktop after "popping out" Lady Gaga's music player. It's in a separate window, and I am able to surf away from her profile.

Assuming you've set your player settings to allow others to add your song to their profiles and playlists, you will see a big plus (+) sign next to your song (see Figure 11.4).

The bottom buttons on the artist's music player are Albums, Videos, and Playlists (see Figure 11.4). When you upload your music, you can designate it as part of an album and provide relevant information. When fans click on the Albums button, details about each album appear over the music player (see Figure 11.5).

The Videos button operates in similar fashion to the Albums button. Any videos that you upload to your musician account will be represented in the Video section of your music player, as in Figure 11.6.

Artists can create their own playlists of well-loved songs. Those playlists they designate as public appear in the music player under the Playlists button. Like albums and videos, a list of playlists will appear over the music player. When you choose a playlist, it takes you to that playlist's page (see Figure 11.7).

We'll explore playlists more in the next section.

Lastly, a little color wheel appears to *you only* when you view your music player on your profile. Choose the color wheel and customize the look of your music player (see Figure 11.8). You can coordinate it with the layout and color scheme of your album, MySpace profile, or other branding factors.

Figure 11.4   The artist player for Prince Damons (www.myspace.com/princedamons) details the number of plays for each song, as well as the day's plays and all-time plays. This artist has set each song as "addable" to fans' playlists. The buttons at the bottom of the player let fans check out the artist's albums, videos, and any playlists he may have created.

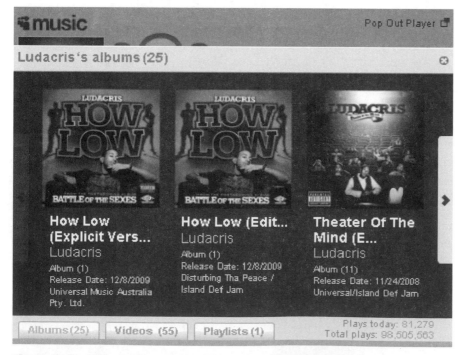

Figure 11.5   Click on the Albums button for artist Ludacris (www.myspace.com/ludacris), and each of his designated albums comes up with information about the album, as well as the album cover.

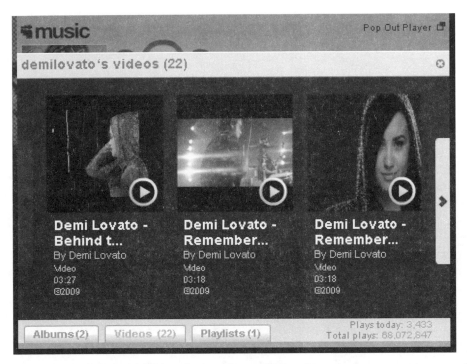

Figure 11.6   Select the Videos button for artist Demi Lovato (www.myspace.com/demilovato), and the videos uploaded to her account will pop up. Clicking on a video takes you to the page within MySpace Videos where the video resides.

Artists whose music is sold through Amazon.com will see a Buy button next to each song on their music player that is also available on Amazon. Artists with ringtones sold through Jamster will have a Ringtones icon on their music player as well. Since this is not a setting you can access and change (MySpace's systems detect whether a song is sold on Amazon or Jamster), it's not a foolproof method of selling one's music on MySpace. And, it favors artists with some type of major distribution channel, who are probably more likely to get detected through the MySpace/Amazon/Jamster system. For more information on how to sell music on MySpace, check out Chapter 20, "Now What? MySpace and Your Marketing Plan."

The artist's music player has been streamlined in recent months to offer more than just songs for the fan to listen to. Now, users can check out the artist's albums, videos, and playlists and in some cases buy MP3s and ringtones from this one central location, making it a one-stop shop for the fans' multimedia experience.

The Playlist

Remember when you used to create tapes, and more recently CDs, with your favorite songs? The playlist is the modern-day version of the old-school mix tape. Today, you and your fans can share favorite songs with friends online via this new digital "mix tape."

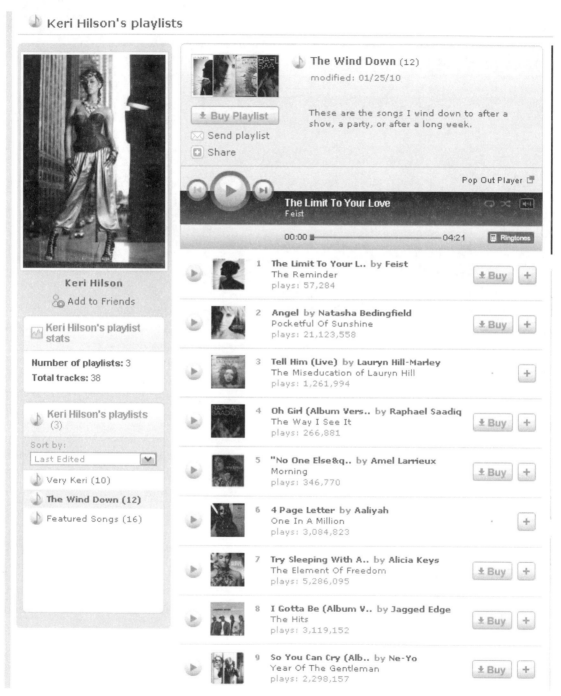

Figure 11.7 Keri Hilson's playlist of music to chill to, appropriately titled Wind Down, shows her selections of songs she enjoys and recommends to others (www.myspace.com/kerihilson).

Figure 11.8 Choose the color wheel at the bottom of your own music player, and you can change the color settings of your player.

In the previous section I mentioned the little plus sign next your song in your music player, which allows fans to add your song to their playlists. When a fan clicks this symbol, they are given the option to add the song to the profile playlist, to add it to another previously created playlist, or to create a new playlist with this song. They can also choose to make their new playlist private, meaning only they can access it from within their home control panel (see Figure 11.9).

Once a fan has added your song to his or her profile's playlist, every visitor to that person's page has to the opportunity to hear your music playing, which exposes your songs to hundreds, even thousands, of pairs of ears, depending on how much traffic that profile gets. Multiply this by the oodles of fans that all have your song playing on their profiles, and you can quickly see the potential for viral promotion and free exposure. When a fan adds your song to his or her profile, it will appear in that fan's friends' update feed. That means that Joe Fan's friends now know he is listening to your music and may decide to check you out (see Figure 11.10).

This can't happen unless you activate the add option in your artist music player. As a rule, you should always allow listeners to add your song to their profiles and playlists. You are presented with this option when you upload music to your profile's player. But, you can always go back anytime to correct the oversight if you neglected to allow listeners to add your songs to their profiles.

Figure 11.9 When choosing to add a song to one's profile, the user is presented with several options (www.myspace.com/kesha).

 Detroit Music & Entertainment Authority added a new profile song:

(▶)**The Laymans Heart**
by **Manna and Quail**

Figure 11.10 Now the fan's friends can see the songs that have been added to the profile playlist.

As a quick reminder of how it's done, log into your MySpace account. In your home control panel, click Edit Profile, then go to the Manage Featured Songs tab. Here you'll see the main settings for your player. The first check box in the Page Settings section is Allow Users to Add Songs to Their Profile. Always make sure this is checked, as in Figure 11.11.

Obviously, the whole point of having an artist profile is to show off your songs. So be sure to upload your best creations. Personally, I believe in keeping songs short and sweet to leave listeners wanting more. Some artists even just put snippets—short 35-second to 1-minute clips.

You can change the order your songs appear in your player anytime you like by going back into the Manage Featured Songs section of your profile editor. And you can designate any song to play first and automatically when a visitor loads your page, which is really helpful when you are promoting a particular single.

Add a Song

These song settings apply to all songs uploaded to your Artist profile.

Song Settings
☑ Allow users to add songs to their profile
☐ Automatically play the first song for visitors that are logged-in.
☐ Randomize the songs in my featured playlist.
Update Settings

Figure 11.11   Make sure the first option (to allow users to add your songs) is checked in your account settings.

A playlist that a MySpace user displays on his profile can hold up to 10 songs, making it pretty important real estate on a fan's profile. However, playlists that are private or not embedded into the profile can house up to 100 songs. Users can buy songs available on Amazon.com. And, the fan who created the playlist can email it to friends and share it on more than 220 places online, including Facebook, Twitter, Virb, and other hot spots (see Figure 11.12).

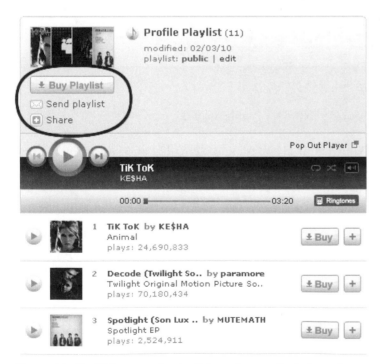

Figure 11.12   This person's playlist can be emailed, shared across the Internet, or purchased from Amazon.com.

Artists Can Create Playlists, Too

The first playlist an artist creates on MySpace is his own. The songs you upload to your player go into a playlist entitled Featured Songs. To view your playlists, click on Profile on the medium blue navigation bar and then choose My Playlists (see Figure 11.13). The main playlist displayed is your Featured Songs.

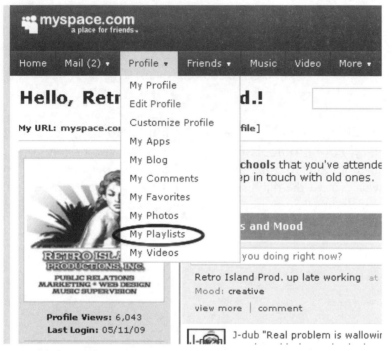

Figure 11.13   Access your playlists by going to the My Profile drop-down menu.

You can see in Figure 11.14 that your featured songs can be emailed and shared online just like any other playlist. When you have new songs added to your player, be sure to go to this page and alert fans and friends by emailing them your list and posting to your other properties online!

While regular MySpace users simply hit the plus button next to a song they want to add to their profile or other playlist, the artist is restricted from this. At this time, you cannot, as an artist, go to other artists' profiles and add their songs from their music players (by clicking the plus button). Nothing happens. Instead, what follows is the process you can use to create your own playlists either for your private listening pleasure or to share with others.

On the right side of the page, a little ways down, is a section called My Playlists. Here you will see the list of playlists you have actively created, not including the songs you have uploaded. Choose New Playlist to begin the process of creating a list of songs you enjoy listening to (see Figure 11.15).

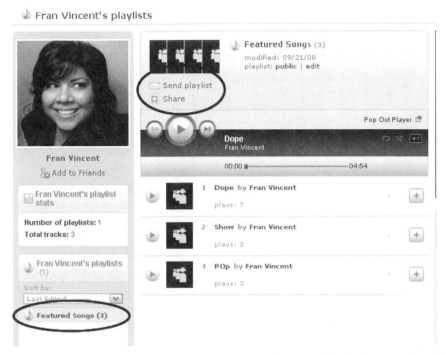

Figure 11.14 This artist's Featured Songs are shown in playlist form and can be emailed and shared with fans.

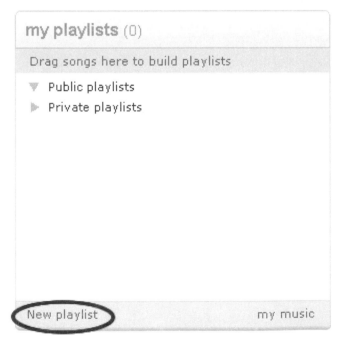

Figure 11.15 The New Playlist link in the My Playlist section.

Now name and describe your playlist and designate it private if you don't want anyone else to see it (see Figure 11.16). Let's assume for a moment that you will keep it a public playlist.

Figure 11.16   Create a new playlist and give it a description.

The playlist you just created now appears in the My Playlists box under Public Playlists. Highlight your new playlist and click on the Edit link that appears to the right of the playlist name. The edit page for your playlist should now have loaded.

Click on the Browse button to choose from Recently Added Songs by Friends and Top Songs in the Major, Indie, and Unsigned charts (see Figure 11.17). These are the songs available for you to add, which you can do by clicking the plus sign next to the song you want and choosing your new playlist as the place you'd like to add the song to. The songs are automatically placed in your designated playlist. Unfortunately, you are limited in the songs you can add to your personal playlist by choosing tunes from the aforementioned categories. Right now, there's no way to choose genres, search for your favorite artists or fellow indie artists, and be more selective in the songs you choose to add. Once, and if, MySpace resolves this, the playlist creation function will have much more marketing promise.

To view your playlists, click on the My Music link in the My Playlist section (refer to Figure 11.15). The playlists will come up on the right side of the page. Here you can also delete your playlists, manage your featured songs, and view the playlists of select major artist (see Figure 11.18).

Personally, I find the process of creating a playlist in an artist account to be awkward, clunky, and complicated. Hopefully this is something MySpace will improve upon in the future.

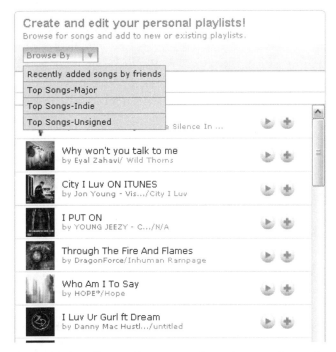

Figure 11.17 Choose from songs in various predetermined categories to populate your list.

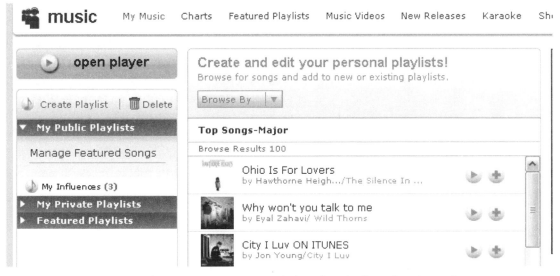

Figure 11.18 Delete playlists, manage songs, and view the playlists of major artists from this section.

The public playlists you create will appear in your Playlists button on your music player for all to enjoy (refer to Figure 11.7). You can also email or share your playlist with others. You may wonder why you would want to do this. Well, first, you can create new playlists of your favorite songs every couple of weeks so your fans can hear what you're listening to. This also gives you a reason to interact with fans, ask their opinions on your song choices, and describe why you like your picks and how the individual songs or artists have influenced you. Bulletin and post your new playlists to your blog, and even send your playlists to your individual email lists outside of MySpace. Post notices on your other social networks, Twitter it (or tweet, if you prefer), and invite fans to come take a listen. To take it a step further, you can even get out a camcorder and video blog about it.

Second, there may be other artists out there who you can team up with and work together to create mutual playlists and cross-promote to your individual fan bases.

Getting Fans to Share Your Music

Profile songs are crucial page elements for many active MySpacers. The songs one chooses for his or her page not only are reflective of that person's musical interests at that time, but they also sometimes hint at the person's social and emotional moorings and values. They might coincide with the visual theme of the person's MySpace profile (for example, the Beach Boys with an island theme). The song a person chooses is a very personal choice and says something about the person, even if the person himself is unconscious of an overt revelation. We often make judgments about a person we don't know based on what the person looks like, what his profile looks like, what he writes in his blogs and profile text, and what kind of music and videos he features. It's a first impression of sorts.

A person doesn't need to be your MySpace friend to add your songs to his profile. Any fan in the MySpace community can feature your songs on his page. Your job as a marketer is to encourage visitors and friends alike to listen to your songs and add them to their profiles. Post bulletins, send emails to friends, post a "flier" or notice on your page, blog about it, have a contest or some kind of incentive for people to add your music to their profiles . . . Tell people if they add your song to their profiles and keep it there for at least a month, not only will you leave a comment on their profile, you'll list them as a top friend and enter them into a drawing to win merch. If you have a big enough following, fans may even want to win a phone call from you.

As mentioned previously, you can email your playlist to fans. To email your featured playlist, click on Send Playlist and then customize your message and address it to fans on your MySpace Friends list (see Figure 11.19). If you already have friend groups set up (refer to Chapter 9), this can make the process a lot quicker. Plus, you can even add a video you've already uploaded to MySpace right into your email to make it more interesting. Be sure to include a call to action inviting fans to forward the email to their friends and to post their favorite songs to their profiles.

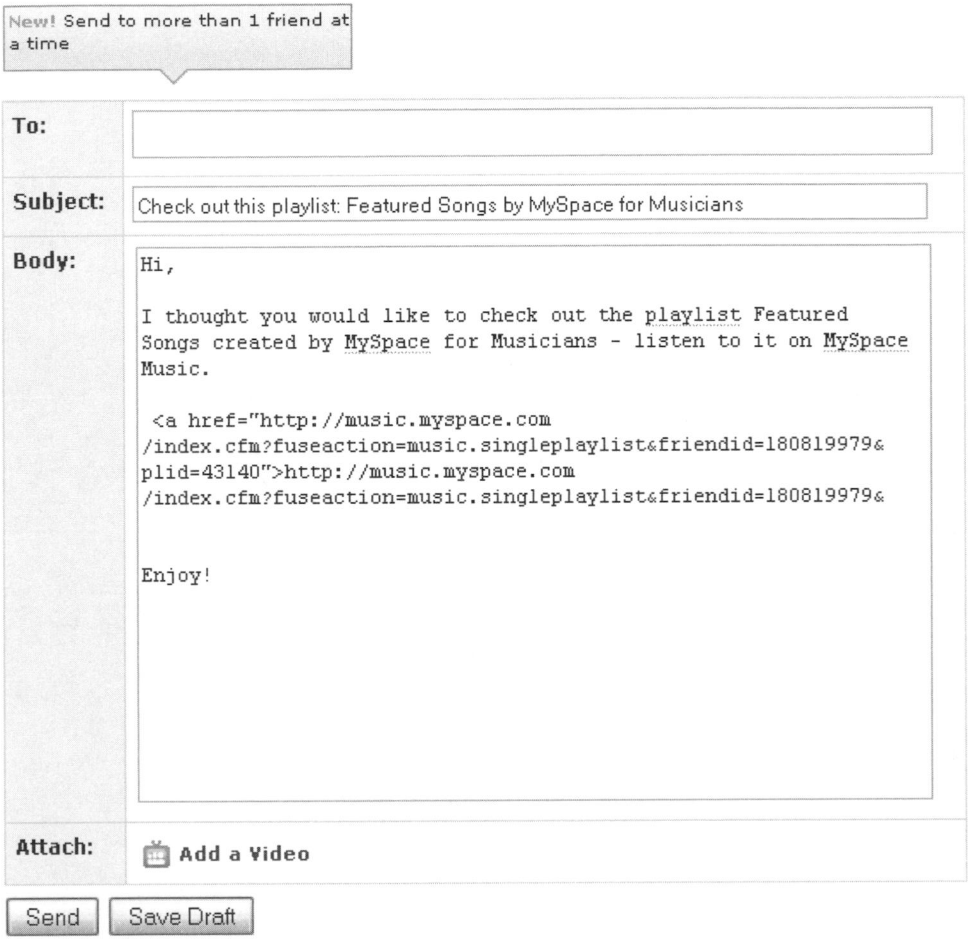

New! Send to more than 1 friend at a time

To:	
Subject:	Check out this playlist: Featured Songs by MySpace for Musicians

Body:

```
Hi,

I thought you would like to check out the playlist Featured
Songs created by MySpace for Musicians - listen to it on MySpace
Music.

 <a href="http://music.myspace.com
/index.cfm?fuseaction=music.singleplaylist&friendid=180819979&
plid=43140">http://music.myspace.com
/index.cfm?fuseaction=music.singleplaylist&friendid=180819979&


Enjoy!
```

Attach: 📺 Add a Video

[Send] [Save Draft]

Figure 11.19 Send your playlist to people on your Friends list. The message in this example was already filled in by the MySpace service, but you can customize it yourself.

Post your playlist by clicking on Share and choosing the services you want to use, such as Facebook or Bebo (see Figure 11.20).

There are a number of ways to encourage people to listen to your songs and add them to their profiles. The key is to be interactive. Just because you have music uploaded onto your profile doesn't mean your job is done. Ask people to listen, comment, and add. All of the suggestions in this chapter are especially important when you are promoting a single and need to build buzz while you're trying to get Internet and other radio play or secure gigs. The number of plays and the kinds of comments you receive can be convincing to the right people that you have a growing audience.

In addition to sharing and sending your music playlist (explored in the previous section), let's take a look at some other ways you can get fans interested in your song clips.

Figure 11.20   Post your playlist elsewhere on the Internet by clicking Share and choosing the destinations.

Ask Nicely

Sometimes we take it for granted that people will know exactly what we want them to do. But unless you ask, a person might not think to add your song to his or her profile. Encourage visitors to your page to listen to your newest song, comment on it, and add it to their profile. Let them know you appreciate their support. You can embed your request right into your profile's text, near the top of the About section. It might look something like this:

> Check out our latest single, "Life in the Afterglow." Let us know what you think.... Tell us what you think by leaving us a comment. If you like it, please add the song to your profile and tell your friends. Thanks again for your support!

Whenever possible, encourage fan interaction with you and your music. An interactive environment makes you seem more real and less like a faceless marketing department behind a profile. This encouragement can be done directly on your profile, in bulletins, through emails, by leaving comments for friends, and in your blog entries. Ask fans to listen to your music and give their thoughts and feedback. Invite them to leave you comments and re-commend you to their friends. Leave them a nice thank-you comment when they take the time to give you feedback. Remember, if you don't ask, you don't get. So ask, and ask often.

You can get would-be and current fans to visit your profile and listen to your songs by using comments, posting bulletins, posting blogs, and adding text to your profile. Following are a few additional ways to use your music player features and profile songs to your advantage using these communication methods:

- **Solicit feedback.** Leave comments on friends' pages and post bulletins. "Hey, we just uploaded a new song, 'Go West Girls,' and we'd really like to know what you think of it! Take a listen and leave us a comment!"

- **Set goals.** Tell everyone via profile text, comments, bulletins, and even email that you're trying to get 100 profile song adds this week. Invite them to listen to your song, add it to their profile, and leave you a comment (see Figure 11.21). Promise you'll comment back for anyone who does this. Then follow through.

Figure 11.21   When fans leave you comments, be sure to comment back to them and thank them for visiting your page.

- **Pick favorites.** Ask friends to vote for their favorite song of yours and leave you a comment with their pick and why it's their favorite. Ask them to add their favorite to their profile.

- **Vote.** Incorporate a poll onto your profile using an application such as PollDaddy (see Chapter 13 for more on apps) and ask fans to vote for their favorite song.

- **Brag.** Have you gotten great comments, feedback, radio play, or even press coverage on your songs? Spread the news and get others interested in seeing what your music has to offer.

- **Post lyrics.** Announce that your lyrics are now available within the music player and that you are responding to the many requests for them. Ask fans to comment on your songwriting.

- **Strive for the top.** Rally your fans and friends to listen to your songs, leave comments, add your music to their profiles, and spread the word…all because you're striving for a spot on the Daily Charts. MySpace editorially decides on top artists based on who's getting the most buzz and contributing interesting music, so it definitely takes a village to catch their eye.

- **Use outside contests, rankings, and awards.** Indie music and ranking sites such as GarageBand.com (see Figure 11.22) and TopsinAmerica.com offer contests, weekly awards, and rankings competitions for musicians. Invite friends and fans to listen to you and vote for you and your music. Then post your award results (see Figure 11.23) in bulletins and on your profile.

ENTER THE CONTEST

Musicians Only : Register Band : Enter Contest : Host MP3s : Sell Album

Get your music heard around the world!

- Every song gets written feedback from listeners
- Top songs climb the charts, win exposure from Clear Channel & more!
- Dozens signed by labels so far

Figure 11.22 GarageBand.com offers chances for artists to enter contests and receive recognition for the best of the week and overall rankings.

- **Offer free downloads.** I don't normally advocate offering free downloads through your MySpace music player. It's better to direct users to your main website, where you can gather some contact information and *then* give a free download. Either way, though, it *is* a great promotional hook. You could even use B-roll type of audio footage, a remix, or an acoustic version of one of your songs instead of the album version. Offer a free

Rank	All-time: <u>#408</u> of 5,136 in Pop Best #46 of 497 on 27Apr2006
Awards!	Track of the Day on 28Mar2006 in Pop #18 Best Female Vocals in Pop, *all-time* #11 Best Love Song in Pop, *all-time* Best Female Vocals in Pop, week of 13Mar2006 Best Female Vocals in Pop, week of 20Mar2006 Best Melody in Pop, week of 6Feb2006 Best Love Song overall, week of 6Feb2006 Best Love Song in Pop, week of 6Feb2006

Figure 11.23   An artist's GarageBand.com awards.

download to the first 150 people who add your song to their profile and post a bulletin on your behalf. Use services like Go-Backstage.com to give out free music, and require an email address for your marketing list in return.

Keep your text conversational, light, and sincere. Encourage friends to repost your bulletins inviting fans to listen to and comment on your songs by including an auto-bulletin button or by simply asking nicely (see Chapter 14, "Bulletins and Event Invitations"). Include auto-comment buttons on your profile so visitors can easily post your requests to their friends (refer to Chapter 10). A mass commenting or friend adder program with commenting capabilities will help you leave many comments at once. Remember, however, to fly under the radar by not posting more than 50 to 100 comments a day. Some say you can do more than that without being caught, but I recommend a conservative approach so as not to risk losing your entire profile and all your hard work. After all, MySpace's terms of use disallow such programs.

You're on your way to building a fan base that helps *you* market your music. Now let's learn more about photos and videos. . . .

12 Photos and Videos

Your career is more than just music. Photos and videos are an integral part of the package and essential to your imaging and branding. When people purchase your music and buy into what you're offering, your image is a part of their decision.

A Picture's Worth a Thousand Words

Photos are an integral part of the artist's image. Often, after the music, the photo is the second thing that people look to when listening to music. Consumers, industry insiders, and media alike know that image is important and it takes effort to package oneself as an artist. A compelling image that fits in with your style of music speaks volumes about your artistry and professionalism.

We've discussed photos in a few places already. Here's a recap:

- **Chapter 6, "Getting Started."** Your main (thumbnail) photo, guidelines for choosing photos, and photographers.

- **Chapter 7, "Signing Up and MySpace Profile Basics."** Uploading photos during the profile setup process.

- **Chapter 8, "Customizing Your Page."** Embedding photos, images, and other graphics right onto your profile.

This chapter will focus on uploading photos into your account and the various features you can tap into. However, before continuing, please reference the photo sections in the aforementioned chapters.

You've seen by now how critical a good picture is to your image as an artist. Without it, an artist looks as though he doesn't take his music or career seriously (see Figure 12.1).

If you haven't already uploaded your profile (a.k.a. thumbnail) photo, click on the Photos: Upload link. Choose the photo(s) you'd like to upload from your hard drive by clicking on them in the upper-left corner. Below the area to choose your photos to upload, you can pick an album in which you'd like to place them. When you're finished, click Upload to send your photo files to the MySpace servers (see Figure 12.2). Note that photo sizes must be less than

217

Figure 12.1   Without a great photo to represent you, your profile looks...well, lame. If you don't care, neither will your fans.

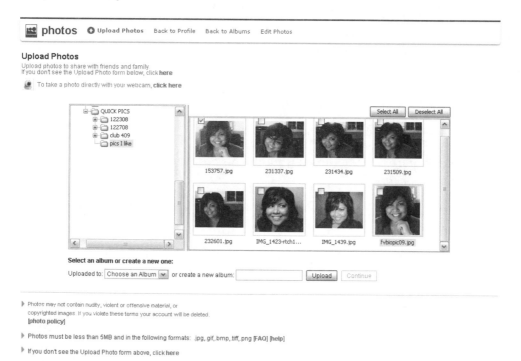

Figure 12.2   This is the main photo upload screen.

5 MB (as of this writing) and in one of five standard formats: JPG, GIF, BMP, TIF, or PNG. Remember, you can only use photos for which you own the copyright or have otherwise licensed the right to use.

A link above the photo browsing window gives you the option to take a photo with your webcam (refer to Figure 12.2). For regular users this might be a fun option. But in my opinion, bands should stay away from webcam photos for their profile, not only because the quality and lighting are often not very good, but also because it doesn't exactly say, "I'm a professional musician who takes my career seriously." If you decide to proceed, click on the link and follow the directions. The MySpace page will recognize your webcam and allow you to take a photo and upload it immediately to the MySpace server.

Back to your uploaded photos... Now that your photo has been sent to the server, you will be asked to add a caption. Enter your caption in the text box provided (see Figure 12.3). You can also "tag" the photo by clicking the Tag Photo link and picking people who appear in your photo from your Friends list (see Figure 12.4).

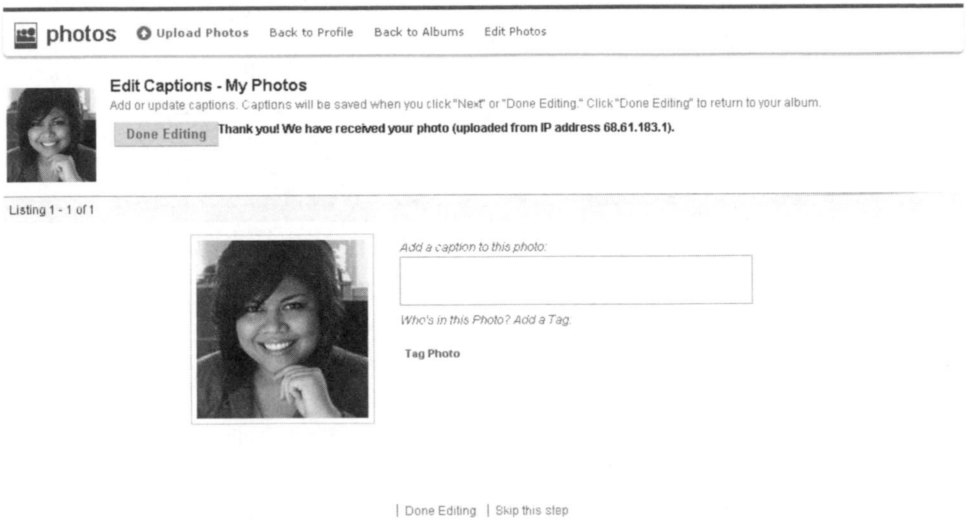

Figure 12.3 Add a caption to your photo. When you have people other than yourself in the photo, click on Tag Photo to add your friends' names and notify them of your upload.

If you prefer not to add a caption, simply skip the step. Otherwise, click Done Editing when finished, and you will see your photo in the designated album (see Figure 12.5).

As you can also see in Figure 12.5, you have a variety of links for things you can do with photos, such as arranging your photos in an album, deleting, moving photos to other albums, and creating slides, collages, and other photo art.

Photos that represent who you are as an artist and are intriguing, fun, or beautiful should be your second priority, right after creating great music!

Video Essentials

How many times have you heard a song and thought, "Meh, it's only so-so," but when you saw the video you completely changed your mind? The strength of the music video is in its

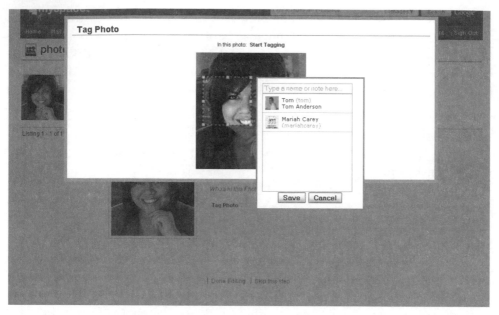

Figure 12.4   The Tag Photo screen: Click on a face in the picture and choose that friend's name from your Friends list.

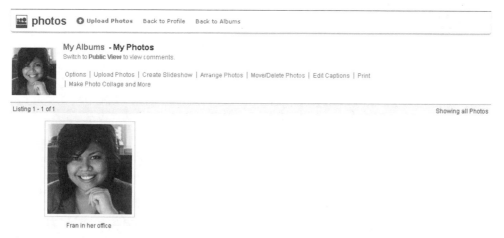

Figure 12.5   Your photo now appears in the folder you chose.

ability to transcend just the music and evoke the imagery of the song or the powerful image of the artist. Suddenly, a song that you couldn't relate to before becomes more three-dimensional. You discern elements of the music, lyrics, and mood that previously escaped your notice. Sometimes it's the artist and the slickness of the production or the moving story embodied in the video that can change one's mind. People learn in a variety of ways, and for the visually oriented, video is king.

Music videos can be expensive endeavors, but indie artists may be surprised by the resources in their community. If you're interested in making a music video, contact local private and university film programs and network with student and indie filmmakers. Many know that music video production can be lucrative and are anxious to have a few under their belt. Some will even direct and produce your video for free and may only require you to pay for film supplies and set materials.

Video blogs and behind-the-scenes footage are also a great way to build a rapport with fans. These types of videos humanize the artist and make him or her more relatable to the audience. And fans love to get an inside peek at what their favorite musicians are up to in the "real" world.

In Chapter 8, we briefly touched on how to embed videos into your MySpace profile. Now let's look in more depth at uploading your videos onto MySpace.

Your MySpace profile control panel has a link near your picture for Videos: Edit | Upload. Click the Upload link to move to the Upload a Video page (see Figure 12.6). Click Browse to locate your video on your hard drive. When you've found it, click Open in the Browse window and then Upload Video. Note that as of this writing, you can upload as many videos as you want into your account, but each must be less than 500 MB. Most major video file types are supported, but like photos, you may only upload videos for which you own the copyright or have licensed use.

Figure 12.6   This is the main screen to upload videos. In the upper-right corner, you can choose to record your video through your webcam instead.

Now you are taken to a page where you are asked to title and describe your video (see Figure 12.7). Pay special importance to the Tags field. Here you will add keywords that best describe your video to aid users in finding it. (For example, add your band name, where you filmed the video, the name of the song, the genre of music, other special words associated with the song, and so on.) Do not put commas between your tag words. Optional settings are also available at the bottom of the page. As a band, you generally will want all your videos to be public and embeddable by users.

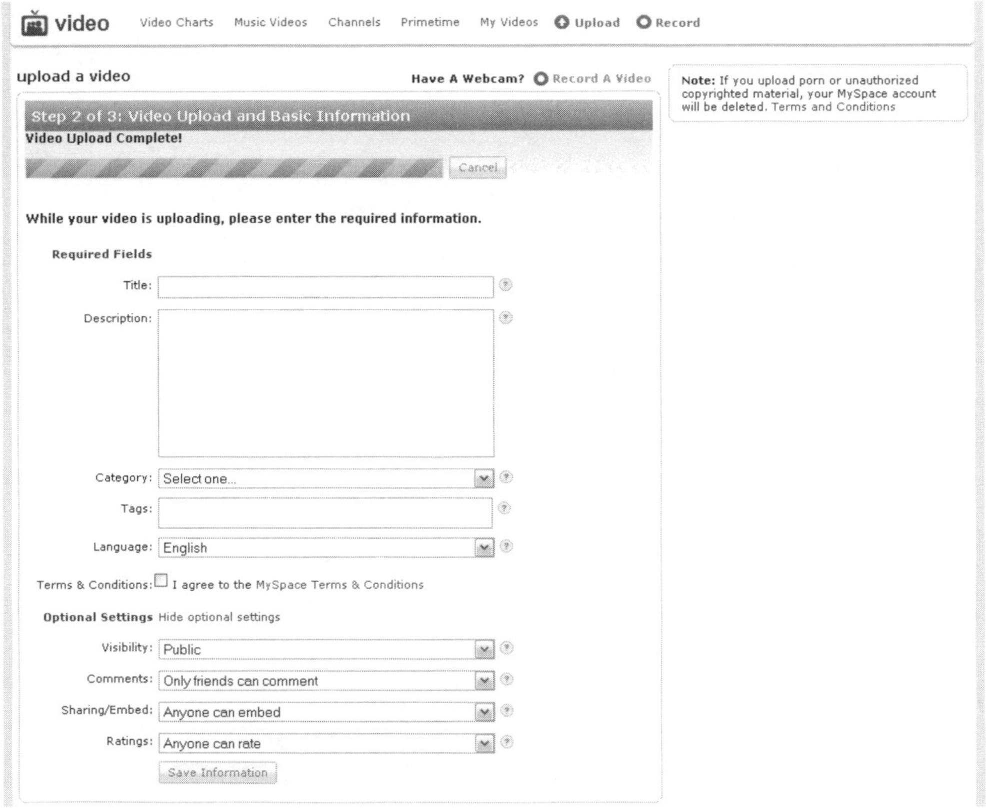

Figure 12.7   The Upload a Video screen allows you to title your video, add a description, and make your clip searchable.

When you are finished describing and tagging your video, click Save Information. This will send the video to the MySpace servers. It will take a few minutes for it to upload and then be converted to a playable web format. You'll also be provided with embed code and a link to the video that you can email to friends (see Figure 12.8). When it is complete, a thumbnail of the video plus additional information will appear on your My Videos page (see Figure 12.9).

To access your Videos page from your home control panel, simply click on the Videos: Edit link below your main photo. Each video has settings you can manipulate (see Figure 12.9). Click on the appropriate links to post your video to your profile, bulletin, or blog; edit the

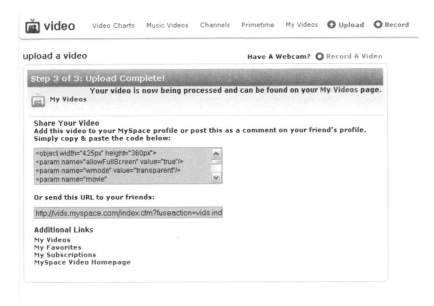

Figure 12.8   Your video is now ready to plug into a comment or your profile.

Figure 12.9   On your My Videos page, you will see all of your uploaded videos.

description and tags; or even delete it. When you click on the Add to: Profile link, your video will be added to the music player that appears on your profile. Notice in Figure 12.10 that the number of profile videos available appears at the bottom of the music player, and when you click that link, the videos appear in a window in the player.

You may have noticed the red Record link in the upper-right corner of all the video pages we just discussed. This is a great tool to record video blogs and speak directly to your fans. Assuming you have a webcam connected to your computer, click on this Record link. It will take you to a MySpace screen that, with your permission, can access your computer's webcam (see Figure 12.11). From this page you can record and save your video blogs (20 minutes or less each) right to your MySpace account!

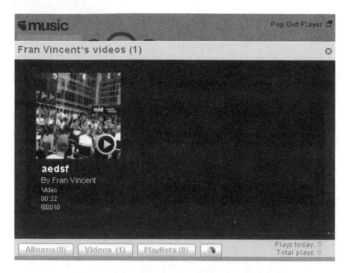

Fran Vincent's Latest Blog Entry [Subscribe to this Blog]

Figure 12.10   The videos you elect to add to your profile will be playable from your music player.

Figure 12.11   The Record screen may ask you to allow or deny this page access to your webcam. To use this feature, click Allow.

Recording and posting video blogs regularly is a fantastic way to communicate with your fans. Better than just writing them a note or a blog, they can see you, hear you, and feel like you're talking directly to them. Moreover, you can allow users to comment on your videos, which makes it a two-way interaction! Do video blogs regularly and make them available to fans. Be sure to bulletin, blog, and email fans to let them know when new videos are up.

More Video Tips

A great touch for your profile is to embed one of your music videos right into the layout, and then below it provide the code in a text box. Encourage users to grab that code and embed it on *their* pages by copying and pasting the code into their profile. Make it easy for them by showing the code in a scrollable text box (see Figure 12.12).

Figure 12.12 Fans can copy the video code in your text box and then paste it right into their profiles. It's free advertising for you!

The code will look like this:

```
<textarea cols="30" rows="5" wrap="hard" readonly="yes">INSERT YOUR VIDEO CODE HERE</textarea>
```

You can change the column height and row width to make the box smaller or larger. Since the text box is set to read only, users can only copy the code from it; they cannot alter it in any way.

Try this same tactic when displaying banners that you want users to grab and embed onto their profile. (This is great for when you are posting banners touting a new album, single, or tour.) For more on banners, see the section "Profile Banners" in Chapter 8.

Be aware of conflicting audio and video on your profile. If your music player is set to begin playing automatically, you should not have any videos on your profile that also play automatically. Obviously, it creates a sound collision when everything starts playing at once. Should your embedded videos play as soon as your page is loaded, and you don't know how to stop them from doing so, try to edit your settings from within your video hosting service (whether it's MySpace or another site) or switch to a different video host.

Now that you've mastered uploading photos and videos, let's move on to those micro wonders . . . apps and widgets!

13 Apps and Widgets

When people hear the term *social media,* they often think of MySpace, Facebook, Twitter, and other similar services. But social media goes beyond that and includes blogging, content syndication, commenting, and more. In this chapter we'll focus on apps and widgets, what they are, and how they can be used to promote your music.

From Games to Microsites

The average user may not know the difference, but those who work in the web space distinguish between widgets and apps, and we will do the same in this chapter. Widgets and apps (short for *applications*) are similar—at the basic level they are small, portable, viral programs that serve a function in either the web or mobile space.

However, web widgets are basically graphical interfaces rendered by blocks of code that can then be plugged into any web/HTML environment. They generally display a predetermined set of information and/or allow the user to input data or interact in a very strict fashion.

In many cases, apps tend to be more complex and interactive, much more like a computer program whose output varies depending on the input of the user. Let's take a look at some examples:

■ An artist generates an email widget through their ReverbNation.com (see Figure 13.1) or VerticalResponse.com (see Figure 13.2) account and plugs the code for this widget into their MySpace profile or website. Fans can then enter their email addresses (see Figure 13.3). It's a one-way input of information.

■ Bands create promotional widgets that display their videos, bios, and music clips (see Figure 13.4). These widgets act as mini (or micro) websites. The band then copies the code for their promotional widget into their MySpace profile and website. While users can input their email address into the widget to join a fan mailing list, the content offered by the widget is preset, and, as on a regular website, the user can only click and view the information (see Figure 13.5).

227

Figure 13.1   This email widget from ReverbNation.com allows fans to input their email address, which is then sent to the artist's account on ReverbNation. The artist can then send the fan updates and other email promotions.

Figure 13.2   VerticalResponse.com is primarily an email marketing site where users can build widgets like this one that are capable of gathering fan-inputted email addresses for future promotions. The widget can be customized in color and the fields you'd like your fans to fill out.

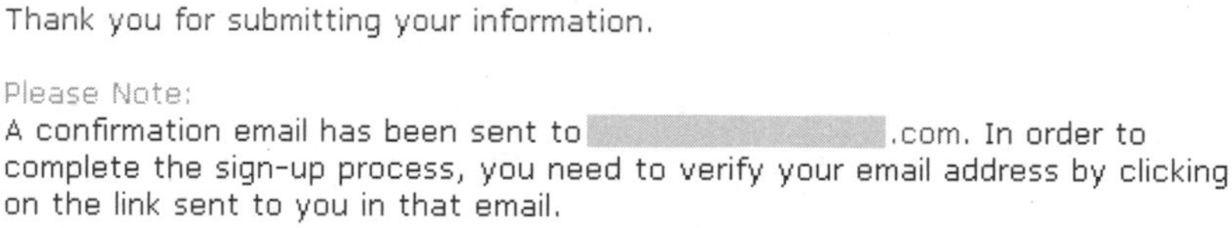

Thank you for submitting your information.

Please Note:
A confirmation email has been sent to ▮▮▮▮▮▮▮▮▮▮.com. In order to complete the sign-up process, you need to verify your email address by clicking on the link sent to you in that email.

Figure 13.3   After entering their email address into a VerticalResponse widget, the fan receives a message confirming their request was received.

- In both MySpace and Facebook, users play games such as Mafia Wars (see Figure 13.6) and YoVille (see Figure 13.7) and take quizzes and tests (see Figure 13.8), posting the results to their profiles. Their friends see these game activities and often want to play too, so they load the same app onto their profile, play the games with their friends, and compare quiz results. The cycle repeats amongst the next set of friends, allowing the app to spread via profile word of mouth.

- Users with iPhones and other similar mobile gadgets can download all kinds of apps (see Figure 13.9) in the form of games, work and life tools, social networking (such as accessing one's MySpace or Facebook account on the road), and even music apps (see Figure 13.10). These applications are downloaded to the gadget, installed, and used similar to desktop computer programs but on a smaller scale.

Now that we have differentiated between apps and widgets, let's explore them individually and discuss how you can use them in your musical endeavors.

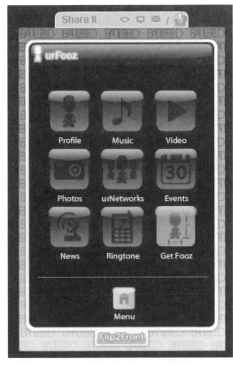

Figure 13.4   urFooz bills itself as a portable profile, which is what an artist widget is. This Jordin Sparks urFooz widget allows the user to click on the artist's bio, music, videos, events, and more.

Figure 13.5   While fans can enter their email address into the Goldfrapp widget, you can see that up top are links to view artist info, and the bottom showcases links to buy and more.

Figure 13.6   Mafia Wars is a popular game on social networks such as MySpace and Facebook.

Figure 13.7   YoVille, another popular social networking game, allows users to build their own little worlds and interact with their friends.

He Ain't Heavy . . . He's Just a Widget

Widgets are small, light, easy to move around.... They're meant to be the opposite of cumbersome. You've probably seen dozens of widgets in your web adventures already without realizing it. For instance, ever been to a blog or a site with a scrolling or constantly refreshing block of news headlines or video clips? News and video widgets are common now, and they allow bloggers and other sites to offer up-to-date content to their readers. All they had to do was go to a site such as Reuters.com, copy the block of code, and plug it into their site (see Figure 13.11). And like that *<snap>*, the widget adds new and interesting content.

For artists, there are probably hundreds of different types of widgets you can use to promote your music, gather information about your fans, and interact with them. Check out

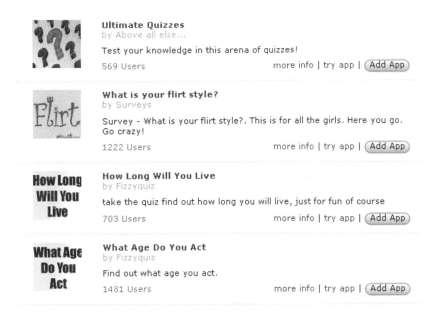

Ultimate Quizzes
by Above all else...

Test your knowledge in this arena of quizzes!

569 Users   more info | try app | (Add App)

What is your flirt style?
by Surveys

Survey - What is your flirt style?. This is for all the girls. Here you go. Go crazy!

1222 Users   more info | try app | (Add App)

How Long Will You Live
by Fizzyquiz

take the quiz find out how long you will live, just for fun of course

703 Users   more info | try app | (Add App)

What Age Do You Act
by Fizzyquiz

Find out what age you act.

1481 Users   more info | try app | (Add App)

Figure 13.8   Quizzes are a perennial favorite on social networks and even some dating sites. Users post their results to their profiles and invite friends to take the quiz or even challenge them to beat their scores.

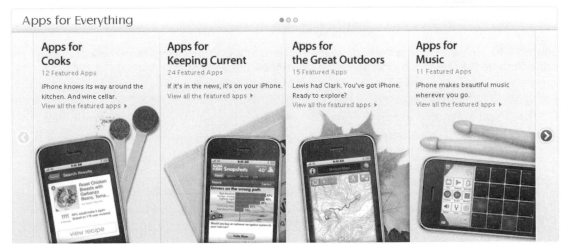

Figure 13.9   This is a quick snapshot of the iPhone app gallery.

Appendix A for a list of some of those widgets. Choose one or two from the list and build your own widget to display on your MySpace, website, Facebook, and more.

Most artist promotional widgets act like mini websites and contain much of the same information, only shortened. When you're getting ready to build your own widget, first gather the information you'll need.

Figure 13.10   iPhone users can also download various music applications, from those that play music to some that record, create, and even identify music heard on a radio!

- **Bio.** (You may need to edit it down to a few short paragraphs.) Widgets don't lend themselves well to endless pages of reading!

- **Music clips in MP3 format.**

- **Music and promotional videos.** This can also include video blogs, acoustic versions, behind-the-scenes footage, goofing around, clips from the studio or songwriting with band members, and concert footage. Some widgets are able to display the videos you already have uploaded to your YouTube account, so be sure to have your YouTube account page address readily available.

- **Photos and graphics.** Gather your promotional photos, graphics from your website or MySpace profile (some widgets will allow you to use these as the widget's background), and the cover(s) of your albums and singles. If you have extras, such as wallpapers, avatars, and icons for your band, pull those as well.

- **Events and gig dates.**

Embed Code:

`<script src="http://nmp.newsgator.com/NGBuzz/buzz.ashx?bu`

Reuters widgets allow you to view, read and interact with Reuters content on your social network, blog, web site or personalized homepage.

A widget is a free, quick and simple way to have Reuters content available on the web sites you visit most often.

Figure 13.11   Reuters is just one of many news sites to offer widgets that display the day's top stories. Here is an entertainment news widget from Reuters suitable for use on any website, social network, or blog.

- **Links to buy music** (from iTunes, Amazon, or wherever you are selling your music from), ringtones, and merch.

Sites such as ReverbNation have options for artists to build widgets that are very specific, such as a widget that only displays upcoming shows. Poke around some of the suggested sites in Appendix A and do your own research to find the widgets that work for you (see Figure 13.12).

Figure 13.12   This artist widget was created through Sprout Builder (sproutinc.com), which gives you complete artistic control of how your widget looks and functions, which is essential for a truly custom, branded look.

Posting and Sharing Your Widget

Once you have your widget built, you can publish it to your MySpace by using the share or embed functions in the widget. Here you'll see links to MySpace and other social networks and blogs where your widget can be posted (see Figure 13.13).

Figure 13.13   When a user clicks on the Share link in this widget, a screen comes up with various options for posting and emailing.

Click on the MySpace icon, and a MySpace window will pop up, showing you what can be done with the widget. As you can see in Figure 13.14, you can post it to your blog, bulletin, or About Me section.

Figure 13.14 The widget for the motion picture *Up in the Air* can be posted to your MySpace with the click of a button.

Let's say, however, that you don't want to embed the widget in your About Me section of your profile. Maybe you want to put your widget on the left side of your profile in the Band Members section. In this case, you'll have to abandon the one-click method and paste the widget code directly into the section you desire.

In my opinion, the best way to do this is to go back to the widget, click on Share, and instead of clicking on MySpace, simply copy the "embed code" noted in the widget (refer to Figure 13.13) and paste it into the section in which you'd like it to appear on your profile (see Figure 13.15). (Refer to Chapter 8 on customizing your page.)

At the bottom of Figure 13.14, you'll notice the text Add the MySpace Link by Copying the Code. Click here, and you'll see the screen with the widget code and instructions on how to embed your code (see Figure 13.16). I find this a less reliable way for most non-HTML-savvy users to deal with the code, but if you're game to try it, go ahead. Basically, you will take the code that you've copied and paste it right into the field where you want it. Developer guidelines give you more tips on how to do this.

Figure 13.15   The *Up in the Air* widget embedded into a MySpace profile General Interests section.

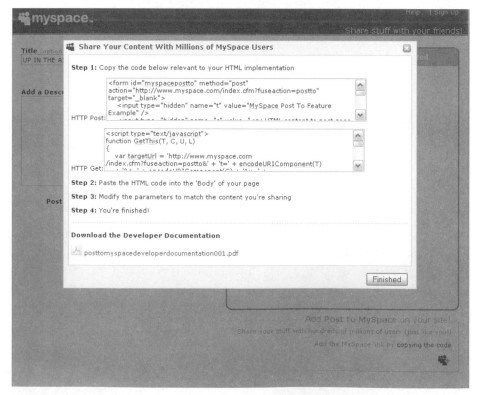

Figure 13.16   This is another, more complicated option for handling your widget.

Once you've finished your widget and posted it into your profile, be sure to email it to your fans and contacts, post it to your blogs and bulletins, and send it out to all of your social networks, not just MySpace. Keep your widget fresh and interesting by updating content and adding new music and videos regularly. It's important to keep reminding fans of your widget and asking them to repost and send to their friends. This is how you will get more fans and more awareness of your music.

Apps for Artists

MySpace has a gallery of apps that you can use for the promotion of your music, as well as the enjoyment of others' music. Find your apps gallery by going to the navigation bar at the top of the MySpace page and then click on More > Apps Gallery. You'll see there are hundreds, if not thousands, of options across an array of categories. If you look at the Music section, you'll see a host of apps, including artist widgets, music discovery modules, music and video playlist creators, and even DJ beatmakers (see Figure 13.17)!

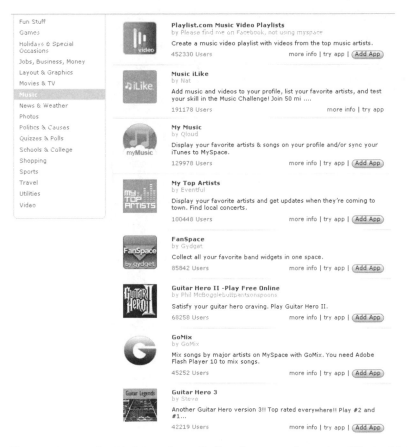

Figure 13.17   The MySpace Apps Gallery has a music section filled with lots of music apps for artists and enthusiasts.

Don't limit yourself to the Music section. Apps in the Events section can help promote upcoming gigs. Get some glittery graphics for your page from Layout and Graphics apps. Sync your Twitter and MySpace updates by downloading an app from the Utilities area. Or even create a poll on your profile with PollDaddy, found in the Quizzes & Polls section.

When you find an app you like, click on that app in the gallery and then on the Add this App button. A screen will pop up asking you what you want to do. Add the app to your profile for all to see or just to your home page (home control panel) for your private use, and alert your friends that you have added an app (see Figure 13.18).

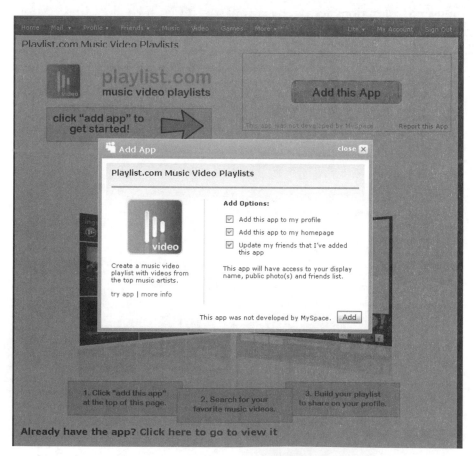

Figure 13.18 The Playlist application can be added to your profile, home page, or both.

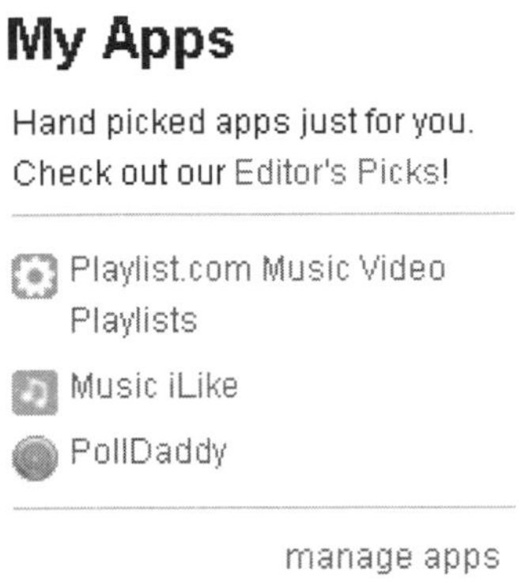

My Apps

Hand picked apps just for you.
Check out our Editor's Picks!

Playlist.com Music Video
Playlists

Music iLike

PollDaddy

manage apps

Figure 13.19   Manipulate your applications from My Apps.

To access your apps, delete them, or change their settings, see the My Apps section in your home control panel (see Figure 13.19).

Now it's time to take a look at bulletins and event invitations....

14 Bulletins and Event Invitations

In this chapter, we'll take a look at using bulletins to communicate with your friends and fans, as well as using event listings and invites to get people to your gigs.

Your Virtual Bulletin Board

In your MySpace home control panel, you'll notice your Stream toward the middle of the page. This area houses the activity of your friends, including bulletins your friends have posted (see Figure 14.1). Much like an actual bulletin board, people post messages and announcements that are viewable only by those on their Friends list (or another subset they designate). This is a quick and easy way to communicate with all your friends at once.

When MySpace was but a youngster in social networking, bulletins were very effective in getting the attention of friends and encouraging them to check out a profile, hop over to the official website, or attend a local gig. Over time, however, many argue that bulletins have lost some of their impact. Most people have a fair number of friends, and the more friends a person has, the more bulletins he'll see in that little window in the control panel. This saturation of real and spam bulletins and the tendency to over-post have caused some users to glaze over when they see posts... or ignore them entirely.

This doesn't mean, however, that you shouldn't bother using bulletins. They can still be effective if approached correctly. We'll look at how to post and how to strike a proper balance between getting on the radar of your audience and keeping in their good graces.

Figure 14.1 Keep track of all of your bulletins in the Bulletins section of your Stream.

241

The Basics of Bulletins

The first thing we'll do is look at where your bulletins are located, how to access them, and how to create and post your own. Then we'll explore how you might use them in your marketing endeavors.

You'll notice that your Bulletins section only holds a limited number of posts at a time (see Figure 14.2)—20 to be exact. It sounds like a lot, but it may be only a small fraction of the total bulletins from one's friends. If there are a lot of bulletin posts going through, some will never see the light of day in this window. When that happens, the poster has to rely on the viewer clicking the View All Bulletins link to see the rest of the posts (see Figure 14.3). You'll need to post often enough to get into the window and be seen, but not so often that you're sending out meaningless bulletins that aggravate your audience. We'll tackle this more later in this chapter, in the "Bulletin Ideas" section.

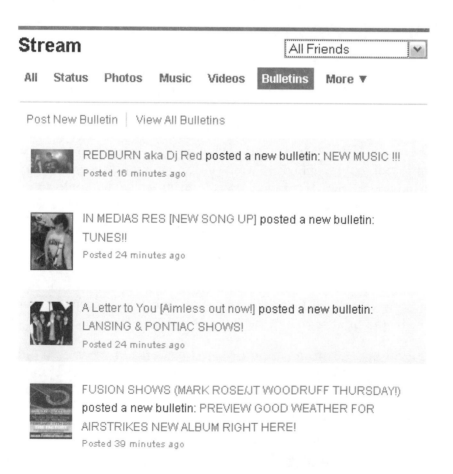

Figure 14.2   Your Bulletins window only holds 20 bulletins at a time, making it prime real estate. In the interest of space, this example shows only five bulletins.

Figure 14.3   The rest of your bulletins are accessed by clicking View All Bulletins at the top or View More at the bottom of the Bulletins area.

For now, let's learn how to post our first bulletin. It's really quite a painless process. In your Stream > Bulletins section, click on Post New Bulletin, as shown in Figure 14.4. Here you are presented with a subject and body field to enter your bulletin text (see Figure 14.5). As of now, MySpace does not provide an HTML editing interface to allow you to customize your bulletins. You can do that on third-party editing sites (addressed later in this chapter, in the "Spicing Up Bulletins" section). But for now, we'll just work with a simple text bulletin in the provided text editor.

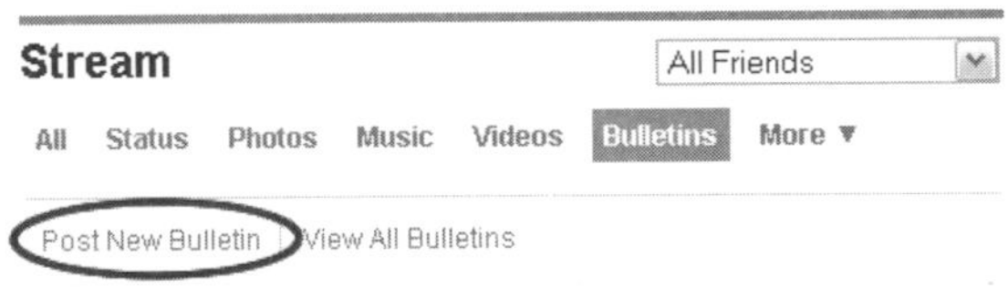

Figure 14.4   Send out your own bulletins any time by clicking Post New Bulletin in your home control panel.

First enter your plain text. You can also add a video to your bulletin if you desire. Click on the little Add a Video icon at the bottom of the bulletin text box (as shown in Figure 14.5), and you can choose a video you've uploaded into your MySpace account (Figure 14.6) or another video that has been uploaded onto MySpace by any user. The system will then embed it into your bulletin. This is great for announcing video blogs, new music videos, and live footage, sharing fan videos, and more.

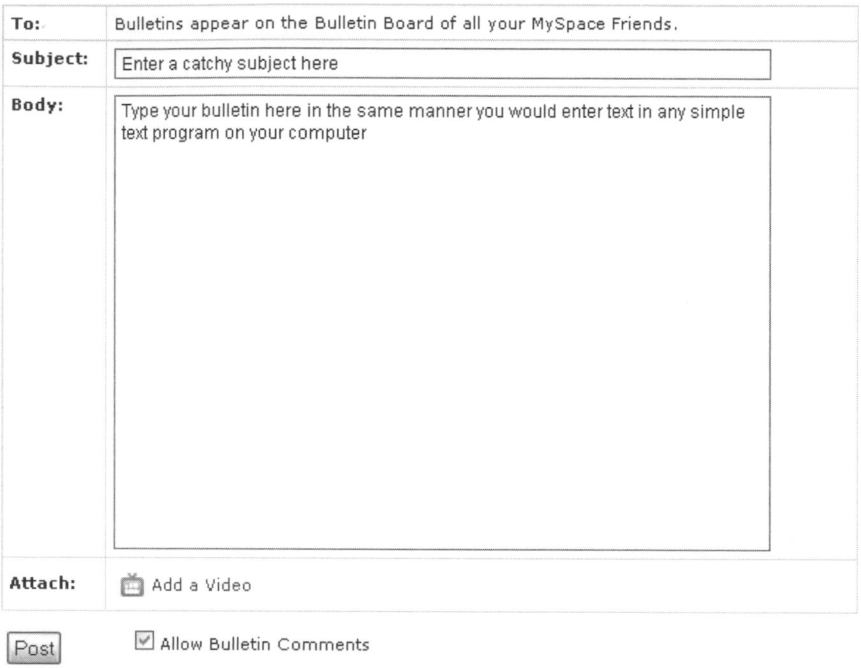

To:
Bulletins appear on the Bulletin Board of all your MySpace Friends.
Subject:
Enter a catchy subject here
Body:
Type your bulletin here in the same manner you would enter text in any simple text program on your computer
Attach:
Add a Video
Post
Allow Bulletin Comments

Figure 14.5 This is your MySpace bulletin editor, where you can enter text and code.

Home
Mail (1)
Profile
Friends
Music
Video
More
«Back to Bulletin Board
Post Bulletin
Add a Video
Search MySpaceTV
Search
close
My Videos
Featured
Top Videos
Uploads | Favorites | Subscriptions
Parrots Dancing
by: Frannie
add
Displaying 0-1 of 1
Page 1 of 1
Post
Allow Bulletin Comments

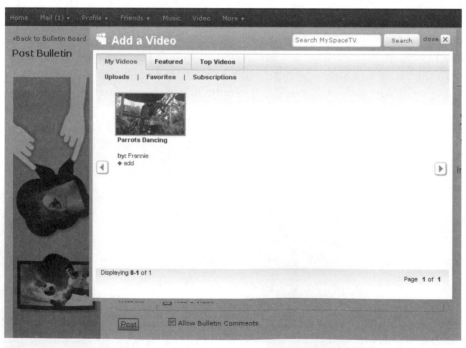

Figure 14.6 You can choose a video that is currently uploaded onto MySpace and embed it into your bulletin.

Also notice in Figure 14.5 that there is a little checkbox to Allow Bulletin Comments. These function like any other comments on MySpace. (Refer to Chapter 10 for a rundown of the most common types of MySpace comments.) If you click this box, people will be able to leave their feedback and thoughts, good and bad, right on your bulletin for all to see (see Figure 14.7).

Comments

Write your comment here...

Submit

Figure 14.7   A comment box will appear beneath your bulletin if you choose to allow friends to give feedback on what you have posted.

After you've entered your simple text, double-check it to make sure it is exactly how you want it to appear. Then click Post. MySpace used to give you a chance to confirm and edit plain text before it posted. Now it posts these types of bulletins immediately to everyone on your Friends list! So, if you make a mistake and want to change it, you will have to delete the bulletin and then re-post it.

It sometimes takes a few minutes for your post to become available as a bulletin (see Figure 14.8). When it does, it will look like Figure 14.9. When a friend clicks on your post, he'll see something that looks like Figure 14.10.

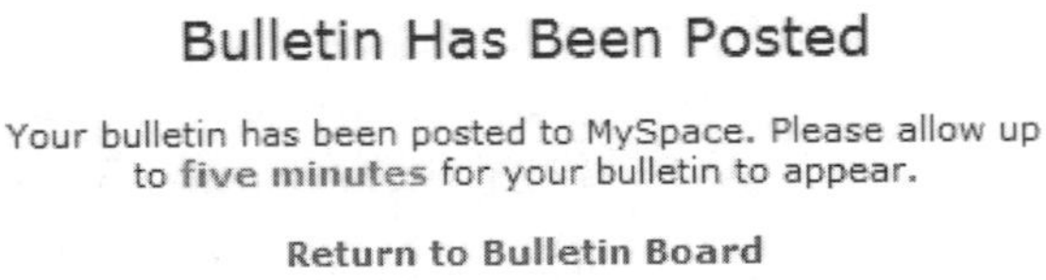

Bulletin Has Been Posted

Your bulletin has been posted to MySpace. Please allow up to **five minutes** for your bulletin to appear.

Return to Bulletin Board

Figure 14.8   MySpace shows you this screen to let you know your bulletin has been successfully entered.

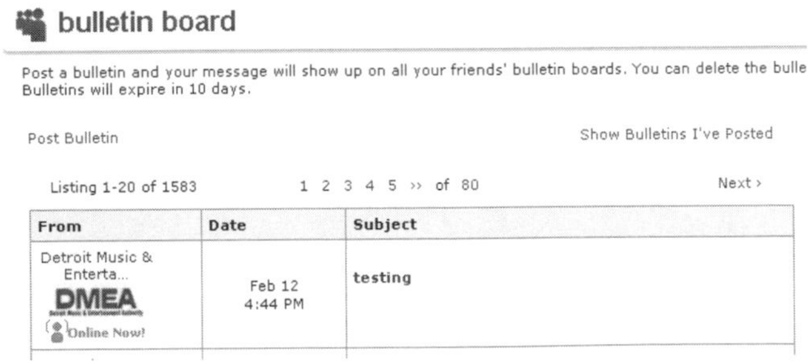

bulletin board

Post a bulletin and your message will show up on all your friends' bulletin boards. You can delete the bulle Bulletins will expire in 10 days.

Post Bulletin   Show Bulletins I've Posted

Listing 1-20 of 1583   1 2 3 4 5 » of 80   Next ›

From	Date	Subject
Detroit Music & Enterta... **DMEA** Online Now!	Feb 12 4:44 PM	testing

Figure 14.9   Your bulletin goes into the queue and hopefully will appear in everyone's Bulletin Stream depending on how many other bulletins it has to compete with. In this figure, you see the bulletin posted in the traditional MySpace Bulletin Board section (the precursor to the Stream). You can still access this classic view by going to bulletins.myspace.com/index. cfm?fuseaction=bulletin while logged in.

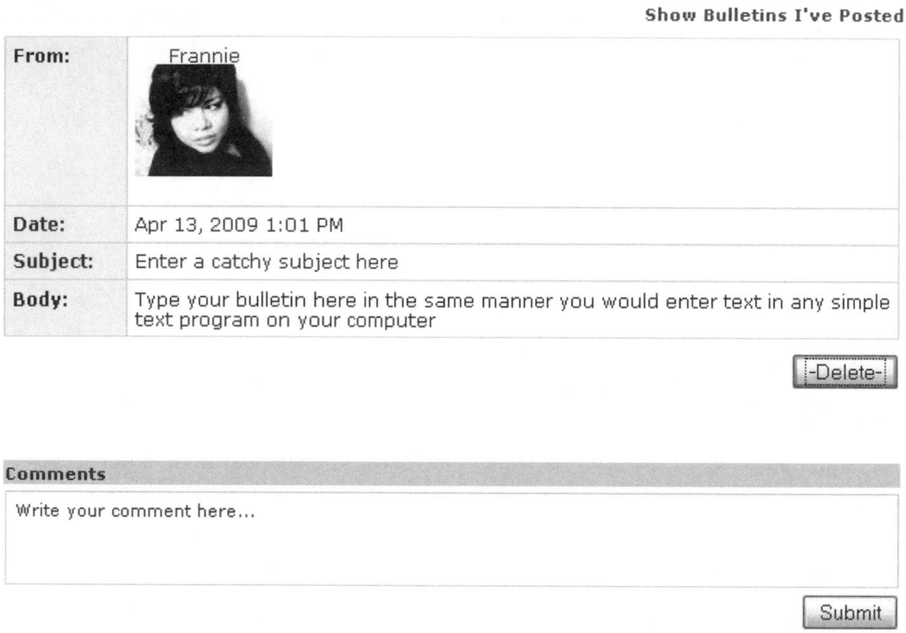

From:	Frannie
Date:	Apr 13, 2009 1:01 PM
Subject:	Enter a catchy subject here
Body:	Type your bulletin here in the same manner you would enter text in any simple text program on your computer

-Delete-

Comments

Write your comment here...

Submit

Figure 14.10   Your bulletin post looks like this to your friends.

So now, let's say you have changed your mind and you want to remove your post. Not a problem. You can access all of your bulletin posts in a few ways. If you are on the page where you view all bulletin entries, click on the Show Bulletins I've Posted link on the right side (see Figure 14.11). Here you'll be able to see all of your bulletin posts and mark the ones you want to delete (see Figure 14.12). You can also reach this page from your home control panel in your Stream. From here, click View All Bulletins and follow the directions in the beginning of

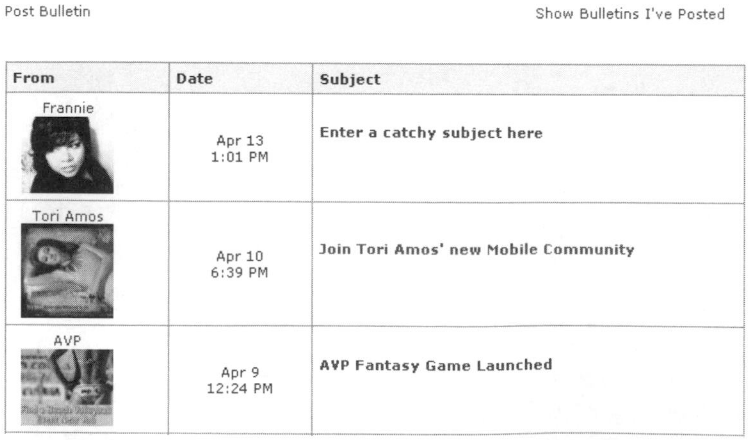

Post Bulletin   Show Bulletins I've Posted

From	Date	Subject
Frannie	Apr 13 1:01 PM	Enter a catchy subject here
Tori Amos	Apr 10 6:39 PM	Join Tori Amos' new Mobile Community
AVP	Apr 9 12:24 PM	AVP Fantasy Game Launched

Figure 14.11   While viewing your list of bulletins, you may decide you want to withdraw one of your posts. Click on Show Bulletins I've Posted to view your entries only.

Post Bulletin   **Return to Main Bulletin List**

	From	Date	Subject
☐	Fifi	Apr 3, 2007 12:33 PM	**Enter a catchy subject here**

☐ Select/Deselect All

[❌ Delete Selected]

Delete selected bulletins.
You can only delete your own bulletins.
Regular bulletins expire in 10 days

Figure 14.12 Delete any or all of the posts you've written. Use the check boxes to choose the ones you want to mark for deletion.

this paragraph (see Figure 14.13). This link will take you to the same place. Or, you can delete your post while you are reading it, utilizing the Delete button below the post (see Figure 14.14). Note, however, that although you can delete your own posts, you cannot delete bulletins posted by others. They'll stay in the system for 10 days.

Figure 14.13 You can also access your bulletin posts from your home control panel.

In the same way that your friends view your posts, you also view theirs. You'll notice that there is a button at the bottom of every post you're reading that lets you reply to the poster (see Figure 14.15). This makes it easy to ask a question or put in your two cents on the topic at hand, unless you find the poster irritating. In that case, you can hit the Delete from Friends button!

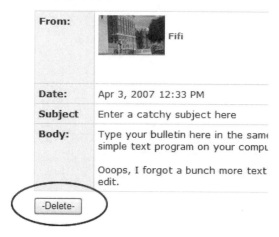

Figure 14.14   While reading a post you've written, you can simply hit the Delete button to get rid of it.

Figure 14.15   The Reply to Poster button allows for instant interactivity.

You've now mastered the technical basics of bulletin posting. But what if you want to jazz up your post with videos and pics? Read on!

Spicing Up Bulletins

There are a number of ways to snazz up your bulletins with pictures, videos, bold text, and more. In Chapter 8, we went through how to add these elements to your profile and tweak your text. The process is the same for bulletins.

If you are comfortable with adding in HTML tags on your own to customize your text and embed visual elements, then you can do so right in the bulletin body field in MySpace (see Figure 14.16). An interesting thing happens when you enter HTML tags. The MySpace system *knows* that you have added HTML. So instead of posting the bulletin immediately (like it did for plain-text bulletins), it will give you a chance to preview your bulletin and make changes. You'll even notice the Post button change to a Preview button when HTML tags are entered.

So now when you click Preview, you are presented with the confirmation screen. Here you'll see the HTML tags you entered executed into a visual display (see Figure 14.17).

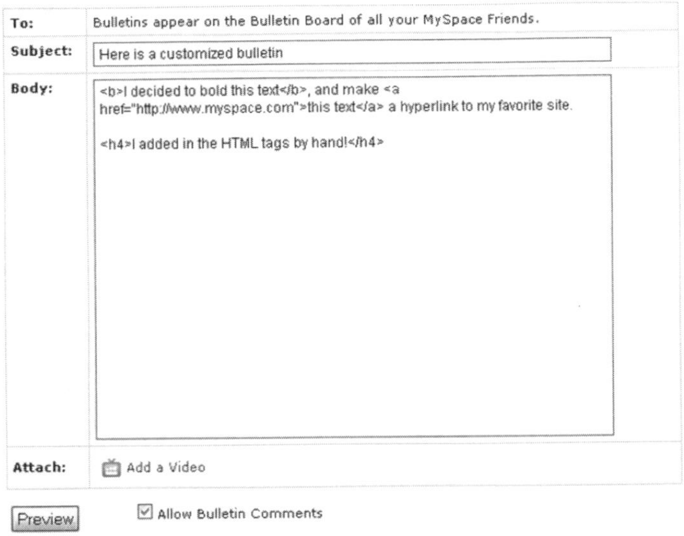

To:	Bulletins appear on the Bulletin Board of all your MySpace Friends.
Subject:	Here is a customized bulletin
Body:	<b>I decided to bold this text</b>, and make <a href="http://www.myspace.com">this text</a> a hyperlink to my favorite site. <h4>I added in the HTML tags by hand!</h4>
Attach:	☐ Add a Video

Preview   ☑ Allow Bulletin Comments

Figure 14.16   HTML tags have been added to this bulletin by hand in the provided bulletin text box.

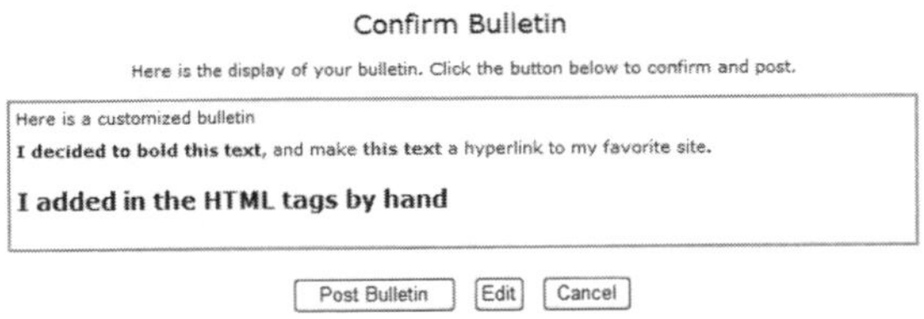

Confirm Bulletin

Here is the display of your bulletin. Click the button below to confirm and post.

Here is a customized bulletin
I decided to bold this text, and make **this text** a hyperlink to my favorite site.

I added in the HTML tags by hand

Post Bulletin   Edit   Cancel

Figure 14.17   Once you click Preview, you'll be able to see your HTML tags rendered on the confirmation page.

But if you're not ready to take that DIY route, you can always try out one of the many bulletin editors available on the Internet. A good one is located at www.acelayouts.com/bulletin-editor (pictured in Figure 14.18). I like this one because it has most of the HTML editing bells and whistles you might need in one convenient online application. All you do is

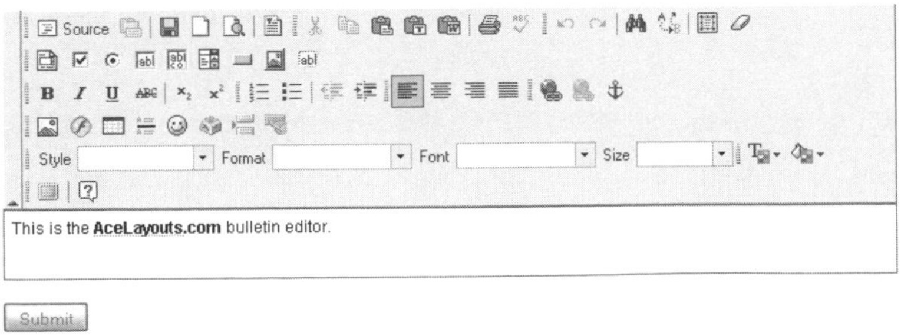

This is the **AceLayouts.com** bulletin editor.

Submit

Figure 14.18   The bulletin editor from AceLayouts.com is a great tool for customizing your bulletins.

enter your text and then manipulate as you please. You can change the font, size, style, and text color; boldface text; add bullets and indents, tables, and hyperlinks; and do more with the press of a button. You'll see the changes in real time, as you would in a word processing program (see Figure 14.19). The downside is the editing window is very small. If you are entering more than a couple of lines of text, you'll have to scroll to see it all.

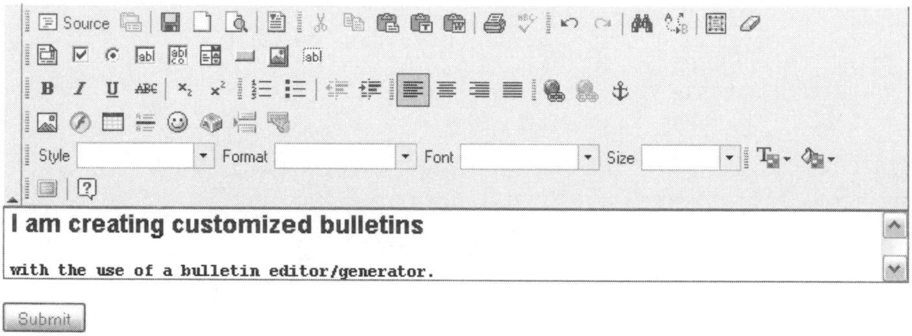

I am creating customized bulletins

with the use of a bulletin editor/generator.

Submit

Figure 14.19   In this bulletin editor, what you see is what you get.

You can also embed photos and Flash animation in your bulletin. (Remember that your photo or Flash module must already be stored somewhere on the Internet first.) When you are finished sprucing up your bulletin, click Submit, and the code will be generated for you. You can copy and paste this into your MySpace bulletin body or use the Post Bulletin Direct to MySpace button, and the application will post it for you (see Figure 14.20). Note, however, that MySpace sometimes blocks these types of actions by third-party sites, and posting directly may not always work. Be ready to rely on good old-fashioned copying and pasting instead (see Figure 14.21). Should this recommended bulletin editor not suit you, simply do a web search for "myspace bulletin editor," and you'll find many others from which to choose.

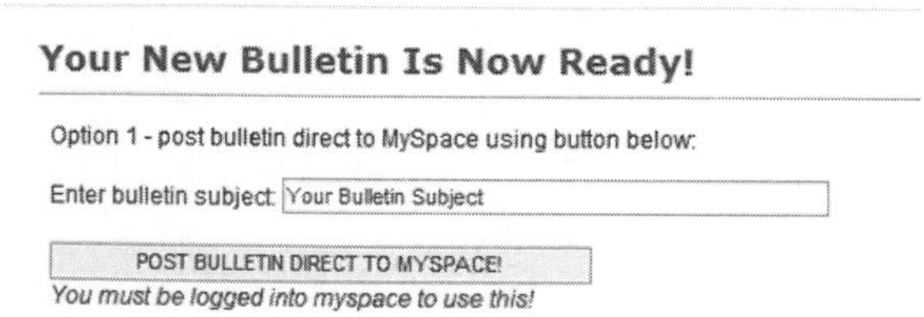

Your New Bulletin Is Now Ready!

Option 1 - post bulletin direct to MySpace using button below:

Enter bulletin subject: Your Bulletin Subject

POST BULLETIN DIRECT TO MYSPACE!
You must be logged into myspace to use this!

Figure 14.20   This bulletin editor gives you the option of letting them post the bulletin for you. The editing module at BumLine.net will post the bulletin for you.

One other item to note when using outside bulletin editors: Most do not have a quick-and-dirty button for embedding video codes. It's easy to get around this. First, you can paste the editor-generated code into your MySpace bulletin, *then* click on the Add Video icon (as described previously) and choose a MySpace video to embed. And voila! You'll have an embedded video.

Please copy and paste everything in the box below into your bulletin

```
<h2>I am creating customized bulletins</h2>
<strong><font face="Courier New">with the use of a
bulletin editor/generator.</font></strong>
<br><br><a
href="http://www.AceLayouts.com">AceLayouts
Bulletin Editor</a>
```

Figure 14.21   You can also simply copy and paste the code into MySpace yourself. You may want to remove the reference to the editor site, just to make your bulletin clean and free of outside advertising plugs.

If your video of choice is not housed on MySpace, you can simply get the code for the video you want to post (as shown in Figure 14.22) and then paste that into your MySpace bulletin body at the point where you want the video to appear (see Figure 14.23). The video should then appear at the place you specified. It works the same way as embedding video into your profile or comments. Please refer to Chapter 8 for more details on editing HTML.

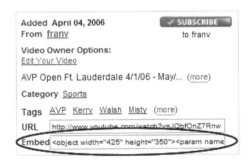

Figure 14.22   This circled code from YouTube.com is needed to embed your video into a bulletin.

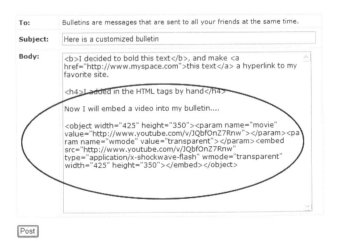

Figure 14.23   Here's what the embedded video code looks like in a bulletin.

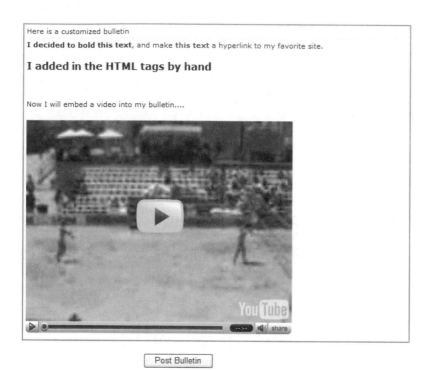

Figure 14.24   When processed, the HTML code now pulls the video into the bulletin for all to see.

Repost Buttons and Automated Bulletins

One way to encourage friends to repost your bulletins to *their* friends is by using auto bulletins and repost buttons. A repost button involves creating and embedding a button or other mechanism in your profile or bulletin post that another user can interact with. They click on the repost button and are able to post that same bulletin to their friends.

I should tell you first that although auto bulletins and repost buttons were easy to do in MySpace for a long time, the service now often blocks these. This means that the repost and auto-bulletin code you generate may not work at the time you try it. Still, it's important for you to know that these options exist so you can employ them when and if MySpace lifts their sometimes ban on certain types of code.

A repost button could be used at the bottom of your posted bulletin, encouraging friends to repost your message to their Friends list. You could also use a repost button right in your profile and ask people to post your bulletin announcement to their friends. This is useful for when you've got a gig coming up, and you need to pack the house, or if you've got a new release available for download.

Creating a repost button is best done by using a code generator website, such as www.htmlgens.com/fields/auto-bulletin.php (shown in Figure 14.25). The code will make a handy little button that, when pressed by a logged-in MySpacer, will plug your predetermined

Myspace Bulletin Repost Button

Bulletin Subject:

Button Text:

Bulletin Post:

Button Only?   ○ Yes ◉ No

Generate

Figure 14.25   This auto-bulletin generator from htmlgens.com will create a handy button for you that, when pressed, generates a new bulletin with text you've specified.

bulletin text into the MySpacer's bulletin editor. All that person has to do is submit it. It will then go out to all of his or her friends.

In lieu of a repost button, you can also ask your friends to spread your bulletin by simply copying and pasting it into a bulletin post of their own (see Figure 14.26). This works well with text posts only. The more people who see your bulletin, the better. But remember to ask sparingly and for things that really matter. Too many posts about trivial topics may cause people to stop taking notice.

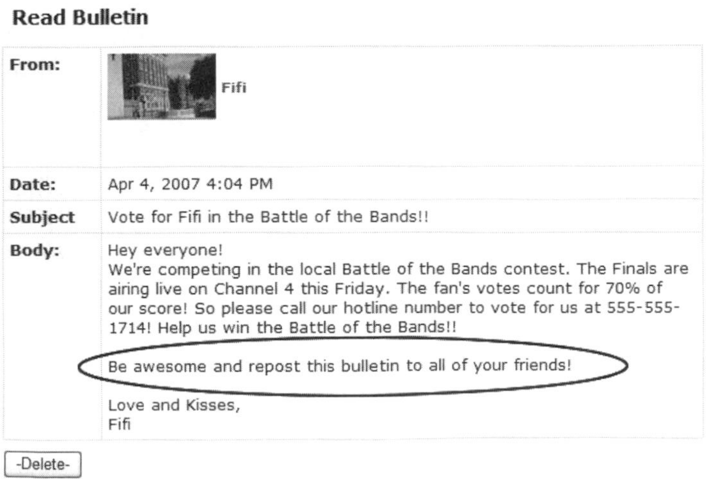

Read Bulletin

From:	Fifi
Date:	Apr 4, 2007 4:04 PM
Subject	Vote for Fifi in the Battle of the Bands!!
Body:	Hey everyone! We're competing in the local Battle of the Bands contest. The Finals are airing live on Channel 4 this Friday. The fan's votes count for 70% of our score! So please call our hotline number to vote for us at 555-555-1714! Help us win the Battle of the Bands!! Be awesome and repost this bulletin to all of your friends! Love and Kisses, Fifi

-Delete-

Figure 14.26   Because auto-bulletin buttons don't always work properly in the MySpace environment, simply asking friends to repost can do the trick.

In Chapter 9, we touched on the existence of adder programs. Many of these programs also offer automated commenting, messaging, and bulletins. In the case of bulletins, you can enter your bulletin text or code into the adder program and even tell it how often to post the bulletin and at what intervals (such as every four hours). Keep in mind, as I mentioned before, that use of these types of programs is prohibited by MySpace. If you choose to use them, you do so at the risk of losing your profile. And if you don't know what you're doing and you decide it's a good idea to post the same bulletin every two minutes, you risk losing fans and being seen as a spammer (or was someone with waaayyyy too much time on their hands). That leads us into the next section. . . .

Bulletin Spam

Bulletin spam falls into two categories: actual posts by devious hackers who have commandeered your account, and people who post so many bulletins to their own Friends list that it's downright obnoxious (hence making them look like inconsiderate spammers).

The former type of bulletin spam is a reality on MySpace. You may notice a friend sending out unusual posts that seem out of character. Or, you may notice bulletins appearing in *your* name that you know you didn't post! When hackers or phishers get access to your account, they post spam bulletins to your friends, commonly for ringtone offers, surveys, mortgages, or sexy pictures and videos (that when clicked lead to a hacker site). If you see an unusual post by a friend, email your friend right away and let him know you thought the post was odd and that he should look into it. Should you be the victim of a hacker, immediately change your MySpace password and delete the offending posts. You may want to then make a follow-up post to your Friends list, letting them know those bulletins for erectile dysfunction drugs were not made by you! And if you see a private message sent to you that also looks suspicious, please alert the friend who sent it and *don't* click on anything!

As far as avoiding becoming a spammer yourself . . . There are people on MySpace who think it's a good idea to post bulletin after bulletin, sometimes just seconds or minutes apart. If you're going to post more than one bulletin a day, at least space them out and cap yourself at a reasonable amount. Post every few hours, not every few minutes. More than three to five a day, and you're just becoming a nuisance. Plus, overposting causes people to tune you out; your posts lose their efficacy. If a fan sees 20 posts from you each day, how can any of them be all that important?

Bulletin Ideas

Bulletin topics are similar to blog topics. (See Chapter 15, "Blogging in the MySpace World.") In fact, you can also use bulletins to direct traffic to your blogs. Notify your list that you've entered a new blog entry and what it's about, especially when you have a blog that is a bit lengthy. Some don't like this approach, but I think it works.

Try to keep your bulletins short and sweet. Nobody wants to read pages and pages of a bulletin. That's what blogs are for! Here are a few topic ideas:

- Advertise your gigs and public appearances.

- Ask friends to listen to your newly uploaded songs, rate them, and vote for their favorites.

- Encourage people to add your new single to their profiles.

- Let everybody know that your music is available for sale and download and how they can get it.

- Tout new profile features.

- Announce promotional partnerships, merchandise for sale, ringtones, and fan contests.

- Post album and performance reviews, plus favorable news clips.

- Embed new video clips or direct fans to your profile to view them.

- Dispel rumors or address gossip.

- Herald new official website features.

- Ask fans to sign up for your official email list and be eligible for special offers.

- Recruit a street team.

- Solicit votes for contests in which you may be entered.

- Check in with fans while you're on tour, offering tidbits about your experiences.

- Post links to new photos.

- Ask fans to leave you comments.

There are additional ideas peppered throughout this book, and you'll likely be inspired by posts from other bands on your Friends list, too. Some artists, such as MySpace queen bee Tila Tequila, who boasts almost four million friends as of today (see Figure 14.27), post often and post personal topics that many people can relate to (see Figure 14.28). She doesn't send out just messages about her career, but also regular musings on how she's happily put on a couple of pounds, what she's doing for the weekend, and even goodnight messages in which she recaps her day and encourages fans to be thankful for all they have in their lives. This might not sound like what most entertainers do, but that's the beauty of it. Tila relates to her audience on a personal level and draws them into her life, portraying herself as a regular girl despite her model good looks, celebrity friends, gritty rap style, and controversial image. She also makes for a very interactive artist, something that fans love and don't often find.

Figure 14.27   MySpace celebrity Tila Tequila is a master of gathering friends and making a name for herself in this cyber-environment.

Figure 14.28   Her posts are often personal, and she talks to her audience like she would her closest friend. This helps to build a loyal fan base.

One of the keys to keeping yourself in your fans' good graces is to post relevant topics, even if they're personal, and to stay away from "junk" posts; too many or redundant posts; inflammatory, hateful, or derogatory tirades; and controversial, irrelevant content. People do indeed delete others off their Friends lists because of ridiculous posts. And you don't want to be one of those who is kicked to the curb.

So, here are a few tips to help keep you in the clear:

- **Keep your hatred and vitriol to yourself.** Nobody likes a Negative Nellie. If you've got a problem with a real-life friend or acquaintance or you despise some celebrity or government official, just put a lid on it. It's a bad reflection on you. I once kicked off an artist who posted a series of rants that were vulgar and disgusting, detailing what horrible, violent things he'd like to do to a media figure he hated. Not cool. The exception is if you're commenting on really bad behavior (a la Kanye West swiping Taylor Swift's moment on stage). Even then, do so with some class.

- **Set politics aside.** It's okay to get on your soapbox about music and entertainment industry issues, but be careful about political issues. Remember that half your audience off the bat will likely be on the opposite side. And most of your fans are entertaining themselves on MySpace in the hopes of escaping the daily media saturation of partisan politics. Let your music speak your views for you. If you must comment on a political issue, at least work hard to make it positive while still conveying your viewpoint. Realize as well that you may lose fans over it.

- **Don't post for everyone a message meant for one.** This is particularly annoying. A post that starts with "Hey Jimmy, here's that video I promised I'd send you" should have been sent to Jimmy only, not the 2,000 friends on your list who don't know Jimmy and couldn't care less.

- **Be careful of posting a lot of acronyms.** I know it's how kids write. However, not everyone on your list may get your text-message speak. So use real words and sentences, please. That goes for writing in plain, proper English, too. I've read messages and bulletins from artists whose colloquial slang is so specific that I had no idea what they were talking about. Aim to be easily understood by all.

- **Steer clear of junk posts.** These are posts that are completely meaningless and bulletins you only sent out because you were bored. Things like, "Dude, I made mac and cheese, and it was awesome." Yes...and? Now you've just sucked up a precious piece of real estate in the bulletin window that someone else could have had. Plus, the fans who clicked on that bulletin and were disappointed by its lack of content are lamenting that 30 seconds of lifespan they'll never get back. Keep it interesting.

- **Don't mislead.** Keep your bulletin subject lines germane to the content. Posting an intriguing subject line that has nothing to do with the bulletin post, in a desperate attempt to get people to click on your bulletin, just makes you lame. And not credible.

- **Plan out your posts.** If you've got a gig coming up, you definitely want to advertise it. But you don't want to be the guy who posted "Come to my concert Friday" five times a day for a week. That's overkill. Figure you can safely post once or twice a day the week before the concert. For more stretched-out projects, say months down the road, once a week or less will do.

- **Don't overpost.** Along with the previous tip, think about your overall number of posts in a day. *Relevant* content three times in one day is all right, but shouldn't be done every day. Usually one relevant post a day is considered tolerable. Irrelevant content over and over again is just going to train your fans not to click on your posts anymore. If you've got a ton happening in one day, think about how you might be able to break it up over a three- or four-day period if possible. Perhaps not every topic is urgent for that day.

Bulletins are a type of email marketing because they go to everyone on your Friends list. You want people to remain open to what you have to say. Respecting their time and resources is the first step. You should also take your bulletin entries and post them as blogs so new friends and page visitors can see what they've missed.

People also often wonder whether they can block all posts or posts by certain people. If you don't want to read posts by a certain someone, that person probably shouldn't be on your Friends list. As for a reliable, easy way of blocking posts, I haven't found it. There are probably programmers out there who could accomplish this, but I haven't yet found a simple way to do this that the average MySpacer could implement.

Event Planning

Now let's check out the use of event invites for getting friends and the public at large to attend gigs and other promotional shindigs.

To access your events page, click on More on the blue menu at the top of your MySpace home page and scroll down to Events (see Figure 14.29). This link transports you to your MySpace Events page, where you can view events in your area and post your own (see Figure 14.30).

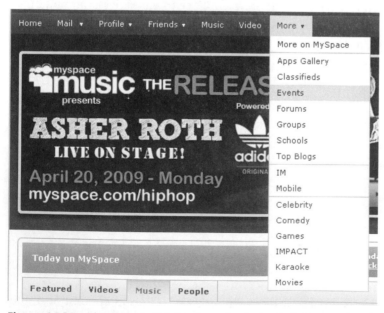

Figure 14.29 This Events link leads to the hub of all the local social activity.

Figure 14.30   This main page of MySpace Events gives you many tools to browse events and create your own invitations. You have many tools at your disposal to spread the word about your gigs.

The tabs at the top of each Events page allow you to go back to the main Events page (Home), or create, view your calendar, or browse events.

To see the dozens of events in your area alone in categories such as Concerts, Sports, Nightlife, and Art, click on Browse (see Figure 14.31). Going out of town? Just change your location and find out what's hip and happening in any area you plan to visit. In this same way, fans will locate events that you post.

Looking at others' events is a good way to get familiar with what others are doing and how they're doing it. Then you can tweak and improve your event listings as needed.

Click the Create tab to develop your own event listing and invitation (see Figure 14.32).

On the Create page, fill in the details of your event (see Figure 14.33). The more information you provide, the better. You can keep your event private and viewable only by those you specify, or you can make it public so anyone searching events in your area can access the invitation. This works well for gigs and CD release parties, because you usually will want as many people as possible to attend. Additionally, note whether you want your guests to be able to invite others and so on.

When you begin to enter your event's title, two drop-down menus appear. Here you can choose the Music and Art category for your event and then the subcategory (such as Concert). Categorizing your event helps others find it.

Figure 14.31   Discover shows and events in and around your area of choice.

Figure 14.32   Click Create to begin your event invitation and listing.

Be sure to enter a great description to entice people to attend. The next page will allow you to customize your invite, so at this time you cannot use HTML tags in your text description. Click Save and Continue to go on to the Customization page. Here you'll see templates you can pick to snazz up the background. You can also alter the text colors, fonts, and sizes and upload a thumbnail and even a banner to really make your invite branded to your band (see Figure 14.34).

Save your changes and head over to the final screen . . . adding guests. Choose the friends you want to add to your guest list (see Figure 14.35). You may also import contacts from several popular email programs and add emails from other friends outside of MySpace.

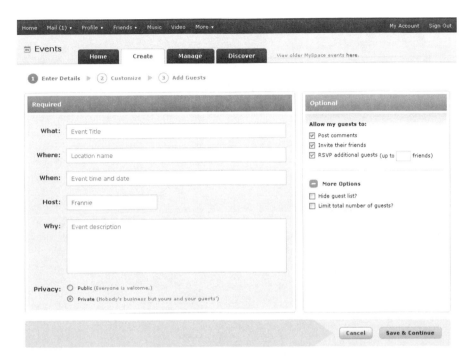

Figure 14.33 This invitation page asks for all the info on your event. Fill in as much as you can so even strangers will have the details they need to come to your show.

Figure 14.34 Customize your event invite with template backgrounds, banners, artwork, and your choice of colors and fonts.

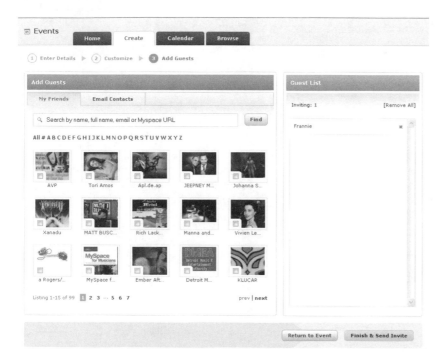

Figure 14.35   Choose your MySpace friends you want to invite. Click on Email Contacts and add the emails of other friends you want to come to your event.

Click Finish and Send Invite, and you'll have an opportunity to craft a personal message (see Figure 14.36). When you are finished, the system will send your invitation to your customized guest list. It will also post the invite as a bulletin if you choose this option.

When you're finished, your invite will look something like Figure 14.37. Of course, I've chosen a busy background for mine, but you can make it a solid color, white, or a different pattern altogether. Be sure to upload an image, such as your band photo or album cover, to really make the invite stand out. And if you want to craft a header banner, you can use that as well.

Your invite also keeps track of RSVPs and encourages people to post your event to their own bulletins or blogs.

Managing Events

You can always edit your event or invite more people at any time, or you can even cancel it if your plans change. The Home tab on your Events page offers a host of tools to manage not only events you've created, but also invitations you've received from others (see Figure 14.38).

From here you can click on your events, edit them, and add information and guests. When viewing an event you created, click on the Admin button for more tools (see Figure 14.39).

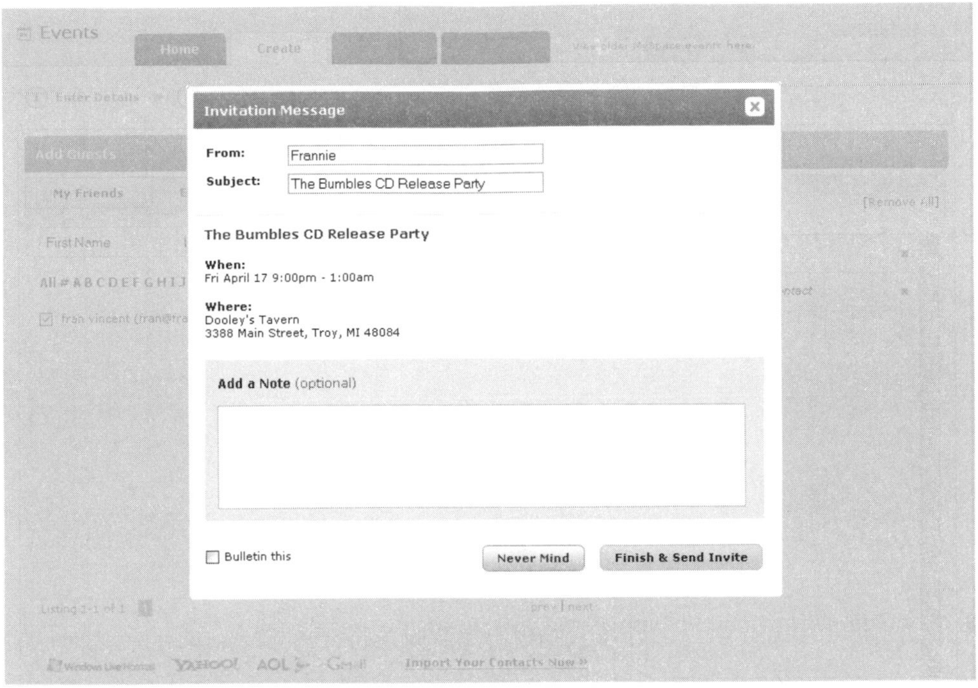

Figure 14.36   Write a message to your invitees.

Figure 14.37   A finished event invitation.

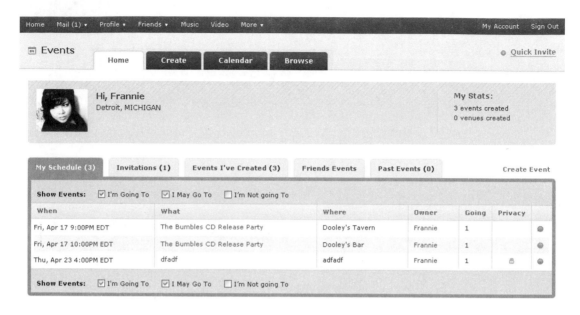

Figure 14.38   Your Home tab on your Events page lists items you are planning.

Figure 14.39   The Admin button appears in the upper right of your invitation.

The Admin panel allows you to see your RSVPs in graphical mode and even how many times your invitation page has been viewed (see Figure 14.40). Here, you can send a message to all your guests, remind people of your upcoming show, post the event as a bulletin, reuse the invite for the same event at a later date, export the event to a file, and even delete the event from the system. As of this writing, some of these features were not yet functional (as they

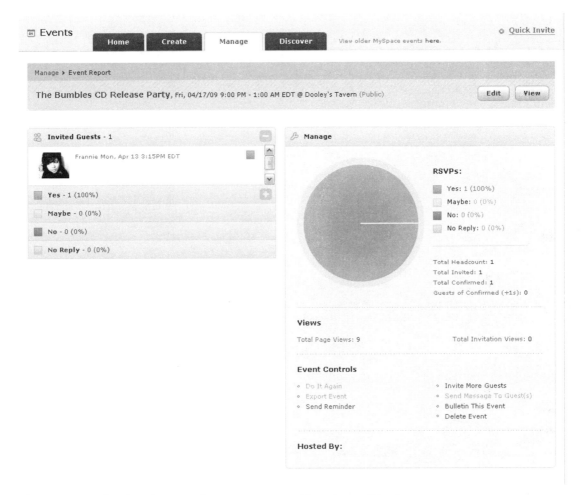

Figure 14.40   The Admin area of your events provides a host of tools for you to track and promote your show.

were still in beta testing). So you will have to try them out for yourself to see whether they are out of beta release and fully usable.

When you're invited to an event, you'll receive an email in your MySpace account (see Figure 14.41). Or view your invites by clicking on the Home tab and then the Invitations link in your MySpace Events page (refer to Figure 14.38). Plus, events that you post or confirm as a guest automatically appear in your MySpace calendar (see Figure 14.42)!

Event invites are an excellent way to get friends to gigs, parties, and appearances. But more than that, they can be used to gain exposure within the MySpace public at large. By using public event invites, people who aren't already your friends can have a chance to see you perform.

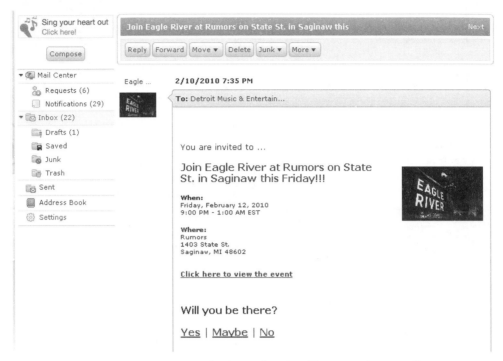

Figure 14.41   Event invites appear in your Inbox just like any other email.

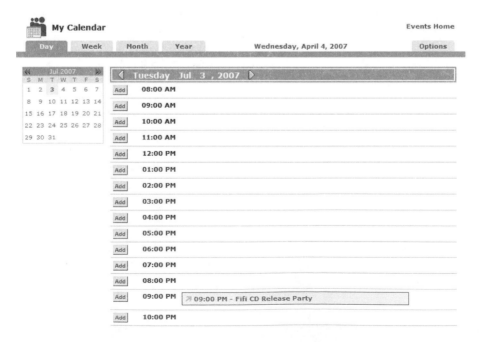

Figure 14.42   Your MySpace calendar is automatically updated with your events. You can keep your calendar private or make it public for all to see.

15 Blogging in the MySpace World

Before MySpace, blogging became an Internet phenomenon all its own. Short for "web log," a blog is a user-generated webpage that is updated often with short news blurbs, commentary, or journal entries. Blogs typically allow comments from readers, making them an interactive format. Blogs can be standalone websites or components of a larger web presence. What started in the mid-'90s as a fledgling movement has grown today into hundreds of millions of blogs worldwide. Popular blogs often center around technology, politics, celebrities/entertainment, and news, but they also include other genre-specific topics and even personal musings from witty individuals.

Do-it-yourself blog sites and software programs such as Blogger.com, WordPress.org, TypePad.com, and LiveJournal.com have made it simple for anyone and everyone to have their own blog. Media moguls and grandmas into gardening alike share their thoughts with readers on blogs. And today blogging has become a cultural force as writers act as pseudo-journalists to uncover big national news items and even the latest hot bands.

MySpace offers its own blogging tools to members. Entries are posted right on the user's profile page and are searchable by other community members. Here are a few differences between blogging within MySpace and using another third-party service:

- You can limit access to your blogs by creating private lists. Each entry you make is customizable and can be open to all MySpacers, just your friends, or just the people you specify.

- Your MySpace blog entries remain within MySpace and can be made accessible to members only. This can be good because you have ready access to millions in the community. You can also set certain blog entries to be accessible by a preferred list of friends, such as your street team.

- Your MySpace blog's public entries are searchable by the community and are included in topic-specific directories.

- Your MySpace blog can be ranked within the service, giving top-ranked blogs even more exposure.

- The MySpace blog interface is easy to use and can embed photos; however, it's not quite as flexible or customizable design-wise as other services.

- The MySpace blog is ideal for short announcements and the latest news. It can also be set to private and used as a personal diary for your eyes only.

- Both MySpace and third-party blogs give you room for user-generated comments. You can decide whether you want to allow user comments in your MySpace blog entries.

You can categorize your MySpace blog, making it searchable by members. And readers/fans can subscribe to your blog so they will receive notice each time you post a new entry.

Why Blog?

You're probably wondering what you would use a blog for. There are many topics suitable for a blog. While it can definitely be an online journal of sorts, it doesn't have to be that deep. Here are just a few ideas for blog entries:

- Announce gigs and tours.

- Post press releases and news items.

- Use it as a brag book for positive reviews and media interviews.

- Reveal new album/record releases and where to order.

- Tell fans about personal band member tidbits, such as congrats to a member who got married.

- Boast about sales and rankings. Did your album reach the 10,000- or 1,000,000-sold mark? Are you rated the best garage band on your favorite music site?

- Alert fans to new videos on your page or other music sites, such as Yahoo! Music and YouTube.

- Bring website and profile changes to the attention of readers. If you just added new features or redesigned your page, let people know.

- Showcase new merchandise, such as T-shirts, caps, and posters.

- Clear up any rumors or gossip. Let fans hear the truth directly from you.

- Ask fans to rate songs and review your latest records. Interactive blogs are great for bonding with fans. They love to leave comments and tell you what they think!

- Create a tour diary to give fans a sneak peek into life on the road.

- Video blogs are huge today. Get a camcorder and take regular video of you talking about new things with your music and career, what you're up to, and even things happening in your personal life. Post these to your main profile *and* create a blog entry and embed your new video blog in the post.

Sift through blogs of MySpace artists to get even more ideas!

A blog is best used with your bulletins. When you post a new blog, announce it through a bulletin to your Friends list. Refer to Chapter 14 for more information.

Basics of Blogging

Let's get started on your first blog. It can be for practice only, because you can delete your blog entries at any time. I'll walk you through the steps.

Posting Your Blog

First, log on to your account. In the box where your thumbnail picture appears, you'll see links to Manage Blog and View My: Blog (as shown in Figure 15.1). The latter link will allow you to view blogs you've already posted, so instead click on Manage Blog. You will be presented with several options. In the main part of the resulting page, you'll see a link to view

Figure 15.1   Your home control panel contains links to access and manage your blogs.

the most popular MySpace blogs. Skip over that for now and instead look to the left and notice the links above and below your picture (see Figure 15.2). This panel is where you will control most of your blogging experience.

	Today	Week	Total
Posts	0	0	22
Comments	0	0	7
Views	0	0	441
Kudos	0	0	3

My Controls

Post New Blog

View Blog

Customize Blog

Blog Safe Mode

Figure 15.2 This panel in your Manage Blogs section allows you to navigate through your blogging experience.

Click on Post New Blog, as shown in Figure 15.3. The next screen is the default interface for entering your blog (see Figure 15.4). It gives you all the tools you need to create or edit your blog. Type the bulk of your blog in a text or Word file *first*. This way you have it saved in a separate file in case your browser crashes, your electricity blows, or MySpace spits out an error. You won't lose all of your hard work. If you choose to type up your entry in the MySpace blog editor, at least copy and paste it frequently into a text or Word file as you edit. Enter (or copy and paste) your blog text into the Body field. The default view is a WYSIWYG design editor; however, you can switch to an HTML editor to tweak the code by clicking the HTML button.

Let's stick with the default design view and learn how to modify your text!

Figure 15.3   Post a new blog by clicking here in My Controls.

Customize Your Blog Text

The editing options you see probably look familiar. They are similar to those you find in popular word processing programs. Highlight the text you want to change and click on the design options, such as the Bold, Italic, Underline, and Strikethrough buttons (see Figure 15.5). There are also alignment buttons for left/right/full justify and centering, as well as indent/outdent. And finally, there are text coloring tools, emoticons, and symbols.

The bottom links allow you to add photos, videos, and links to the blog. Highlight the text in your blog that you wish to link to another website. Then click on Add a Link. A pop-up will appear, in which you can type in the address, or URL, of the webpage you wish to link to (see Figure 15.6).

To add a photo or video, position your cursor at the point in your blog where you want to insert it. Click on the Add a Photo or Add a Video link. A pop-up will appear, in which you can choose from photos (or videos) already uploaded to your MySpace account or another upload location (see Figure 15.7). The editor will insert the media so you can see it in real time (see Figure 15.8). To center or right justify the picture or video, click on it and then click the appropriate alignment icon.

Figure 15.4   The default blog editor appears when you click Post New Blog.

Figure 15.5   To bold this text, highlight it and then hit the B (for bold) button.

Although not as frequently used, you can add symbols to your blog text. The icon at the top of the blog editing bar that looks like a sort of cube or paperweight is the Symbols button. Click here to see a list of symbols that you may want to insert into your blog, such as a copyright or registered trademark symbol or even a heart or a spade (see Figure 15.9).

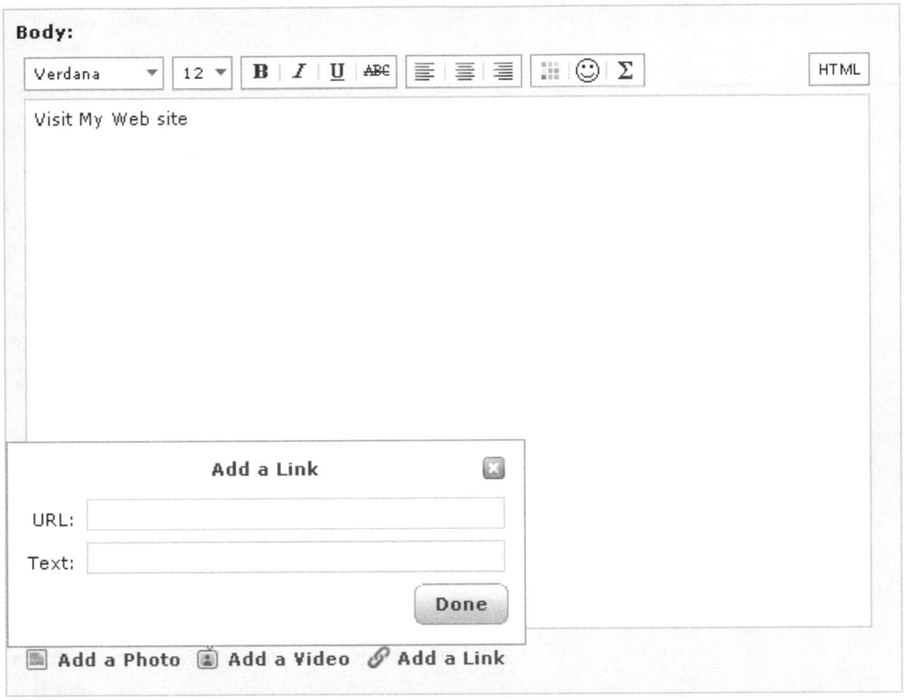

Body:

| Verdana ▼ | 12 ▼ | **B** *I* <u>U</u> ᴬᴮᴱ | ≡ ≡ ≡ | ⊞ ☺ Σ | HTML |

Visit My Web site

Add a Link   ☒

URL: _____

Text: _____

Done

🖻 **Add a Photo** 🖼 **Add a Video** 🔗 **Add a Link**

Figure 15.6 Hyperlink text within your blog by filling in the URL.

Of course, sometimes you just need a smiley face! Clicking this pulls up an assortment of emoticons that you can pop into your blog. Use these to express your emotion behind a sentence or thought you typed. Some of the smileys are animated, and there are even a few unusual ones, such as a green alien face and a little red devil (see Figure 15.10).

The drop-down menus on the editing bar allow you to additionally modify the look of text. Your options are Font and Size.

Highlight the text you want to alter and then choose the font and the point size.

Introductions, Please
The intro fields for your blog appear at the top of the editing page (see Figure 15.11). Your date and time of blog creation are automatically entered, but you can customize them if you prefer. Your subject is the next field to fill out. Keep it to the point, but don't be afraid to be playful. Just know when it's appropriate. Avoid misleading headlines. You may think it is clever of you to type in "Giving Away Free Tix" (or something more outrageous) so more people will click on your blog, but when they find out it was all a ploy, you will have broken that trust and alienated your audience. Who would click on any of your blogs again?

You should also choose a category for your blog. For most of you reading this book, the category will be Music. This allows readers looking only for music-related blogs to pull up yours in a search.

Figure 15.7 Embed a picture into your blog by choosing an already uploaded graphic or upload a new one to the MySpace server.

You're Almost Finished...

Now skip down to the bottom of the editing page. This last section contains some fun fields as well as those related to privacy and commenting. Tell Us What You're Reading, Viewing, or Listening To and Current Mood are not essential to fill out, but they make for an interesting touch (see Figures 15.12 and 15.13). You can even specify what you're listening to or watching.

The most important part of this section is the Privacy settings (see Figure 15.14). Note the different options: Public, Diary, Friends, and Preferred List (see Figure 15.15). As a music marketer, Public, Friends, and Preferred List are the settings you'll stick with. Most of your posts should be Public, meaning any MySpacer can read them. You can use the Friends and Preferred List settings to restrict blogs about special offers or street team info.

The Preferred List, sometimes called a *Private List,* is great for informing street teamers, fan club members, and other select groups only. By restricting access, you can create a VIP aura

Body:

Visit My Web site

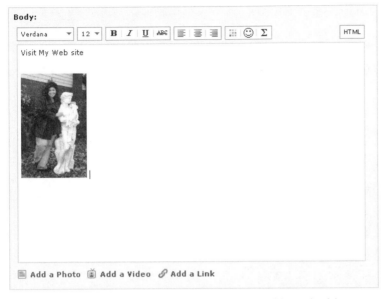

Add a Photo   Add a Video   Add a Link

Figure 15.8 In this example, a photo is inserted into the blog copy.

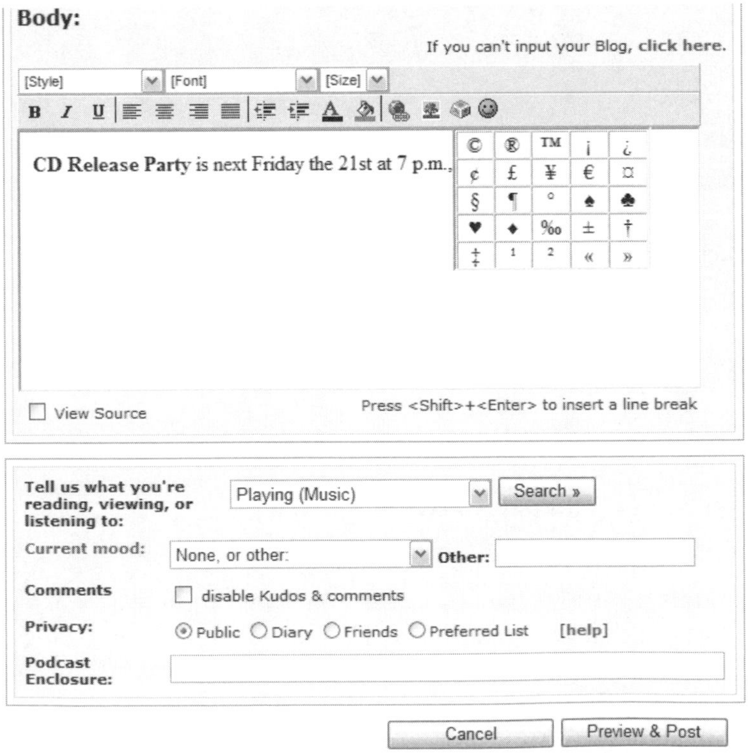

Body:

If you can't input your Blog, click here.

[Style]   [Font]   [Size]

CD Release Party is next Friday the 21st at 7 p.m.,

View Source   Press <Shift>+<Enter> to insert a line break

Tell us what you're reading, viewing, or listening to: Playing (Music)   Search »

Current mood: None, or other: Other:

Comments   disable Kudos & comments

Privacy: ⊙ Public ○ Diary ○ Friends ○ Preferred List   [help]

Podcast Enclosure:

Cancel   Preview & Post

Figure 15.9 Choose from a variety of symbols to insert into your blog.

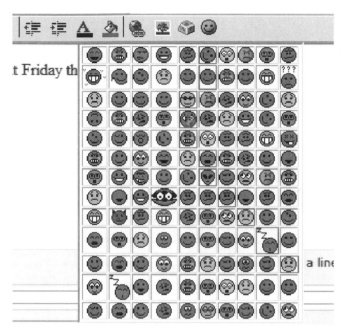

Figure 15.10   People love smileys, also known as emoticons. Pick from this huge assortment to convey your emotions. Just don't overdo it!

Posted Date:	Feb ▾ / 1 ▾ / 2010 ▾
Posted Time:	2 ▾ : 47 ▾ PM ▾
Subject:	
	(max 95 characters)
Category:	None ▾

Figure 15.11   These fields introduce your blog to readers.

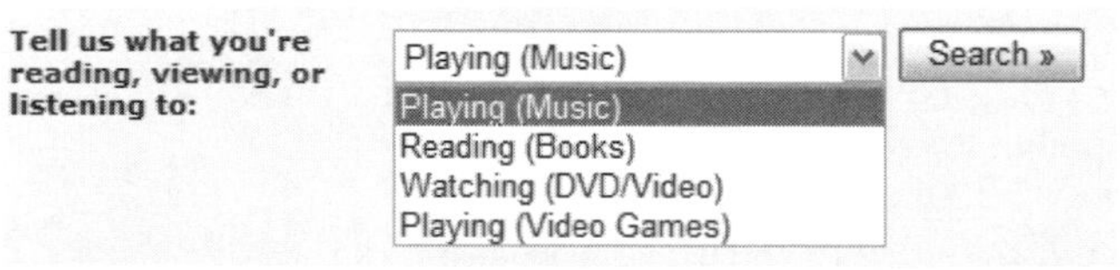

| Tell us what you're reading, viewing, or listening to: | Playing (Music) ▾ | Search » |

Playing (Music)
Reading (Books)
Watching (DVD/Video)
Playing (Video Games)

Figure 15.12   Specify what you were doing at the time you wrote your blog.

and use this to build a "signup only" group to whom you send private messages. Have a signup on your profile for a fan club that can gain unrestricted access to all your blogs, special offers, and private messages. Each blog entry can have different settings, so while one might be for public consumption, another might be for select fans only. It's easy to build a Preferred List—you simply choose the users you want to include. They appear in a list like the one in Figure 15.16. Your blog entry will be viewable only by these specified users.

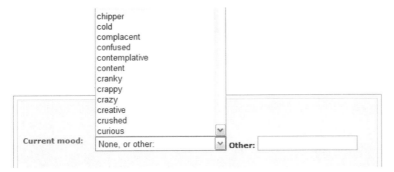

Figure 15.13   The Current Mood list contains tons of options so you can convey your emotional state at the time you penned your blog.

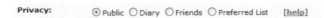

Figure 15.14   Privacy settings in your blog creation page.

Figure 15.15   MySpace's help pop-up describing the different blog privacy settings.

Also in this section you should specify whether to allow user comments. Because your goal is to be as interactive as possible with fans, allowing comments is an important component of that objective. Therefore, you'll probably want to keep that box unchecked (see Figure 15.17). Blog comments appear in a similar fashion as any other profile or image comment (see Figure 15.18).

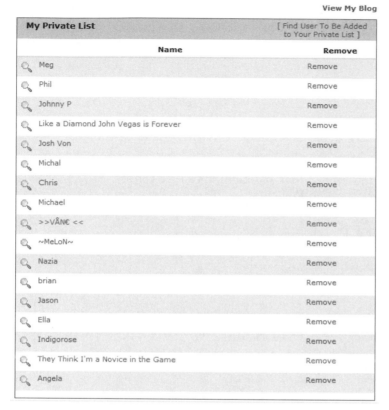

Figure 15.16   A sample preferred reader list.

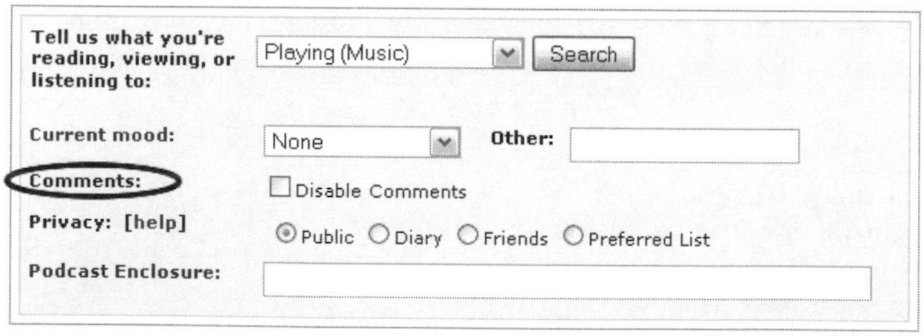

Figure 15.17   In most circumstances, you'll want to allow users to post comments on your blog.

Lastly, you may attach a podcast by entering its URL location in the Podcast Enclosure field (see Figure 15.19).

When you are satisfied with your blog entry, click the Preview & Post button. You'll be presented with a confirmation screen. Review your blog's text once more. Edit if necessary. Otherwise, click Post Blog to process your blog entry (see Figure 15.20).

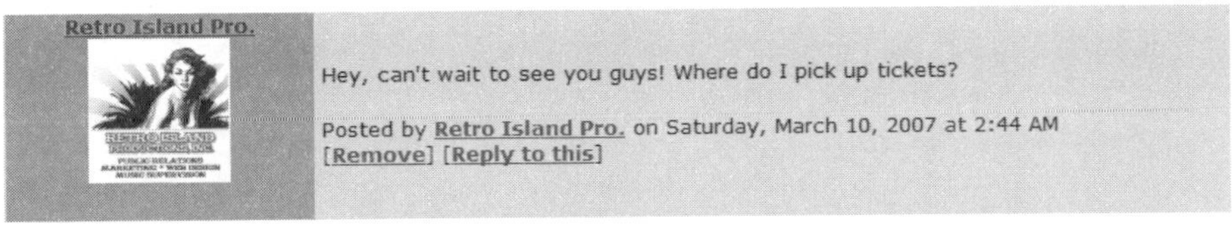

Figure 15.18   A sample of blog comments.

Figure 15.19   The Podcast Enclosure field.

Figure 15.20   This is your confirmation page. If you're not happy with your blog text, you can always edit before proceeding.

Your posted blog will resemble something like Figure 15.21. Notice the bottom of the blog. You'll see a link for readers to add their two cents, as well as the number of comments you've received so far. You can also edit or remove your blog.

Designing Your Blog Space

MySpace provides a mechanism by which you can customize the overall look of your blog pages (see Figure 15.22). This is helpful when you want your blog to look similar to your profile. Click on the Customize Blog link in your blog control panel. Here you'll see a page that contains fields related to every aspect of your blog's design. Change the page's colors, fonts, and table alignments or add image backgrounds and custom headers. You can even add looping music and paste in custom style sheets, similar to how you change the look of your main profile (as described in Chapter 8).

Click on Blog Safe Mode (see Figure 15.23) to edit your blog without pulling up all the design changes. This mode also shows your blog entries in source code (see Figure 15.24). People

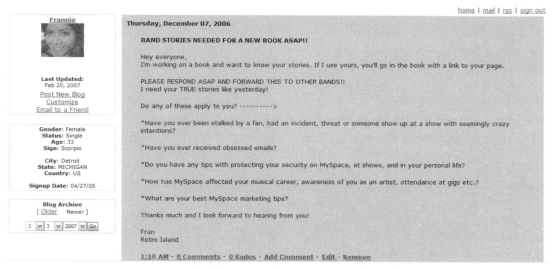

Figure 15.21   A sample blog in a default page design will resemble this.

often find Safe Mode editing helpful when their blogs contain lots of images, colors, and custom designs, and they only want to make a few simple edits without having to reload the page each time. It's quicker and cleaner.

More Blog Features

You will also see in your blog control panel links to My Subscriptions and My Readers. If, while browsing around MySpace, you find a blog that you like and want to read again, you can click the Subscribe link next to the blog (see Figure 15.25). This will place it in your My Subscriptions section and will alert you when new entries are posted. Likewise, if a MySpacer likes your blog and wants to keep abreast of your posts, he can subscribe to yours as well. Those who are subscribed to your blog will appear under My Readers (see Figure 15.26).

The inconspicuous links in the upper-right corner of your blog entry contain a link for RSS, which is a type of web feed used to publish often-updated digital content. This link allows users to add you as an RSS feed, which means your blog content is downloaded directly into the user's computer and viewed on their RSS-capable web browser or other RSS-reading program (see Figure 15.27). This is convenient for the reader because he doesn't have to go back to your MySpace profile and click on your new blog . . . it is automatically downloaded for him.

You can also email a blog to anyone. Click on Email to a Friend and follow the instructions (see Figure 15.28).

You can also translate any blog entry into a number of different languages. The available translation options are available just below each blog entry you read (Figure 15.29).

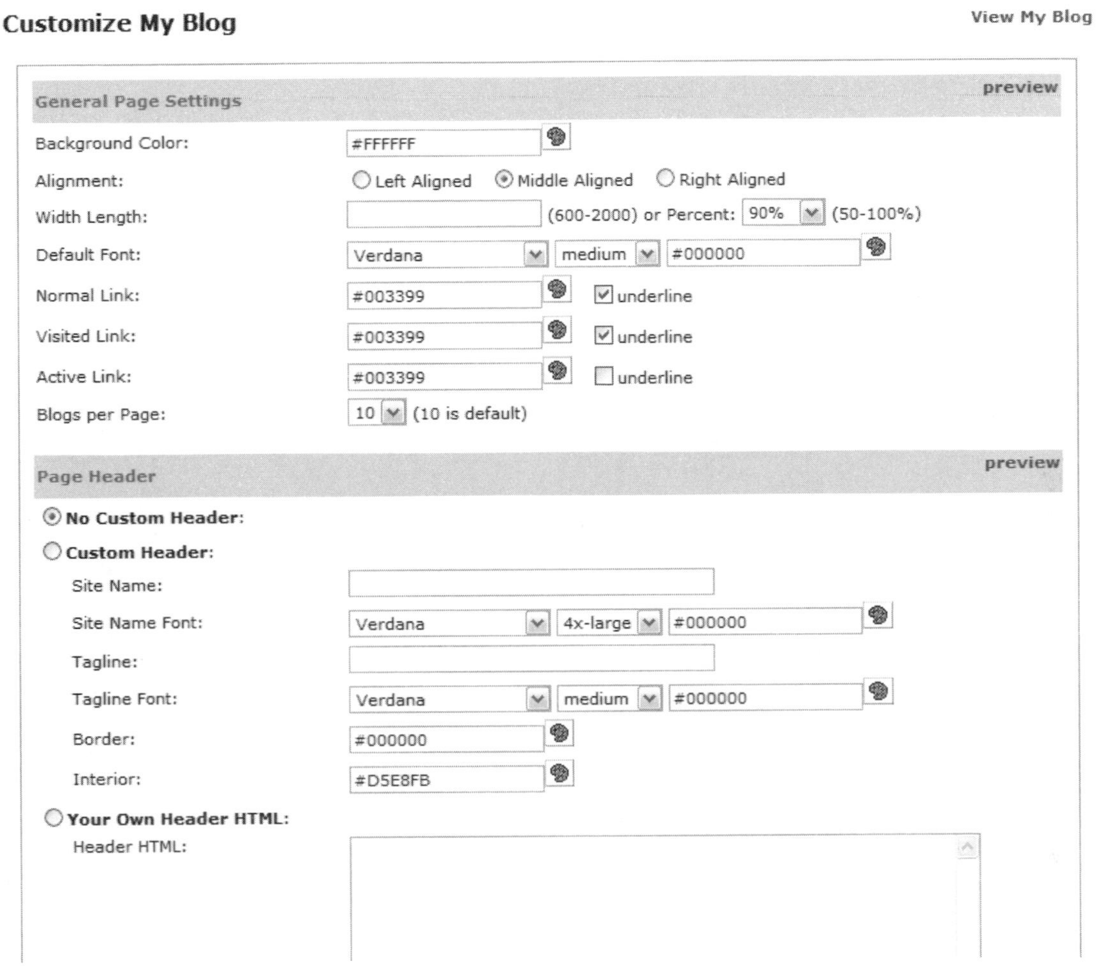

Customize My Blog

View My Blog

General Page Settings

preview

Background Color:	#FFFFFF
Alignment:	○ Left Aligned ● Middle Aligned ○ Right Aligned
Width Length:	(600-2000) or Percent: 90% (50-100%)
Default Font:	Verdana medium #000000
Normal Link:	#003399 ☑ underline
Visited Link:	#003399 ☑ underline
Active Link:	#003399 ☐ underline
Blogs per Page:	10 (10 is default)

Page Header

preview

● **No Custom Header:**

○ **Custom Header:**

Site Name:	
Site Name Font:	Verdana 4x-large #000000
Tagline:	
Tagline Font:	Verdana medium #000000
Border:	#000000
Interior:	#D5E8FB

○ **Your Own Header HTML:**

Header HTML:

Figure 15.22 This interface helps you customize the look of your blog pages to correspond with the look of your main profile.

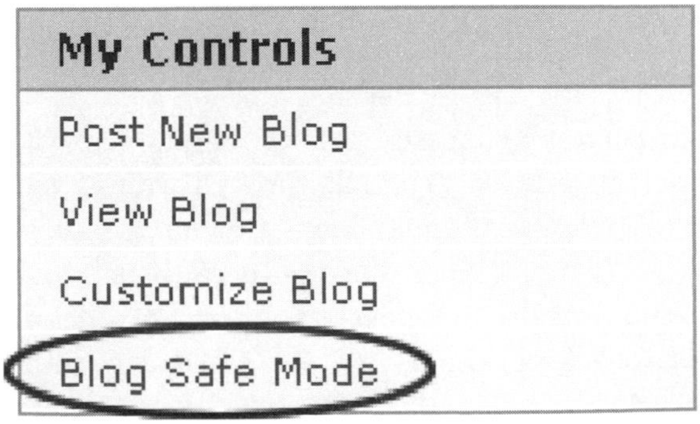

My Controls

Post New Blog

View Blog

Customize Blog

Blog Safe Mode

Figure 15.23 Find the Blog Safe Mode option in your control panel for editing at the source.

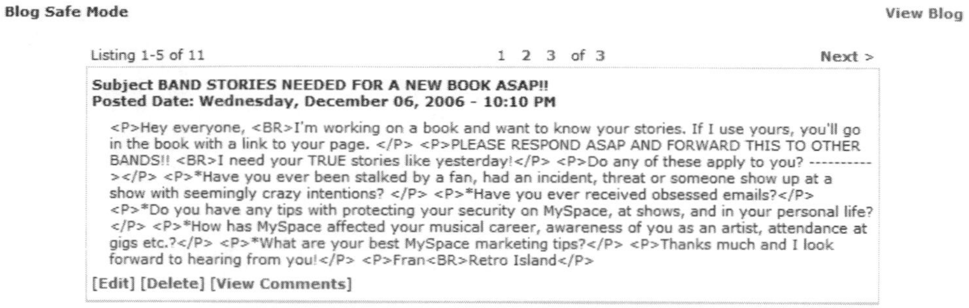
Blog Safe Mode
View Blog
Listing 1-5 of 11
1 2 3 of 3
Next >
Subject BAND STORIES NEEDED FOR A NEW BOOK ASAP!!
Posted Date: Wednesday, December 06, 2006 - 10:10 PM
<P>Hey everyone,
I'm working on a book and want to know your stories. If I use yours, you'll go in the book with a link to your page. </P> <P>PLEASE RESPOND ASAP AND FORWARD THIS TO OTHER BANDS!!
I need your TRUE stories like yesterday!</P> <P>Do any of these apply to you? ----------></P> <P>*Have you ever been stalked by a fan, had an incident, threat or someone show up at a show with seemingly crazy intentions? </P> <P>*Have you ever received obsessed emails?</P> <P>*Do you have any tips with protecting your security on MySpace, at shows, and in your personal life? </P> <P>*How has MySpace affected your musical career, awareness of you as an artist, attendance at gigs etc.?</P> <P>*What are your best MySpace marketing tips?</P> <P>Thanks much and I look forward to hearing from you!</P> <P>Fran
Retro Island</P>
[Edit] [Delete] [View Comments]

Figure 15.24 This is what the no-frills Blog Safe Mode looks like.

Retro Island Prod.
RETRO ISLAND
PRODUCTIONS, INC.
Last Updated: 12/17/2008
Send Message
Instant Message
Email to a Friend
Subscribe
City: DETROIT
State: Michigan
Country: US

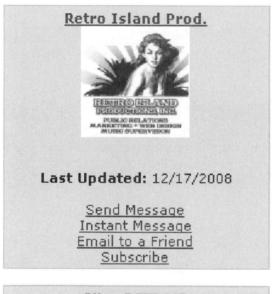

Figure 15.25 Subscribe to your favorite blogs to keep on top of new entries.

If you click on one blog entry at a time (as opposed to viewing all blog entries on one page), you will also notice that next to the translation link is an icon that shows various other networks where you can post this blog. This allows you to share a blog with your friends on other networks, such as Facebook (see Figures 15.29 and 15.30). This is especially helpful if you have multiple profiles on various services. You can click and post to your own profiles on Facebook, Twitter, Bebo, and even other social bookmarking sites, such as Delicious and Blogmarks.

Figure 15.26   As a blogger, you can view the people who have subscribed to your blog.

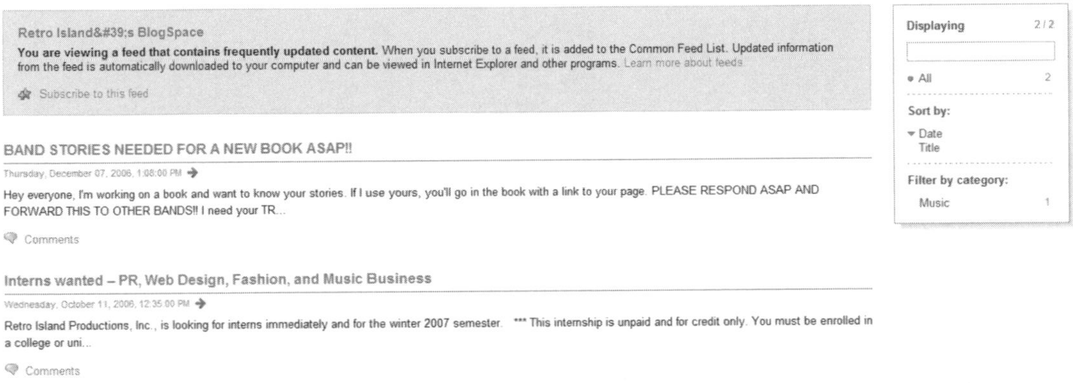

Retro Island's BlogSpace

You are viewing a feed that contains frequently updated content. When you subscribe to a feed, it is added to the Common Feed List. Updated information from the feed is automatically downloaded to your computer and can be viewed in Internet Explorer and other programs. Learn more about feeds.

Subscribe to this feed

Displaying   2 / 2

• All   2

Sort by:

▼ Date
   Title

Filter by category:

   Music   1

BAND STORIES NEEDED FOR A NEW BOOK ASAP!!

Thursday, December 07, 2006, 1:88:00 PM ➜

Hey everyone, I'm working on a book and want to know your stories. If I use yours, you'll go in the book with a link to your page. PLEASE RESPOND ASAP AND FORWARD THIS TO OTHER BANDS!! I need your TR...

💬 Comments

Interns wanted – PR, Web Design, Fashion, and Music Business

Wednesday, October 11, 2006, 12:35:00 PM ➜

Retro Island Productions, Inc., is looking for interns immediately and for the winter 2007 semester.   *** This internship is unpaid and for credit only. You must be enrolled in a college or uni...

💬 Comments

Figure 15.27   This is what your blog looks like in an RSS feed.

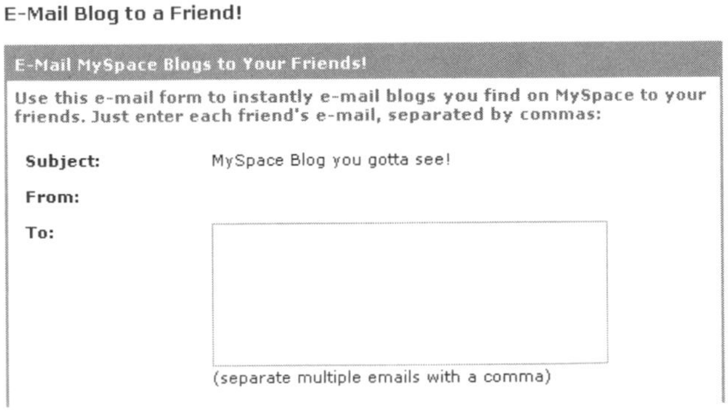

E-Mail Blog to a Friend!

E-Mail MySpace Blogs to Your Friends!

Use this e-mail form to instantly e-mail blogs you find on MySpace to your friends. Just enter each friend's e-mail, separated by commas:

Subject: MySpace Blog you gotta see!

From:

To:

(separate multiple emails with a comma)

Figure 15.28   When you see a blog that you think will interest a friend, you can forward it to them directly.

Figure 15.29   You can translate any blog into various languages. And, click on Share to post your blog to other networks and services.

Figure 15.30   Click on More in the Share menu, and you'll get a page with all the places you can post/share this blog.

	Today	Week	Total
Posts	0	0	11
Comments	0	0	1
Views	0	1	274
Kudos	0	0	1

Figure 15.31   Check out your blog tallies to see how much exposure you're getting.

Your blog's control panel tallies your blog's posts, comments, views, and kudos. You can keep track of how many hits you're getting that day, week, or all the time (see Figure 15.31).

Blogs can be an effective public relations tool for both bands and businesses to communicate with fans and customers. Today's consumers, however, demand sincerity and won't take to constant sales pitches. Be real and write clearly and concisely. And don't be afraid to speak from the heart.

Now that you know everything you need to post blogs on your profile, let's move on to learning the ins and outs of using groups and forums.

16 Using Groups and Forums

Groups and forums have been a staple of Internet interactions almost from the 'Net's birth. MySpace offers both. This chapter will introduce you to groups and forums, explain how to interact when using them, and give you tips for starting and marketing your own.

Groups versus Forums

In most places on the web, the words *group* and *forum* are interchangeable and are both used to denote a place where netizens gather to hold discussions and post their thoughts on any given subject. On MySpace, however, forums and groups are distinctly separate areas. Although both allow MySpacers to generate topics of discussion, individual groups are created by MySpace users, while forums are made (and the topics determined) by the MySpace powers-that-be.

Forums recently became searchable, a welcome addition to help you find information easily. However, the visual design cannot be altered by users (see Figure 16.1). Groups, on the other hand, can be customized in a similar fashion as profiles and have always been searchable. Forums are limited, but they are useful because they gather people on a particular topic in one place. There may be dozens of groups about hip-hop music and its related artists, but there is only one forum on this topic (see Figure 16.2).

MySpace forums, while buzzing with activity and discussion, contain far fewer categories and subcategories than groups. There are millions of MySpace groups. Music and entertainment groups alone number more than 750,000, and the Other category contains more than one million individual groups (see Figure 16.3). Forums are open to everyone, while groups can be deemed private and available only to a select few.

The process of starting a discussion and replying to posts is the same in both forums and groups, so once you learn how to use one, you can try the other with no problem!

Getting into Groups

Click on More in the blue navigation bar atop your home control panel, and there you will find the Groups (and also the Forums) link. This is where you can access the Groups

Forum Home

Change Language: English ▼ [what's this?]

Forum Category	Rooms	Topics	Posts	Last Post
Automotive Talk about your ride. We did it for TheBoz.	Chat	46752	786828	Thu Apr 5, 2007 6:15 PM by: **I LUV MY BLUEBERRY!!!!!!** » **View Post**
Business & Entrepreneurs Need advice or a partner for your latest venture?	Chat	59114	99322	Thu Apr 5, 2007 6:14 PM by: **Mandy** » **View Post**
Campus Life Study partners, PARTIES, and alumni.	Chat	24829	213122	Thu Apr 5, 2007 6:14 PM by: **Ørganism ²¹²** » **View Post**
Career Center Career advice, discussion and opportunities.	Chat	15502	43571	Thu Apr 5, 2007 6:04 PM by: **Angel** » **View Post**
Comedy Forums for comics and lovers of comedy.	Chat	11737	302108	Thu Apr 5, 2007 6:15 PM by: **SERPY** » **View Post**
Computers & Technology From PCs to iPods; technoid congregation.	Chat	41394	262327	Thu Apr 5, 2007 6:04 PM by: **Mandy** » **View Post**
Culture, Arts & Literature The finer things in life be here.	Chat	35290	413960	Thu Apr 5, 2007 6:15 PM by: **Đrëdd Hœded Pòe†™** » **View Post**
Filmmakers Forum for Filmmakers	Chat	26608	101370	Thu Apr 5, 2007 6:08 PM by: **FREETHESOULS** » **View Post**
Food & Drink Best food in town is where...?	Chat	14083	129574	Thu Apr 5, 2007 6:12 PM by: **1/2 PINT** » **View Post**
Games Video games improve motor reflexes and strategy skills.	Chat	86895	702368	Thu Apr 5, 2007 6:13 PM by: **Herzog des Gottes Daevion** » **View Post**
General Discussion Whatever doesn't fit everywhere else.	Chat	9677	648297	Thu Apr 5, 2007 6:15 PM by: **soggy bread** » **View Post**

Figure 16.1   These are just some of the forum topics available to everyone.

directory, search function, and links to help you create and manage your groups (see Figure 16.4). Groups are organized by categories including Music, Entertainment, Pets & Animals, Money & Investing, and more than 30 other categories. While you can join groups based on any number of interests you may have, let's stick with music- and entertainment-related topics for now.

Enter the Music category, and you'll see lists of groups spanning more than 40,000 pages (see Figure 16.5)... obviously too many to browse through! So let's start searching for what we want. On the right, there is a search box that allows you to find groups by keyword, name, and even proximity to your local area (see Figure 16.6). Let's start with the keywords "music in film."

The resulting page gives you a variety of possible groups to join, from the Musicians Resource Center to one aptly named Music in Film. Another search for "emo music" yields about 1,400 groups of those who both love and hate the genre. As discussed in Chapter 9,

Forum Home » **Music**

Forum Sub Category	Topics	Posts	Last Post
Acoustic	15933	133599	04/05/2007 6:14 PM by: drawler » **View Post**
Alternative	24380	194258	04/05/2007 6:13 PM by: CC » **View Post**
Electronic/Dance	27593	248835	04/05/2007 6:15 PM by: Sweet X poison INC CO Since 1991[physical] » **View Post**
Emo	26985	503554	04/05/2007 6:13 PM by: wrink lay » **View Post**
General	101922	1077704	04/05/2007 6:13 PM by: Wang chung » **View Post**
Hardcore	15589	147735	04/05/2007 6:15 PM by: anytown » **View Post**
Hip-Hop	127356	1170642	04/05/2007 6:15 PM by: Jesus F. Baby.. » **View Post**
Metal	42850	737193	04/05/2007 6:15 PM by: Dæmonicus » **View Post**
Punk	31249	434722	04/05/2007 6:14 PM by: MoMo the Pirate » **View Post**
Rock	52297	780426	04/05/2007 6:15 PM by: Mistress Nani » **View Post**

Figure 16.2   The Music section of forums.

Figure 16.3   The groups categories are numerous, and so are the subgroups within them.

there are also "add me" groups where you can introduce yourself and ask people to add you to their Friends list.

It usually takes some digging to find groups that really fit you. You'll find that there may be a lot of groups on any particular topic, but maybe only a few are really active and worth joining.

Figure 16.4   Your Groups main page helps you navigate your way through the system.

Figure 16.5   This is just a snippet of the first page of the Music groups section. Notice how many groups and pages there are!

Try searching for groups dedicated to your favorite bands, music business, songwriting, music promotion, or even your particular genre of music. The groups will be either public or private. You can join both to receive updates and group bulletins. Some private groups require you to apply to join and be approved before you are allowed to post any messages. Other groups are by invitation only, and you cannot even view the group's content unless you are invited by a member.

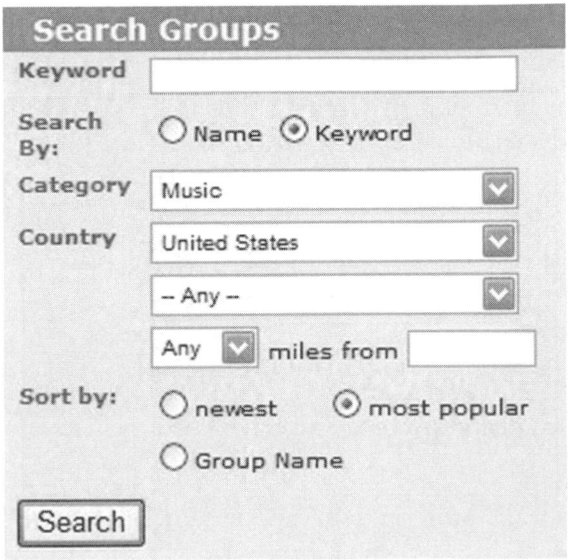

Figure 16.6   The groups search helps you find just what you're looking for.

Group Netiquette

You should join any and all groups or forums you like, but do resist the temptation to post your own topic thread right away. The better approach is to read through some of the threads, get familiar with the "culture" and tone of the group, and then reply to a few posts. People will get to know you that way and see what you're about. Plus, posting "Hey, I'm in a band. Add me!" right off the bat may be deemed spammy behavior (unless you're in an add me group) and get you booted out.

Posting and replying in both groups and forums is just a matter of hitting a button. Clicking on the Post a New Topic or Post Topic links/buttons starts a brand-new thread. When replying to a posted message, Quote includes the original poster's message below yours. Or hit Reply to post your message without quoting the previous poster's message. The Post a Reply button does the same thing as hitting Reply.

When you're ready to post a brand-new topic that others can respond to, click on the Post Topic button or the Post a New Topic link. Again, they do the same thing. You've probably noticed that MySpace gives you lots of ways to accomplish the same task!

Your newly posted topic now appears under the Forum/Forum Topic section toward the bottom of the group page. I know it can get confusing to see the word "forum" while in a group, but don't let the semantics throw you. Below the topic list, you may see Bulletins listed. Like regular bulletins, these are special posts that group members can send out, but others cannot reply to. It's for announcements only. Click on Post a New Bulletin in the group's bulletin section to submit your announcement. Whether members can post group bulletins is at the discretion of the group owner or moderator.

For those of you who are new to groups or the Internet in general, it's time to get good with netiquette, the system of online manners and socially acceptable virtual behavior. Both of these links provide great resources on the topic:

- www.albion.com/netiquette
- en.wikipedia.org/wiki/Netiquette

Some general tips to remember:

- Never type your messages in all caps, which denotes yelling and often hostility in cyberspace.

- Resist the urge to write in "text message speak" or in random caps and lowercase letters...it's irritating to most readers and doesn't speak well for the writer.

- Remember that your online text writings do not have the benefit of communicating your facial expressions, tone of voice, and other body language indicators. So write carefully to avoid misinterpretations.

- Stick to the topic of the group.

- Respect other users and forego posting large graphic files and other bandwidth-sucking media.

- Be sincere, polite, and courteous. Avoid posting advertisements and blatant commercialism.

Once you get comfortable in a group, you may start sending friend requests to other group members. It's always nice to follow up with an email introduction as well. This is another way to help you meet people and build your Fan/Friends list.

In appropriate groups, there will be opportunities to post info about your band and projects, such as new releases or your new music video, request feedback on your songs, and so on. Just use common sense and courtesy when interacting with your group members so that you can help build goodwill and a stellar reputation for your band.

Starting Your Own Group

You may not have found a group that addresses your interests, so start one! In fact, starting a group for your band is a great way to attract new fans. In the main Groups section, click Create Group. After choosing your new group's name and category, you'll specify other details, such as whether your group will be open to the public and a short description of your

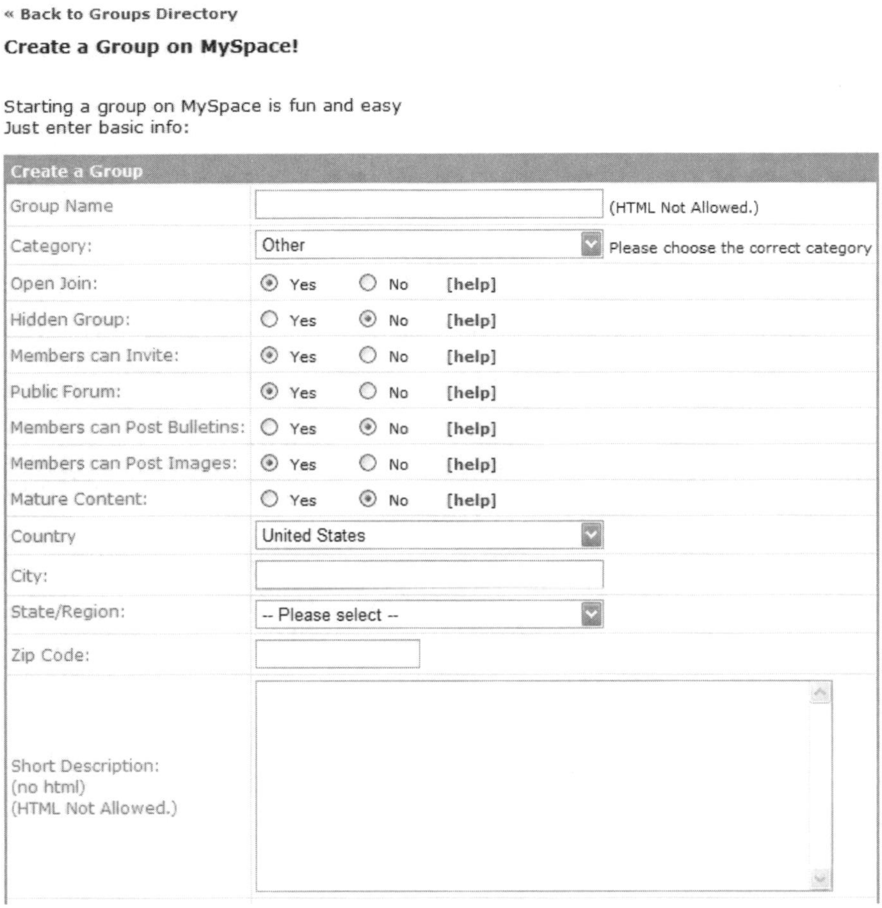

« Back to Groups Directory

Create a Group on MySpace!

Starting a group on MySpace is fun and easy
Just enter basic info:

Create a Group	
Group Name	_____ (HTML Not Allowed.)
Category:	Other ▾ Please choose the correct category
Open Join:	⦿ Yes ◯ No [help]
Hidden Group:	◯ Yes ⦿ No [help]
Members can Invite:	⦿ Yes ◯ No [help]
Public Forum:	⦿ Yes ◯ No [help]
Members can Post Bulletins:	◯ Yes ⦿ No [help]
Members can Post Images:	⦿ Yes ◯ No [help]
Mature Content:	◯ Yes ⦿ No [help]
Country	United States ▾
City:	_____
State/Region:	-- Please select -- ▾
Zip Code:	_____
Short Description: (no html) (HTML Not Allowed.)	

Figure 16.7   The Create Group page helps you start your very own MySpace group.

group (see Figure 16.7). Once you've gone through the initial process, you can customize your profile with graphics and more.

Initially, you will probably invite members of your Friends list to join your group. It's best to do this in batches, because sending out large numbers of invites at once may make MySpace think you are spamming people. If that happens and your account gets deleted, you'll have to start your profile all over again.

Having a group dedicated to your band is a great way to keep people informed and have a dialogue with them outside of your main profile. In fact, one of the nice things about groups is that you can message everyone at once as well as send special bulletins that appear outside of the main bulletin area of one's home control panel. Another idea is to encourage other bands in your area or genre with similar audiences to create a group for themselves as well, and you can cross-promote each other and build your fan bases together.

The key to keeping your fans' interest, like in other social media areas, is to update frequently. New content is king. Yet, do it in a non-intrusive way that's not overwhelming and spammy. You have to test out what works for your audience. If you are posting items every day, and you notice people are starting to flee your group, that may be an indicator that you're overwhelming your audience.

Let's move on now to learning how to contact your audience and the rules of email. . . .

17 Contacting Your Audience

After all the planning and execution of your MySpace profile, contacting your audience is the next step in your marketing endeavors. We've already explored several ways to do this—adding friends, making comments, posting bulletins and blogs, and joining groups. This chapter will touch on the finer points of communication, such as complying with anti-spam laws and crafting a privacy policy. Although this chapter touches on some legal points, it does not constitute legal advice, so make sure to consult an attorney if these issues pertain to you.

Just Say No to Spam

U.S. anti-spam laws went into effect in 2004 and set rules for the sending of all unsolicited *and* solicited commercial email. This is called the *Controlling the Assault of Non-Solicited Pornography and Marketing Act,* but it is commonly referred to as the CAN-SPAM Act. Violators can be slapped with huge fines (such as $250 per message sent) and even jail time, so it's essential that every marketer know and understand these rules. These email rules apply whether you're sending messages the good old-fashioned way or distributing them via the MySpace service. Let's take a look at the major dos and don'ts of the CAN-SPAM Act.

No Fraudulent Headers

Most spam typically comes from forged email accounts, making it difficult to put spammers out of business. But it can be done. Investigators and even regular Joes can determine the origins of an email by sifting through the email's header, which is the collection of information that notes where an email came from, where it has been, and where it's going. An email typically passes through a series of computers and servers before reaching your inbox, and normally the header will reveal the IP addresses of those computers, making it possible to track down where an email came from. Bad guys try to conceal this information by using phony email addresses and names.

The CAN-SPAM Act bans fake, misleading, or missing information in the From portion of your email. You may not create false email accounts using made-up or inaccurate names. Missing header information, such as listing "unknown sender" in place of your return email address or intentionally trying to mask or omit the origins of an email, is a no-no (see Figure 17.1).

From: (Unknown Sender)

Figure 17.1   The From line on this spam email does not allow the recipient to see from where the email came.

You also cannot use bogus contact information to purchase your domain names. When you purchase a domain name, say for your band's official website (www. *insertyourbandnamehere*.com), you are required to give your name, address, phone number, and a working email address. This becomes a part of the public record, and anyone can look up the owner of any domain name, thereby determining who sent emails originating from that domain. Your domain host company may offer services to mask your personal info and list your host company's info instead, but that doesn't exempt you from providing true contact info in the first place.

To stay in the clear, always use a legitimate email account to send marketing messages. It's best to obtain an account separate from your main personal or business one so you don't mix your marketing emails with other emails. You can get an email address from many providers, such as Google or Yahoo!. Or, if you own a domain name, create a special email box just for your marketing activities. Your email account info must be completely accurate and traceable (see Figure 17.2). As far as domain name creation, always use up-to-date contact info and make sure it is updated yearly. Your MySpace profile also must be a real profile and not set up with fake names and pictures. There are plenty of fake profiles on MySpace touting pyramid schemes and ways to make money filling out surveys. These are typically the spammers of the community, and MySpace works to shut them down.

```
The Registry database contains ONLY .COM, .NET, .EDU domains and
Registrars.
Whois Server: whois.opensrs.net
Registrant:
 Microsoft Corporation
 One Microsoft Way
 Redmond, WA 98052
 US

 Domain name: MICROSOFT.COM

 Administrative Contact:
    Administrator, Domain  domains@microsoft.com
    One Microsoft Way
    Redmond, WA 98052
    US
    +1.4258828080
 Technical Contact:
    Hostmaster, MSN  msnhst@microsoft.com
    One Microsoft Way
    Redmond, WA 98052
    US
    +1.4258828080
```

Figure 17.2   Maintaining accurate contact information allows the public to see who owns the domain name from which your email is originating, as in this Microsoft example.

Any email address you use to send marketing messages must remain active for at least 30 days after an email message was sent. So don't close that email account or MySpace profile before that time!

Stick to the Real Subject

You've no doubt received a message in which the subject looked like it might be legit. Perhaps it said something like, "Met you at the club last night," or "Mutual friend." Hmmm . . . maybe it really *is* that friend of a friend who knows a record executive. Or perhaps it looks as if it might be from your bank or credit card provider. So you open the message, only to find it's an ad for pharmaceuticals, stocks, software, or porn. If you're really unlucky, it's not just an ad but something that *looks* like it's from your bank—or it might even contain spyware or a virus. At the very least, it makes you unwilling to ever open anything again.

That leads us to our next rule. The subject line in any email you send cannot be deceptive or misleading. It should clearly state the purpose of your email and indicate the content. Here are a few examples:

- Instead of "See Me This Weekend," be more specific and use "Mary Songstress Appearing Saturday at the Bossa Lounge."

- Rather than "Our Album's Out Next Week," try "The Cleary Band New Album Hits Stores Tuesday."

- "Come to our party!" might be fine for friends and family, but for your marketing list a clearer subject is in order, such as "You're Invited to the JamTones' CD Release Party."

The spam email in Figure 17.3 is a prime example of what you should never, ever do if you want people to take you seriously!

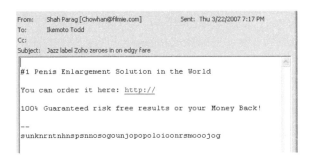

Figure 17.3   This is an actual email I received with a subject line that mentions a jazz label, yet the email is for penis enlargement!

Let Them Opt Out

Every time you send an email, it must contain an opt-out option. Each recipient is entitled to unsubscribe. Your opt-out mechanism can be very simple, such as a notice asking people to reply with the word "unsubscribe" or "remove" in the subject line. Or it can be a special link administered by a third-party email marketing service, such as ConstantContact.com or VerticalResponse.com. Users can click and take themselves off your list. The service will automatically remove them. Figure 17.4 shows a great example of opt-out language. Whatever you choose, your opt-out option must remain in effect for at least 30 days after the marketing email was sent.

Monster respects your online time and privacy. If you no longer wish to receive the Contract & Temporary Newsletter please click here and submit your request.

Requests for unsubscribing or for changing preferences can be made only by clicking on the link above and may take up to 10 days to take effect.

Figure 17.4   Monster.com uses plain but cordial language to describe how to opt out.

Take Them Off Your List

Fans come and go, and sometimes they decide they don't want to receive your emails after all. It's just the ebb and flow of things, and you shouldn't take it personally. You must, however, take uninterested people off your list. The law compels you to remove unsubscribers immediately. You have 10 days to take people off of your list who have requested removal. Below your opt-out mechanism, throw in some text letting people know it may take up to 10 days before they are completely removed. Then make sure you do it. Make a special effort to double-check any multiple or duplicate lists you may be maintaining.

When a person has requested removal, not only can you not send them email, you cannot use a third party (such as a friend or a company) to send emails to them for you.

The benefit of using an outside email marketing service (such as the aforementioned Constant Contact or Vertical Response) is that all the unsubscribes and opt-ins/outs are automatically handled for you.

No Bootleg Emails or Lists

You are probably collecting emails through a variety of methods—your website, MySpace profile, gig signups, and fan club members. These are all legitimate list sources because the recipients have chosen to be added to your list. However, randomly generated email addresses or harvested emails are strictly off limits. Spammers often use bots to comb through forums, newsgroups, and websites to find email addresses, even if those places have notices strictly prohibiting such practices. Or spammers generate random email addresses and hope they belong to actual people (see Figure 17.5). Never do this. Keep it strictly on the up and up by only using emails you've personally collected through opt-in mechanisms.

To...   jones1227@aolyahoo.com; jones1228@aolyahoo.com; jones1229@aolyahoo.com; jones1230@aolyahoo.com; jones1231@aolyahoo.com; jones1232@aolyahoo.com

Figure 17.5   Randomly generated emails, including those in sequential order, are a hallmark of spam scam artists.

You can also purchase lists from a reputable list broker or from a magazine or other website whose audience matches yours. You always take a risk when doing this because the people on that list may not take kindly to having their name/address sold or rented and may see your email as an intrusion. However, this is not always the case. Either way, proceed wisely and with care, making it easy for anyone to take himself off your list if he so chooses.

Honor Thy Privacy Policy

Always post a privacy policy on your website, MySpace profile, gig sheets, and so on. It can be as short and sweet as, "We will never give, rent, sell, or lease your email address to any-one!" And *stick to it*! Under the law, you must honor your privacy policy. If you say you won't give, sell, lease, or otherwise transfer collected emails and information to others, then you must abide by your policy. On top of this, if you do sell a list of email addresses (and it's not in violation of your stated privacy policy), then you may not include anyone who pre-viously requested removal from your list. I find that people are more willing to give their information to you (for the purposes of receiving info about your music only) if you state that you will guard their info fiercely and you will not sell it or give it away. More information on privacy policies can be found further on in this chapter.

Reveal Your Postal Address

Not only is it important to have a valid return email address in your email, it's also im-perative to include your valid postal address. You can pop this into the bottom of the email, below your opt-out statement and near your copyright details. Try not to put your home address, but include a business address instead. Virtual office addresses and boxes that look like street addresses can be had for a reasonable fee. Including your valid postal address reinforces that you are indeed a legitimate entity, and not one of the many anonymous spammers plaguing the Internet (see Figure 17.6).

privacy policy | FAQ | terms & conditions

unsubscribe | cancel membership

For further information, please write us at
Borders Rewards Customer Care, P.O. Box 7002, LaVergne, TN 37086.
Or call us at 800.443.7359.

Figure 17.6   This Borders Inc. email gives the company's address below links to unsubscribe and to view the privacy policy.

Don't Use Protected Networks

Steer clear of using unprotected computers or networks without permission. This means you may not use open-relay or unauthorized computers to send multiple email messages or to conceal your identity. Spammers often do this, unbeknownst to the owners of these net-works. Your very own computer may have even been commandeered by a virus to send spam (making it what is known as a *zombie computer*).

Identify Advertisements

You must clearly identify any unsolicited emails you send out as advertisements. This means that if your recipient did not specifically opt in to your list, then you must clearly note that the recipient is receiving a solicitation from you. For instance, when emailing someone on referral from a friend or a business associate, you can introduce yourself with text such as, "Bob GuitarGuy recommended I contact you because he thought you would enjoy my music, so I hope you won't mind this solicitation! Details about my music are below, and you can even listen to clips on my website. Thanks!"

You may even note the nature of your solicitation at the bottom of the email. This is common when someone purchases a list or trades email addresses with another entity. You may have seen wording such as, "You are receiving this email advertisement because you opted into a list that indicated interest in products and services similar to the above." Always be sure to follow with unsubscribe links.

All of the preceding information assumes you are not a porn marketer—there are additional rules for the dissemination of sexual content and solicitations. For further research, visit www.spamlaws.com/federal/can-spam.shtml or www.ftc.gov/bcp/edu/pubs/business/ecommerce/bus61.shtm.

Triggers

Most ISPs have built-in spam filters that look for a host of things in every email that passes through their gates. And increasingly more people today are adding special software to their computers to further catch any possible spam or scammer emails. Filters search for missing header information, unknown senders, and even words that trigger suspicion. Each and every item is assigned a score, and if your total email score is above a certain threshold, it is deemed spam, even if it isn't.

Marketers and spammers alike often scrutinize their emails in an effort to circumvent the system and get their messages through, making filters more restrictive and less tolerant. We, as music marketers, have to be conscious of what we are putting in our emails to avoid as many of these triggers as possible. Items that comply with the U.S. CAN-SPAM law (such as complete To/From information) are a start. Your word choice is also integral, because some words and phrases common to junk mail will cause a filter to block you out (see Figure 17.7).

The Apache SpamAssassin Project

The Powerful #1 Open-Source Spam Filter

Figure 17.7 SpamAssassin is one of the best-known filters used by email providers around the world.

Don't drive yourself crazy about the words you're using. As a music marketer, it's unlikely you'll be including some common triggers, such as "stock tips" and "cheap software." But, there are a few that you may consider using that are red flags for filters.

- Avoid using the word "free" in the subject of your email. And never, *ever* use it in all caps.

- In the body of your email, the word "free" in conjunction with words such as "offer," "preview," and "sample" can get you banned from an ISP.

- Don't put any text in your email claiming to be in compliance with CAN-SPAM laws or any other law. Spammers do this all the time, and the filters weed them out.

- While you do have to provide an opt-out or unsubscribe mechanism in your emails, using the word "unsubscribe" sometimes causes filters to spit you back into the ether. This is why marketers try to get creative when putting in opt-out language. Try something like, "Don't want to receive emails anymore?"

- Avoid using sales-y words and phrases, such as "Act now!" or "Supplies are limited!"

- "Click here" standing by itself with a link to an outside site can also raise filter eyebrows.

- Resist funky font colors, especially red, yellow, blue, and green.

- Spammers try to trick the filters by misspelling words, but the filters eventually get wise. Avoid intentionally misspelling words or using symbols instead of letters. It gives people the impression that you *are* a spammer, or at least that you are really sloppy.

You're probably wondering how anybody is supposed to get an email through with all these annoying, confusing rules. Remember that filters usually use a point system to decide whether your email is unwanted. Too many points, and you won't get through. Being mindful of some of the triggers will help you draw less filter attention to your emails and will increase the likelihood that your messages will get through to your recipients.

If you want to really go bonkers, you can take a look at a list of spam word triggers at www.wilsonweb.com/wmt8/spamfilter_phrases.htm or www.wordbiz.com/avoidspamfilters.html.

You've Been Tagged as a Spammer!

It's going to happen, so you might as well resign yourself to it. Sometimes you'll know when it does; sometimes you won't. A spam filter may add your domain name or ISP to a blacklist. Email servers consult these blacklists before deciding which messages will be allowed to pass through to their email account holders. That means that, at least for a while (which could be days or even weeks), emails from your domain name or ISP server can be actively blocked.

It happens to every marketer, whether you're sending email from your AOL or Yahoo! account or from your own personal domain name and server. Perhaps you sent an email to someone who forgot they signed up for your list. Then they hit that Report Spam button, and now you're flagged. Sending out lots of emails at once to the same domain name can also get you marked as a spammer. So send out in small batches if you're using a regular email account. If you have a big mailing list, consider using an email marketing service to do the sending for you. And try to keep your marketing emails to no more than one to two times a month at most.

But it might not even be your fault. If someone using the same web-hosting service as you is sending out emails that filters consider suspicious, the IP address of the web-hosting service will end up on a blacklist. Consequently, all emails originating from the offending IP address, including yours, can be blocked by any service that consults the blacklist.

You'll know you've been blocked if:

- The email you sent comes back to your inbox marked undeliverable. Open all undeliverable emails, and if it says the recipient's account or mailbox is "not found," you're okay (see Figure 17.8).

```
This message was created automatically by mail delivery software.

A message that you sent could not be delivered to one or more of its
recipients. This is a permanent error. The following address(es)
failed:

  jared@franvincent.com
    SMTP error from remote mail server after RCPT TO:
<jared@franvincent.com>
    host MAIL.musicianshotline.com [207.12.117.142]:
    550 unknown user <jared@franvincent.com>
```

Figure 17.8   Notice in this returned email that the notes indicate "unknown user." This means the email is no longer valid and should be removed from your list.

- If you see anything in the email that indicates your email has been deemed suspicious or has been flagged by a filter, then you may have been blocked. Look for words such as "abuse," "spam blocked," "spam cop," and so on (see Figure 17.9).

```
This message was created automatically by mail delivery software.

A message that you sent could not be delivered to one or more of its recipients. This is a permanent
error. The following address(es) failed:

  ngpt@franvincent.com>
    SMTP error from remote mail server after MAIL FROM:<SRS0=pylKw1=
2J=franvincent.com=media@franvincent.com>
    host mail.ccsi.com [216.236.168.2]: 553 5.3.0 Spam blocked see:http://spamcop.net/bl.shtml?
65.254.254.78
```

Figure 17.9   In this example, the returned email does not indicate it came back because the recipient's address was invalid. Instead, it shows that the email has been blocked as spam.

- Many emails bounce back to you, and you can't find anything in the returned email indicating that it's due to an incorrect email address.

- The email you sent comes back to your inbox with a subject header stating plainly that you've been blocked.

Once you've determined you've been flagged as a spammer, you should contact your Internet or email service provider immediately. It is their job to get their IP addresses off of blacklists. Be patient and have a backup email account somewhere else. It sometimes takes weeks to get taken off of blacklists.

One quick tip for helping your emails get through to your recipients is to ask them to add your email address to their address book or email safe list. This identifies you to the email server as a preferred sender, and it is more likely that your messages will get through, as shown in Figure 17.10.

© 2007 Borders, Inc. and Walden Book Company, Inc. All rights reserved.
To ensure our messages are delivered properly to your inbox (not bulk or junk folders), add **borders@e.bordersstores.com** to your Address Book or Safe List.

Figure 17.10 This is a capture of a Borders Inc. email asking recipients to add the company's marketing email address to their safe list.

Crafting Your Privacy Policy

Businesses and bands alike post privacy policies (also known as *privacy statements*) to state exactly how they will use information gathered from website visitors and those who submit information to be included in mailing lists. These policies let visitors and customers know exactly what to expect, and as shown in the rundown of the CAN-SPAM law, marketers are expected to abide by their policies to the letter.

Most privacy policies you'll find on the Internet are lengthy dissertations filled with legalese. But yours doesn't have to be. A simply stated policy is fine and actually is much more user-friendly to regular, non-attorney people! For most of you solo artists or bands who only want to collect contact information in order to send notices about your music, gigs, and merchandise, the simplest of privacy policies will suffice. For example:

> The Hard Rockers may collect information that you submit on its websites, through gig signups, and through fan club memberships. We will use this information to distribute content about the band in the form of emails, newsletters, mailings, and other types of updates at the discretion of the band. We will not share, distribute, lease, rent, give away, or sell your information to any third parties not connected with the promotion of the band or the dissemination of band updates and content.

The preceding example assumes you don't use cookies to collect raw data. A good website to consult for a primer on what to include in a privacy policy is www.hooverwebdesign.com/privacy-policy-form.html. You may decide you want a more comprehensive policy, especially if you are an entertainment business that intends to share names and contact data and collect raw info. The Direct Marketing Association has a free privacy policy creation tool that will generate the text for you. Find it at www.dmaresponsibility.org/PPG.

There are many ways to write a privacy policy. Here are a few examples from major and independent record companies and artists:

- Atlantic Records: www.atlanticrecords.com/privacy

- Sony Music: www.sonymusic.com/privacy

- Universal Music Group: privacypolicy.umusic.com

- Virgin Records: www.virginrecords.com/home/privacy.aspx

- Blue Note Records: www.bluenote.com/Privacy.aspx

- Alligator Records: www.alligator.com/privacy.cfm

- Black Eyed Peas: www.blackeyedpeas.com/about/privacy_statement

- Kanye West: www.kanyeuniversecity.com/legal/privacypolicy

Put a link to your privacy policy at the bottom of your emails and official website. Link to it from your MySpace profile as well. On gig signup sheets, include a simple sentence at the top stating how you will or won't use fans' information, such as, "We will never sell or give away your info!"

Quick Tips for Better Email Marketing

There are a lot of ways to craft an email and get it to your audience. We can't cover them all in the scope of this book, but here are just a few tips to make you and your fans' email marketing experience a more enjoyable one:

- **Don't go overboard.** Emailing every day is too much. Every six months is too little. Email no more than one (maybe two) times per month. Any more than that, and you are a nuisance. Don't let too many months go by without an email (no more than 60 or 90 days). Otherwise, people will forget they signed up for your list in the first place.

- **Make it easy for fans.** You don't want to make your fans hunt for ways to join your email list. They will give up and leave in frustration. Put a simple email signup box and submit button right on your home page where people will easily see it without having to scroll all over the place or hunt for a link. Some artists leave the email signup box on every page so fans can sign up from wherever they might be on the website. Be sure to put the same email submission box on your MySpace page as well. You can even use a ready-made widget to do it (see Figures 17.11 and 17.12). And remember to collect emails at shows— have a signup list at your merch table. In fact, you may even want to ask for your fans' MySpace URLs or user names so you can then request them as MySpace friends as well.

- **Keep it simple.** You don't have to spend a fortune on a glitzy email to make your point. Often, simple design is best. Have a strong call to action (directing people to where/how to buy tickets, download your new single, vote for you in a contest, and so on). This is often more effective than lots of glitzy graphics that suck up bandwidth. That doesn't mean you can't or shouldn't embed a band photo or a graphic of your new album. You

Figure 17.11   FanBridge.com helps you collect addresses from fans and create email campaigns. They have a few different signup forms available. This one is a compact signup that can be easily plugged into any MySpace profile or website.

Figure 17.12   ReverbNation.com offers a host of widget options. The one pictured here collects email address submissions from fans. You can even customize yours with the colors of your choice.

can. Just make sure you test it out first so you know it is user friendly and easy to open and view.

- **Emails versus bulletins.** When you post a MySpace bulletin, you are hoping people will see it. You may want to send MySpace emails to your Friends list instead, which increases the likelihood of your message being received and read. One of the ways to do this is to use a friend adder program that has automated messaging capabilities. Of course, this is not allowed on MySpace, and if caught, you will be kicked off the service. So you proceed at your own risk. If you decide to go this route, be sure to only send to those on your Friends list and not random people on the site.

- **Timing is crucial. Or is it?** People often wonder what day of the week is the most effective for email marketing. It depends on so many factors, including your audience and how often you email them to begin with. Some retailers email a lot. Too much in fact, so their benchmark of "good days" is determined differently than that of a music marketer. Test various days to see what is most effective. Using an email service that measures who opened your email, who clicked on a link you provided, and other analytics will allow you to see which emails on which days are most effective. An interesting article on the subject can be found at MediaPost.com through this convenient tiny URL—tinyurl.com/cpofp4.

- **Feed your fans.** One way to bypass email filters is to implement an RSS feed on your website. RSS stands for *Really Simple Syndication*. When you add RSS to your site, you allow fans to choose to download your new content automatically to their web browser,

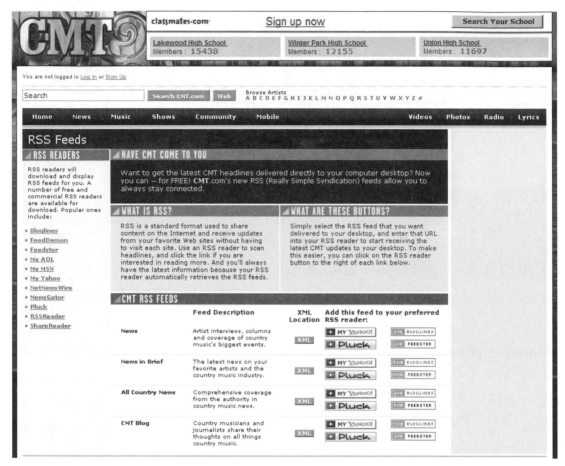

Figure 17.13   Country Music Television (CMT.com) has several options available to fans. You can choose the RSS feed of the content you want to automatically receive and also pick your preferred format. This will drop the newest headlines from the site in that category right into your RSS reader. Offering something similar on an artist site is one way for fans to get your latest content without you having to email it to them. Be sure to visit Appendix A for a list of email marketing providers to get you started.

Outlook, or other RSS reader. In Figure 17.13, Country Music Television offers a host of RSS options to fans. There are various ways for you to implement your own. Do a web search on "create rss feed" for tutorials on how to do this.

Let's take a look now at ways to keep yourself safe on MySpace.

18 Protecting Your Virtual and Physical Security

MySpace and other social networking sites offer almost unlimited opportunities to connect with an audience. Unfortunately, this can also bring unsavory people to your doorstep. Whether you are an artist, a businessperson, or a regular Joe, you must be extremely diligent in protecting your private information and be mindful that personal details you post on your profile should be kept to a minimum.

Regular account users who only use MySpace to keep in touch with friends and family may choose to keep sections of their profiles private and only viewable by members of their Friends list (see Figure 18.1), by going into the Customize Profile mode from their home control panel. As entertainment marketers, this defeats the purpose of having a MySpace profile. Therefore, we must be careful in how we present ourselves.

Too Much Information

When you are setting up your profile and filling in the fields or creating a custom bio, have a trusted friend comb through the info to make sure you haven't revealed anything that could indicate where you live, where you or your spouse work, or where your children go to school. Along with the words you use, the pictures you display also offer the world information about you. Your audience doesn't need to know your children's names or see their pictures, nor do they need to know you live on the south side of town across from that distinctive bank building that many think of as a landmark, as in Figure 18.2. Too much information invites trouble.

Your goal should always be to gain exposure for your product, whether it is music, comedy, films, or other business. Keep this in the forefront of your mind to help you filter through what should and shouldn't be available to the public. Consider these tips when populating your profile with pics, videos, and text:

- **Disguise your city location.** Go into profile edit mode and choose Basic Info. Here, you can specify your city, state, and zip code. Your zip code is used for search purposes. (If a user is looking for bands within 50 miles of your zip, you will pop up in the results.) However, you can actually make the city and state whatever you want. If you don't live

307

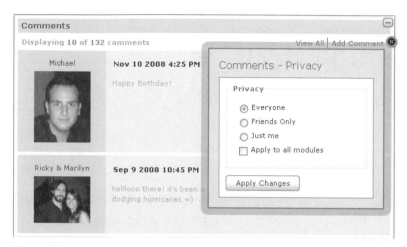

Figure 18.1   MySpace no longer allows regular users to make a profile completely private with one click. Instead, you have to make each section private if you wish to hide it from public view.

I have an awesome city pad. This is the view from my garden apt window

Figure 18.2   This photo of the view from a person's window gives away the location of a home without listing an address, making it easy for stalkers to find.

in a metropolitan area, choose a major city in your area instead. For instance, if you live in Clermont, Florida, choose Orlando, Florida as your location. This is especially important if you are using your real name as your stage name and you or your family is listed in the phone book. For those of you who already live in a large city, you can keep the city/state intact if you are sure no one in your family is listed in the phone book. Or, you may want to put a general region identifier instead, such as South Florida or Northern California.

- **Adopt a stage name.** Although this option may not be for everyone, for some it makes sense to keep your personal and stage identities separate.

- **Do not post your actual phone number.** You may be looking for bookings and contacts, but using actual phone numbers is not a good idea. Instead of posting your home, business, or cell phone, use a disposable phone number or a remote voicemail box. There are several providers that can be found through an Internet search. In my opinion, the better, more flexible ones are those that you have to pay for. You can get a voicemail number in your area code that will never show up in a phone book and is not traceable to your address. Anyone can leave messages for you 24/7, and those voicemails are accessible by phone and often website and email as well. If you must post a phone number, use this type of throwaway voicemail. If you have an agent or manager, he may prefer you list his number for booking instead.

- **Do not post your address.** Never list where you live or work. If you absolutely must put an address, use a P.O. box in a nearby city (not your own), or if you have one, use your manager's business address.

- **Create a special email address only for MySpace.** Use a unique email address to receive messages through your MySpace account and from fans. Never post your usual email address on your profile. If you must post one, use the dedicated email address instead. This way, you can maintain some separation between personal and stage messages. And, if your "performer" email account is ever compromised or a stalker type is bombarding you with hate messages, you can easily close the account and start fresh without disrupting your other personal email flow.

- **Mask your website Whois info.** Have you bought your own domain name for your personal/music website and posted the URL on your profile? You may be surprised to know that anyone can do a Whois search on your domain name to find out about the registrant (that's you), including your full name, address, phone number, and email address. U.S. law requires that accurate information on domain registrants be kept up to date and available to the public. However, it is permissible to allow the Internet company you used to register your domain to list itself as the administrative contact, thereby taking the place of your info and protecting your identity. A domain name registration company will provide this service, usually called *Whois privacy,* for a nominal fee. As an alternative to Whois privacy, consider renting a postal box that has an actual street address (instead of PO box). You can use this in lieu of your home address when you register domain names.

- **Get unlisted.** When you're out there gigging and attracting attention online, getting your name out of the white pages is the first step in keeping stalkers guessing. Although it may not be possible to wipe your information off of every directory in the world, your local white pages are the logical place to start.

- **Keep it all business.** Keep your profile clear of very personal details, such as places of work; frequent hangouts; children's names, info, pictures, and school locations; birthdates; friends and significant others' info; sexual details; drug/alcohol use; and location of where you worship, shop, and so on.

- **Pick photos carefully.** Like the text you write, the photos you display are important in protecting your personal life. Refrain from taking or displaying photos of you or your band outside your house, school, or other places you frequent. Stay away from posting family pictures, especially those that might give away where you or your family lives, works, or learns. Also, be discreet with provocative photos. Outright porn is prohibited. If you have a provocative act, simply be restrained online, keeping in mind that young people of all ages are able to see your profile. Portray yourself as a professional by using photos that are separate from your personal surroundings. It may be as simple as going to another location or using a backdrop, such as a white sheet, to mask your setting.

- **Don't be pressured.** You should never feel as if you have to give out information about yourself that has nothing to do with your product, service, or business. You are not obligated to disclose your sexual orientation, your religion, your political preferences, whether you are in a relationship, your day job, or how much money you make. Although these and many other personal information fields appear in the regular, comedian, and filmmaker MySpace accounts, you do not have to fill them out, nor do you have to volunteer this info in a musician profile.

The more exposure you get, the more wary you need to be about public access to your information. There are many other ways people can find out where you live, such as DMV and voter registrations. Check with your local authorities and department of state to find out how you might limit the information available to the public.

Employers and MySpace

There's another reason to be discreet with life details you disclose online, including nightlife habits, alcohol and drug use, provocative photos, and lifestyle choices. More and more employers are checking out their workers and potential hires online, and this includes web searches, blogs, and social networking sites such as MySpace. Because aspiring musicians usually keep day jobs, this can be cause for concern (see Figure 18.3).

A recent Ponemon Institute survey found that 25 percent of employers use sites such as MySpace and Facebook to screen potential hires. And, about 30 percent of those employers say the information they found affected their hiring decision. While this can pose a legal

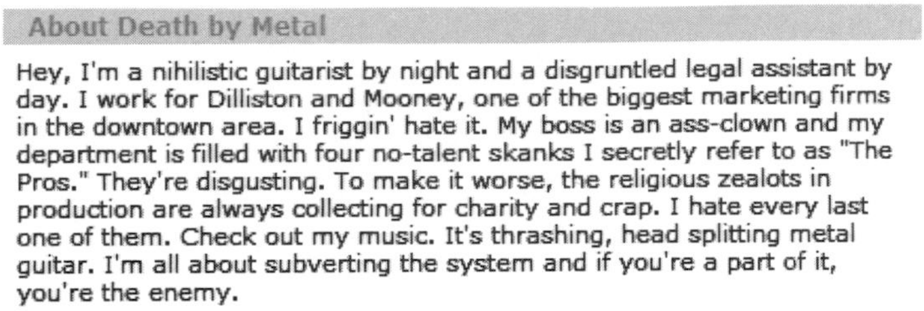

About Death by Metal

Hey, I'm a nihilistic guitarist by night and a disgruntled legal assistant by day. I work for Dilliston and Mooney, one of the biggest marketing firms in the downtown area. I friggin' hate it. My boss is an ass-clown and my department is filled with four no-talent skanks I secretly refer to as "The Pros." They're disgusting. To make it worse, the religious zealots in production are always collecting for charity and crap. I hate every last one of them. Check out my music. It's thrashing, head splitting metal guitar. I'm all about subverting the system and if you're a part of it, you're the enemy.

Figure 18.3   Would you want to hire this person?

problem for the employers if a candidate suspects their religion, sexual orientation, or other protected status was used against them, it's hard to justify half-naked and stumbling drunk photos to a new boss.

These are pretty sobering numbers, especially since the use of social networking sites to vet candidates is still a relatively recently development. What does this mean for you as an artist and a music marketer? It doesn't mean you shouldn't aim to build your personal brand on MySpace, but it does mean that if your intended image is a risqué or controversial one, employers may find it incompatible with their company and decide to pass on your employment.

So how do you make your artist image compatible with your work persona? First, use a stage name in your act and online. Joe Smith, mild-mannered computer programmer by day, can be Vampiro by night, channeling Marilyn Manson and Ozzy Osbourne at raucous, fake-blood-filled gigs.

Your boss or potential employer can use your name and email address to search for you on MySpace, but if you're not using your real name and they don't know your stage name, it will be awfully difficult to find you. Second, use a completely separate, dedicated email account for your MySpace activities. If you use a special email known only to you (because all you use it for is to log into MySpace), then others will not be able to do a successful email search. Get a free email account from Yahoo!, Hotmail, Gmail, or the like. Under no circumstances should you use a work email for your MySpace account. Not only will that make it ridiculously easy for your boss to find you, but once found, it will make you look like a horrible moocher who uses company resources to promote his band.

In addition to your artist or business profile, you can create a completely personal profile that is "clean" and speaks only wonderful things about you as a person and a professional. No mention of your moonlighting, no off-color language, and no links to your artist profile. Instead, it will have information about you as a professional, possibly your resume (no phone or address), maybe even a work bio, some lighthearted banter, and a flattering picture of you. For this profile, use the same email address you put on your resume, and if you feel very confident that your profile supports your professional image, you can even put the URL right on your resume. You may decide to hide your friends as well if you're worried about tidbits on your other life popping up on other people's profiles.

This may sound deceitful, but really it is a marketing tool to help you get a job or keep the one you have. Just as you market your music, so must you promote yourself in your chosen field. If someone wants to do a MySpace search on you, then at least let that person find something that says you are a person who takes his job seriously. When the person in question has found your personal/professional profile that supports your resume claims, hopefully he will be satisfied and end his snooping there.

Some of you may be lucky enough to work in an industry or at a company that is very footloose and fancy free and doesn't care that your act is a little out there. Consider yourself fortunate. Or perhaps you are at a stage where you want to let it all out in the open. If you are already employed, you may find that being upfront with your boss is the best preemptive action. At least she won't be shocked when she is at the water cooler and hears about your activities.

As for potential employers, pay close attention to various clues that tell you this company does not approve of employees taking second jobs or moonlighting or that they feel employees represent the firm 24/7 in everything they do.

Many employers couldn't care less what you do on your time, but there will be some who will care very much, especially if you're employed as a teacher, a childcare provider, a government employee, or a city official or if you work for a charitable or religious organization or you are in law enforcement. Be aware that it's not always possible to reconcile who people want you to be at work with who you want to be onstage. All you can do is try to protect your stage identity, be forthright when asked or confronted about what you're doing, and be willing to accept that sometimes it simply won't be okay with the boss man, and it may mean your job.

In every case, watch for colorful, racist, or sexual language and jokes, derogatory comments, lewd or revealing photos, and info about drug or alcohol use—both in what you put in your own profile and in comments you leave for others and those you allow to be left for you. All of these can be construed as an indication of your character.

Gig Notices and Stalkers

Any performer, regardless of whether he uses the Internet, should always be wary of his physical security while performing in public. However, using MySpace and/or your personal website to advertise gigs can bring so many more people to your audience. They connect with you online through the image you portray on your profile, the pictures you post, and the blogs you write. For some people, the connection is a very powerful one. And this can sometimes lead to trouble. Women and young people especially have to be very careful because they are sometimes more vulnerable when out gigging late at night. MySpace, like many corners of the Internet, has its share of sexual predators.

There have been many instances in the recent past where dangerous fans with sinister intentions have followed performers to gigs, including the shooting of Pantera's heavy metal guitarist Dimebag Darrell Abbott at a show in Columbus, Ohio in 2004. Crazed fan Nathan Gale shot and killed Abbott while he was onstage with the band Damageplan. It's not known exactly why Gale, who was shot on scene by police, murdered Abbott, although investigators have theorized that Gale believed Abbott stole a song from him. At the end of the killing spree, not only was Dimebag Darrell Abbott dead, so were Damageplan's security guard, a club employee, and a concertgoer. In another well-publicized case of a lunatic obsessed with a celebrity, 22-year-old actress Rebecca Schaeffer was murdered in 1989 when stalker fan Robert John Bardo, who had disguised himself as a flower delivery man, shot her to death.

The more you put yourself in the public eye, the more you must be on guard and aware of your safety. This doesn't mean you shouldn't go out and perform. But you should have a plan in place for protecting your personal welfare.

The first step is being careful with what you post on your profile, as discussed previously. The second step is always having a plan when going to and from performances to ensure you arrive at your gig and back home safely.

Here are a few tips to help you stay safe:

- If you are solo artist without a manager and with no other backup musicians with whom to share the stage, try to take someone with you or at least have one friend in the audience.

- It's especially important toward the end of a gig to have someone around. If you don't have anyone in the audience or backstage looking out for you, then have someone from the venue, such as a security guard, watch out for you while you load up your vehicle. Make sure someone escorts you to your car. Going out into the parking lot alone or packing up in the alley of a bar by yourself is an invitation to thieves and other criminals.

- Always call a family member or a trusted friend when you arrive at a gig and when you are on your way home, so people know to expect you.

- Whenever possible, don't go home to an empty house. When your family or significant other can't be there, go straight to a friend's house first or have someone meet you. If you suspect you are being followed home, go straight to a police station. These tactics are important because obsessive fans who have come to your gig may try to follow you home, and you don't want to be there by yourself. It has happened before, and we don't want it to happen to you.

- Think of gigs as you would a blind date. Even if you live alone, you would certainly let people know where you'll be, who you'll be with, and when to expect you home.

- Keep your wits about you at all times. If you take public transportation home, try not to fall asleep. Those who listen to headphones on the bus or train should keep the volume low so they can hear people approaching. Since iPod thefts are on the rise, some experts advise replacing the distinctive white earbuds with plain, dark-colored headphones, which attract less attention.

■   For tips on dealing with stalkers and the obsessed, visit realtysecurity.com/anti-stalk.php.

Consult Chapter 19, "Managing MySpace," for details on how to handle abusive or obsessive emails received through the MySpace system.

Being diligent about discouraging access to your personal information will help you guard against identity theft and stalking. Now that you've gotten the lowdown on keeping yourself safe, let's take a look at how to more fully manage your MySpace experience....

19 Managing MySpace

B y now your profile is up and running, and you're an old pro when it comes to tweaking and navigating. This chapter will give you some hints on managing your experience—a few little tidbits to make your time in the MySpace world as smooth as possible.

Converting to a Band Profile

You may need to convert to a band profile if, in your gleeful enthusiasm, you accidentally signed up for a regular account instead. Once upon a time there used to be a topic in the MySpace help pages addressing this, but as of early 2007, there is nothing that tells one how to convert an account. Tech forums around the Internet offer advice about how to accomplish this feat by entering a special URL into your browser, but the truth is it almost never works. This URL, which varies depending on the tech forum you consult, takes you to a page that looks like the Edit Profile mode for a band, but when you enter information it never "sticks"—it just fades into the ether once you log out. So until a real—and simple—fix is created by MySpace (if ever), you have one of three options:

- Contact customer service. Many users report that MySpace customer service is not always very helpful, but it's worth a try.

- Email MySpace founder Tom for assistance (www.myspace.com/tom). He probably gets thousands of emails a day, so it's a crapshoot. But some users report that he has helped them on this topic.

- Create a new account by clicking on Signup in the right-hand corner of the home page and choosing a musician account. This is the most reliable solution. Remember, you will need to use a completely different email address for your musician account than the one you used for a regular account.

What the Terms of Use Mean

That inconspicuous little Terms link at the bottom of the MySpace common pages explains what you are agreeing to when you visit the community. It seems like an endless, boring stream of legal jargon, but it's still important to be familiar with the greater points of particular importance to musicians.

Almost since the very beginnings of this relatively young phenomenon, an urban legend has been pervading the Internet and real-world media—rumors claiming that MySpace takes over ownership of your music and graphics when you upload them to your profile. The story goes that MySpace can then license your art and photos to whomever they want, bogart all the profits, and cut you out of the deal, with no recourse or chance to get your rights back.

Although the story still persists today, it is nothing more than an urban legend stemming from a misunderstanding of the Terms of Use, which was initially fashioned with unclear and confusing language. MySpace eventually revamped their posted agreement to make it more user-friendly and absolutely clear. Sections 6 and 7 of the Terms of Use Agreement, respectively entitled "Proprietary Rights in Content on MySpace" and "Content Posted," basically say the following:

- MySpace does not own the material you upload onto your profile, be it music, graphics, text, videos, and so on.

- By uploading copyrighted content, you agree to allow MySpace a limited, non-exclusive license to display, modify, and distribute that content within the scope of the MySpace service.

- Without granting this license, MySpace would not be allowed to permit others to view your content or listen to your music because it wouldn't have the permission to do so.

- MySpace does not have the right to sell your content or distribute it outside the service.

- You claim that you own the copyright in the content you are uploading and you have the right to license it to MySpace, royalty-free. You are also verifying that posting this content doesn't violate anyone else's rights.

- You are solely responsible for the content you post.

- The license ends when you remove your profile and content from MySpace.

Like any non-exclusive license, you still own the copyright, are allowing someone else to use it on a limited basis, and can license your content to anyone else at the same time (for example, another social networking site).

The section further notes that the only copyright MySpace owns is in the proprietary content and coding they provide, as well as the *collection* of user-provided content as a whole, in a similar way that a record label producing a compilation album of oldies owns the copyright in that collection of music as presented, but not in the individual songs or recordings (or user-posted content, in this case).

Here's a quick rundown of some of the finer points of the rest of the agreement. MySpace occasionally updates their terms, so be sure to peruse the actual agreement for yourself to learn about all the other nuances that may not be mentioned here. And if you still are concerned and need additional guidance, please contact a qualified attorney.

- Your profile is technically not supposed to include any phone numbers; physical addresses; last names; or nude, obscene, lewd, excessively violent, or sexually explicit photos. (If you must include a phone number or a mailing address for business purposes, refer to Chapter 18 for tips on minimizing your stalker appeal.)

- No content is allowed promoting racism, hatred, or physical harm against a group or individual, nor any content promoting harassment of anyone or exploitation of people in a sexual or violent manner.

- You may not be younger than 13 years old.

- MySpace is only for personal use, not for commercial use. (Although the terms state this, there is no shortage of businesspeople and their profiles on the service!) They are specifically prickly about using MySpace to place ad links and sponsored ads.

- You cannot gather usernames and email addresses for the purpose of spamming people.

- No posting of pirated content, such as unauthorized music or computer programs.

- You may not post photos of people without their consent.

- Bands, filmmakers, and the like may not use misleading or sexually aggressive imagery.

- Criminal activity, including child porn, fraud, spamming, phishing, and many other activities, is prohibited.

- You may not send more than a certain number of email messages within a 24-hour period (although that number is unspecified and is at MySpace's sole discretion). If you are deemed to be a spammer, you agree to pay MySpace $50 for each unsolicited email/communication sent through the service.

- You are not allowed to use automated scripts and the like (bots) to send messages, add friends, or make comments. (People do use these, but MySpace explicitly states that it is forbidden. You risk losing your account every time you use a bot.)

- MySpace can suspend or boot you out at any time for violating any terms of the agreement.

Spammers, Phishers, Hackers, and Scammers

One of the first things that happens to all MySpacers, usually within two weeks of signing up, is that they receive their first spam email. It's usually a lonely girl named Cami or Jenny who wants you to call her 1-900 number or some irksome mortgage loan offer. There are only two ways the MySpace Powers That Be will know that spammers are out there harassing the community: 1) Cami and her friends exceed the number of emails they are allowed to send in any given day, and 2) recipients hit the Spam/Report Abuse link that appears above every email message (see Figure 19.1). So, when you get emails that are clearly unsolicited and questionable, that aim to get you to fork over personal info, or that try to entice you to click on another profile or outside web link, click on that Spam/Report Abuse link. This lets MySpace know who is being naughty (in a bad way) in the MySpace community. Enough reports, and those spammers, scammers, and phishers will be kicked off the service.

Spam/Report Abuse ▼

Figure 19.1   Don't be afraid to let MySpace know that spammers and scammers are lurking about.

As a marketer, you want to avoid being flagged a spammer yourself. Refer to Chapter 17 for guidelines on contacting your audience.

You also have to be on the lookout for account hackers and virus spreaders. Once your account has been hacked and the password has been stolen, criminals will use it to post fake bulletins selling things such as ringtones and porn or to send spammy or virus-infested messages to all your friends. Your friends may alert you that many identical bulletins are appearing under your name (because criminals often post multiple bulletins) or that they're getting weird emails from you. However you discover it, as soon as find that your account has been compromised, *immediately* change your password. Go to My Account within your profile control panel to do this. Report the incident to MySpace by clicking on Help. Then, delete any offending bulletins sent out by the imposters. (Click on Bulletin Posts to do this.) You should also post a bulletin alerting friends that your account was compromised and that they should delete any spammy emails sent by the hackers from you.

So how does this happen in the first place? Here are some ways that your account can be compromised:

- You received a friend request from someone who is already your friend. You approve the request, and *voilà*—your account is now in the hands of criminals.

- You received a friend request from someone you don't know and you approved it. This is why many regular MySpacers have a policy of not approving friend requests from strangers and people who don't make an effort to send a proper email message introducing themselves. Of course, this is not a realistic approach for a band trying to build an audience.

- You received an email from someone and clicked on an outside website link or what looked like an embedded link that ran a script to steal your password.

- You clicked on a profile that contained some type of script that scammed your password or otherwise hacked into your account.

- You logged into MySpace but then were redirected to a page that asked you to log in again. This turned out to be a spoof page that just stole your login information.

How can you protect yourself and what can you do if you are compromised?

- If you receive a friend request from someone you believe is already on your Friends list, check your list first to verify that the person is indeed already a friend. Send an email to your friend first to see whether he or she really did send you a request. It's possible your friend accidentally deleted you. If the friend didn't send you another request, report the incident to MySpace and let your friend know his or her account has been compromised.

- Although it's not practical for bands and entertainers to require everyone to send an email before requesting an add, it is doable and advisable if you are using a personal profile. In either case, be suspicious of profiles with no photos and those that look odd.

- Be wary of fake login pages. Always look at the web address of login pages. It should be a myspace.com page and will look like http://*[subdomain]*.myspace.com/....

- If you click on a "profile" that doesn't look like a profile at all (but more like an advertisement) or one that unexpectedly takes you to a webpage outside the community, immediately close your web browser and run a virus scan.

- Never click on unsolicited or suspicious-looking links sent to you by friends or non-friends, especially those for ringtones, porn, real estate offers, money schemes, bank loans, pharmaceuticals, or software.

- Never click on a profile whose thumbnail doesn't jibe with what you're looking for. For instance, if you're doing a search on a popular male jazz musician, and a random profile with a picture of a naked girl turns up in the search, it's a sign that the profile is a fake one used to entice curious users into a trap.

- Never disclose any personal or password information to anyone who contacts you through MySpace, including Social Security numbers and driver's license numbers.

- Always report an incident to MySpace (see Figure 19.2). You may be surprised to know that much of the junk email generated in the U.S. originates from a handful of prominent spammers. In January, 2007, MySpace filed suit against a notorious alleged spam king. MySpace claimed email marketer Scott Richter used technology to phish for passwords and post fake bulletins through the accounts of unsuspecting MySpacers.

- If you think you've been compromised, change your password. Run a virus scan on your computer. Empty your Internet cache and clear out all cookies, which can be done within the Internet Options of your web browser.

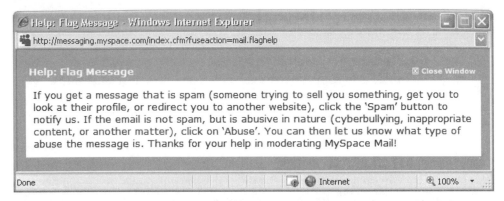

Figure 19.2   If everyone pitches in and reports spammers and abusers, hopefully MySpace will be able to better monitor, delete, and prosecute them.

When spammers, phishers, scammers, and the like are kicked off of MySpace, the thumbnails beside emails they sent you (and in your Friend lists, if you approved them) will appear as grey boxes with big, red Xs through them. The email subject will say something like, "This profile no longer exists." Clicking on these will give you a notice that this person's account is invalid.

You may also notice new friend request alerts, but when you click to see who has sent you a friend request, either there's no one there or the profile thumbnail has an X through it (see Figure 19.3). This means that these MySpace baddies were discovered and removed from the service.

Figure 19.3   Busted! This spammer was kicked off before you ever got a chance to open the email.

Dealing with Abusers

In Chapter 18, we discussed how to protect your physical security. When someone is sending you abusive or harassing messages, MySpace suggests that you report those abusive messages by clicking the Report Abuse link and then ignore further communications from the abuser. If this person is on your Friends list, delete him from your list and remove any comments he has left for you. You can keep that person from viewing your profile by setting it to private, making it viewable by friends only. This is a good option for personal users only, not bands.

You can also block anyone from contacting you by clicking on the Block User link in their profile's contact table (see Figure 19.4). A dialog box will appear, asking you to confirm (see Figure 19.5).

Figure 19.4   The Block User button appears on a user's contact table.

Figure 19.5   Confirm that you want to block a user, and he will be prohibited from contacting you.

MySpace does not like it when people insert profile code to remove the Block User button from their contact tables. You can get around this, however, and still block someone by trying one of the following tactics.

Paste this link into your web browser, and in place of the Xs, paste in the abuser's friend ID. (Review Chapter 8 for details on locating the friend ID.)

www.myspace.com/index.cfm?fuseaction=block.blockUser&userID=XXXXX

The resulting webpage will give you the option of blocking the user.

Because MySpace may have changed its blocking mechanism and web URL since the printing of this book, you can also try to locate the hidden Block User button on the user's contact table. Even though a user can create his own contact table graphic (see Chapter 8), the links remain in the same position. You can remove the words "Block User" from the table or change them to something else, but the link to the Block User function remains fixed in the MySpace environment. The link is still the third down on the right side of the contact table, even if there is no text there at all. Try clicking in the contact table to find it.

Lost Passwords and Defunct Email

Recovering a lost password is easy. The process is the same as it is for almost every registration-driven website—enter the email address you used to sign up, and the password will be emailed to you, as shown in Figure 19.6. Things can get sticky, however, if you have since cancelled that email account. Obviously, MySpace won't be able to email your password, and you are pretty much out of luck in accessing your account ever again unless you remember the password on your own.

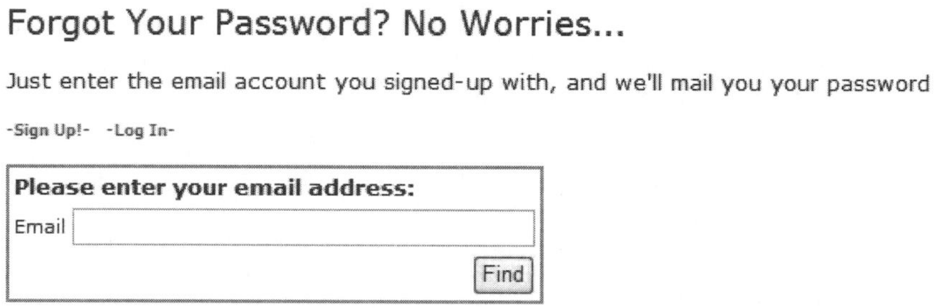

Forgot Your Password? No Worries...

Just enter the email account you signed-up with, and we'll mail you your password

-Sign Up!- -Log In-

Please enter your email address:

Email	
	Find

Figure 19.6   To find your password, you must know what email account you used to sign up for, or previously log into, MySpace.

In Chapter 18, I recommended that you always use an email account separate from your primary personal or work email. Keep this account especially for MySpace and other social networking activities and guard your MySpace password. Never close this email account before starting a new one and changing the email in your MySpace account.

Changing your email address in MySpace is a multi-step process. In My Account > Account, the email address field is at the top (see Figure 19.7). Type your new email address in this field and press the Save Changes button at the bottom of the page. MySpace will send an email to your *old* address containing a confirmation code. You must enter that code into the designated field in My Account before the new email change will take effect (see Figure 19.8). This is why it is so important to not close your old email account before you have fully implemented the change in MySpace. Change your preferred email in MySpace *first*.

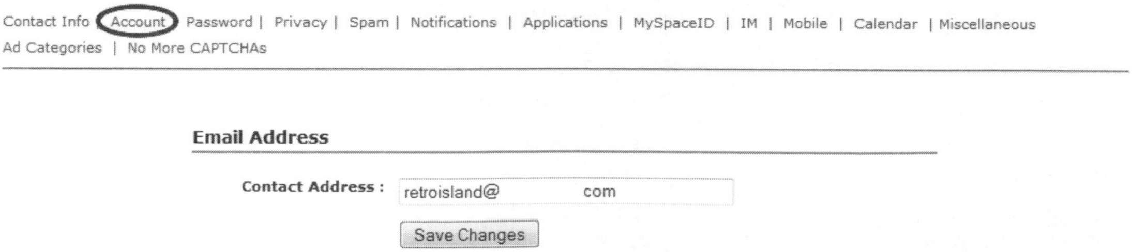

Contact Info | Account | Password | Privacy | Spam | Notifications | Applications | MySpaceID | IM | Mobile | Calendar | Miscellaneous Ad Categories | No More CAPTCHAs

Email Address

Contact Address : | retroisland@ | com |

Save Changes

Figure 19.7   Type your new email address into the field within My Account > Account.

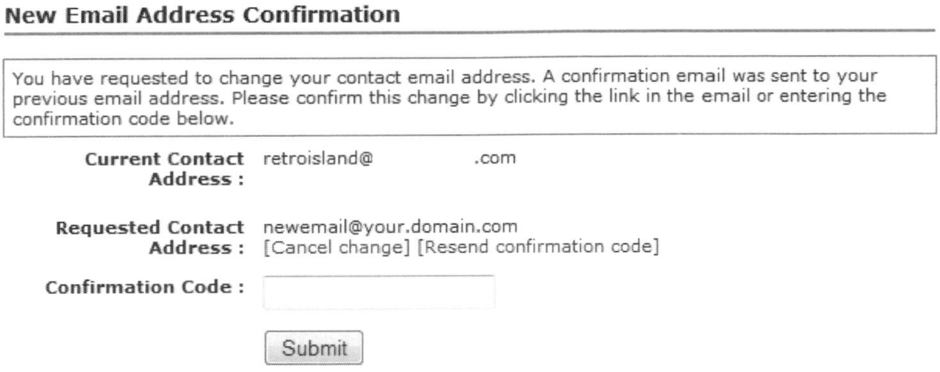

New Email Address Confirmation

You have requested to change your contact email address. A confirmation email was sent to your previous email address. Please confirm this change by clicking the link in the email or entering the confirmation code below.

Current Contact Address : retroisland@   .com

Requested Contact Address : newemail@your.domain.com
[Cancel change] [Resend confirmation code]

Confirmation Code :   [   ]

[Submit]

Figure 19.8 MySpace will send you a confirmation email code, which you must enter into your My Account settings to complete the process.

Away Messages

You can set an email away message in MySpace so that when anyone tries to send you a message, that person is presented with a personal message from you. Your Away Message options can be accessed through My Account > Miscellaneous. While away messages are of course useful if you will be away from MySpace for a while, some musicians and performers use away messages to inform users of how to contact them outside of MySpace. This is most commonly used by the artist who has a manager or an agent who fields all questions, especially those concerning career issues, such as touring and publicity (see Figure 19.9). It is also used to inform fans that the artist does not accept emails through MySpace. Many fans find this off-putting, and I don't recommend it. If you feel you are bombarded by fan emails and you really don't have the time or the resources to answer them all, it's better to put a note on your profile that you try to read all messages and you thank the fans for contacting you, but you may not be able to respond all emails personally.

Music Settings

In Chapter 11, we looked at the artist profile's sound player capabilities. Regular accounts, often used by music business people, such as bookers, publicists, and promoters, also have music settings located in My Account > Miscellaneous (see Figure 19.10). You can disable songs from playing automatically when you visit a band site, and you can disable your player from automatically launching when someone visits your profile. If you've added a band's song to your profile, you may want to disable it from automatically playing. It can be extremely annoying for visitors to be bombarded with sound when visiting other people's profiles, especially if the sound tramples over the music they're already listening to in the privacy of their home or office.

Hiding Online Now

Hiding the Online Now icon that appears near your thumbnail is a must for many MySpacers who like to travel incognito (see Figure 19.11). Your Privacy settings in My Account give

Enter your away message

Message

For all career matters, including booking, touring, personal appearances, publicity, legal, licensing, etc., please email my manager Bob at bobmanager@yourdomain.com.

Thanks!

☑ Show away message when someone wants to send me a message:

Save   Cancel

Figure 19.9   You can direct MySpacers who try to email you to your manager for business matters.

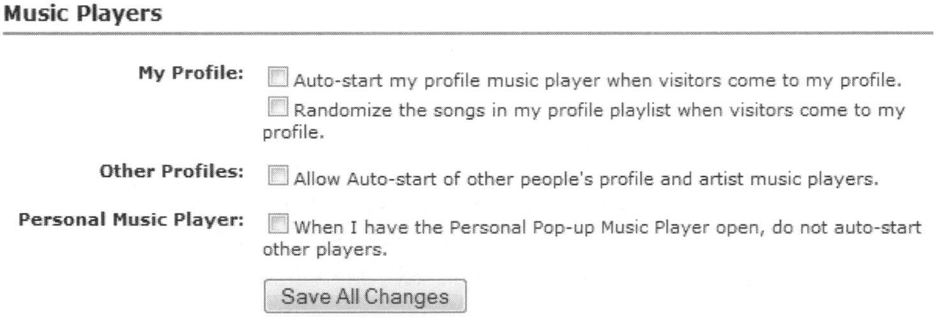

Music Players

My Profile: ☐ Auto-start my profile music player when visitors come to my profile.
                    ☐ Randomize the songs in my profile playlist when visitors come to my profile.

Other Profiles: ☐ Allow Auto-start of other people's profile and artist music players.

Personal Music Player: ☐ When I have the Personal Pop-up Music Player open, do not auto-start other players.

Save All Changes

Figure 19.10   Music settings can keep songs from automatically playing.

 **Online Now!**

Figure 19.11   Your Online Now icon.

you the option to conceal the Online Now icon. This is useful if you don't want to field quickie emails from friends or fans or alert your real-life crew that you are home sitting in front of the computer.

MySpace Mobile

MySpacers can update their status, send photos, and more through their mobile phone. Entertainers and suits who do a lot of networking through MySpace and like to keep their photos updated on the road will love this. They'll never have to miss an opportunity. For more information on MySpace Mobile, please refer to Chapter 4 or go straight to More on your medium blue navigation bar and click down to Mobile. For users without smartphone capabilities, visit My Account > Mobile.

Groups Settings

Along with the spam emails you are sure to receive in your MySpace account, you will also encounter Group Invites. Yes, lonely 1-900 operators and get-rich-quick schemers start their own MySpace groups. You can, of course, block anyone from sending you future invites and spam. You can also keep the system from notifying you when you have a group invite in your email box. Go to My Account > Notifications to turn off group invite notifications.

Instant Messaging and Chat

MySpace offers instant messaging, called MySpaceIM, which is a downloadable program that is similar to other types of Internet messaging software (see Figure 19.12). This downloadable program now also incorporates Skype so you can voice and video chat with your MySpace friends online. Additionally, MySpace offers a web-based IM/chat service. At the bottom of your profile, you'll see a toolbar inviting you to chat with friends who are currently online, through an in-browser pop-up window similar to Facebook's Chat function. Each user can set his IM settings by going to My Account > IM. Here, you can tell MySpace whether you want to allow others to instant message you and who can contact you via IM. To instant message someone, look for the link in the contact table called IM/Call. If you already have the IM software installed, it will open, and you can proceed; otherwise, MySpace will prompt you download their IM software. Bands sometimes find it helpful to restrict IM access to a select group of friends, instead of opening it up to the public or their entire Friends list.

No More CAPTCHAs

You may have noticed that many actions within MySpace, such as adding friends, sending messages, and making comments, often require you to enter an alphanumeric code. This proves to the MySpace system that you are not a script, program, or other malicious software that is automating its spamming activities. You can get around this security measure by showing the system that you are who you say you are. Do this by going to My Account > No More CAPTCHAs and entering your cell phone number (see Figure 19.13). A code will be

Figure 19.12 MySpaceIM is handy for chatting with MySpacers. If you don't already have the MySpaceIM with Skype installed on your computer, you will see this prompt.

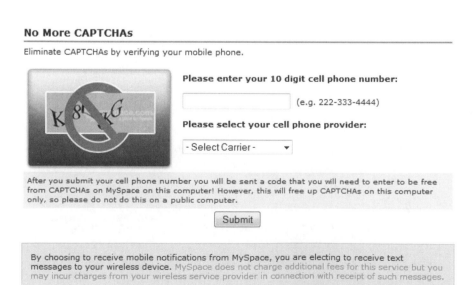

Figure 19.13 The No More CAPTCHAs page will help you verify your identify so you won't encounter the barrage of CAPTCHA codes that most users have to deal with.

texted to you that you must enter on this same page. From then on, whenever you use that same computer to access MySpace, you will not have to enter CAPTCHAs (or at least you'll have to enter significantly fewer CAPTCHAs). If you access MySpace from multiple private computers, you can repeat this process on each computer you use.

This chapter explored many of the most important customization options available to you as an entertainment marketer. Consult your account settings page for additional choices not covered here.

Now that you've customized your experience and privacy settings, let's move on to incorporating MySpace into your overall marketing plan.

20 Now What? MySpace and Your Marketing Plan

Having a MySpace profile is truly a necessity right now. It's considered by the industry to be a marketing must because of its ability to present a quick snapshot of the artist, all within a large, diverse community. But now that you have your profile up, what do you do next? This chapter will illuminate some other opportunities that exist and offer a few tips to help you best utilize your MySpace page for its marketing potential.

Selling Your Music and Merchandise

Some people believe that the MySpace profile exists to sell product. I believe it's there to represent your music and image in a snappy format, making it easy for fans and industry people to access you. If you sell product as well, then it's a bonus. Having said that, it is important to offer your wares (or at least a small selection) through your MySpace page. If someone is ready to buy while visiting your page and listening to your music, then you want to make it easy for them.

The first place to start is to sell your music on your page. When listening to major and some indie artists, you may have noticed that a Buy icon appears beside their songs in the music player (see Figure 20.1). When you click it, you will see an Amazon.com link. MySpace has an affiliate account with Amazon, so every time someone purchases a song directly from the Amazon link in the music player, MySpace gets a little commission. Aggregate this over thousands or millions of MP3 purchases, and MySpace can collect a nice commission check regularly. The catch is, artists cannot add or remove this Buy icon from their music players. MySpace detects whether an uploaded song is already offered on Amazon.com and will automatically link to it. It doesn't always work perfectly, unfortunately, and it takes time for the MySpace system to accomplish this.

For your music to even be considered as Amazon.com linkable through the music player, it must be distributed through a service that can get your music onto Amazon.com. Companies such as TheOrchard.com and CDBaby.com get your music onto Amazon, plus iTunes, Napster, and other sites. This is the best way for indie and unsigned artists to get their music onto Amazon and other major MP3 download sites. For MySpace to recognize your music as being available on Amazon, when you upload your song onto MySpace, you should title it exactly as it appears on Amazon.

Figure 20.1 This Britney Spears MySpace music player has a Buy icon next to each song. Clicking it gives you the option to download the song from Amazon or get the ringtone from Jamster.

Whether or not you have an Amazon link in your music player shouldn't stop you from further encouraging users to buy your music. Once your music is on Amazon through an aggregator, why not open your own affiliate account and add links within your profile to your music? Go to https://affiliate-program.amazon.com to open your own affiliate account. From here you can create special links to your music and embed them into your MySpace layout. Some artists will even make a banner or a Buy button that users can click, taking them directly to a download site (see Figure 20.2). You can do this with your own Amazon affiliate account as well. The bonus is that in addition to making money on the MP3 download itself, Amazon will also reward you with a little commission for every person who purchases by clicking on the affiliate link you created.

Amazon and iTunes are the two major places where users download music. You can't go wrong by creating links (or buttons/banners) on your profile that direct users to your music on these sites.

Ringtones

Like the automatic Amazon link in the music player, MySpace will link to a song's ringtone if it is available on Jamster (a sister company to MySpace). You can't control whether your ringtones are offered on Jamster. However, you can offer your music as a ringtone independently by going to a site such as Myxer.com or MyMusicSite.com. Here you can create an artist account, upload your music, convert it to a ringtone, and sell it to fans. Put links to your ringtones (or directions on how to get them via text message) right on your profile!

Figure 20.2 Artist Ingrid Michaelson (www.myspace.com/ingridmichaelson) encourages users to download her music from Amazon, iTunes, and CDBaby or to visit local stores to get the physical CD. Each icon is clickable and takes users right to her download/purchase page on each service.

Merch

T-shirts, hats, and other band accessories are popular with fans. Lots of places can help you design, manufacture, and even sell your wares. Create e-fliers and post them to your profile so fans know where and how they can get your merch (see Figure 20.3).

For more resources on digital/MP3 downloading sites, mobile, and merch, please visit Appendix A.

Social Media Promotion

Lots of artists are utilizing the many social networking and media tools out there to gain even greater exposure. Twitter, Facebook, external blogs, YouTube, iLike, and many others offer the opportunity not only to disseminate music and videos, but also to carry on a conversation with fans in various communities. Embedded Twitter feeds are quite popular on MySpace at the moment and are becoming a staple for artists (see Figure 20.4). Use your MySpace profile to cross-promote your other social media activities and reach fans wherever they congregate by linking to your other properties (see Figure 20.5).

Figure 20.3 Artist Allie Moss links to her merchandise on MerchLackey.com right from her profile (www.myspace.com/alliemossmusic).

MySpace Advertising and Editorial

MySpace offers opportunities for additional promotion within the service through paid advertising and unpaid editorial.

Reaching Potential Fans through Ads

As you surf through MySpace, you'll see advertisements on every page. They come in all shapes and sizes, from long, wide banners to tall, skinny ones. You'll also notice that some are square and some are quite small. And some are just text (such as Sponsored Links). Each and every one of these placements cost money and is paid for by the advertiser (see Figure 20.6).

MySpace offers two types of advertising services—self-service and traditional. With the traditional service, advertisers connect with an advertising account executive who administers and shepherds all aspects of the client's advertising. Your account exec will work with you one on one to determine the best flight times for your campaign (flights are the days/times each campaign will run) and make recommendations on how to best target your audience. They provide one-on-one counseling as to how your campaign did and how to better

Figure 20.4   Artist Bess Rogers plugs her Twitter feed right into her profile (www.myspace.com/bessrogers).

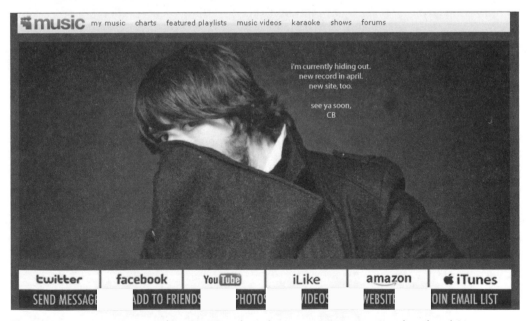

Figure 20.5   Singer/songwriter Cary Brothers (www.myspace.com/carybrothers) incorporates links to his other social media profiles (as well as download sites) right on the top banner of his layout.

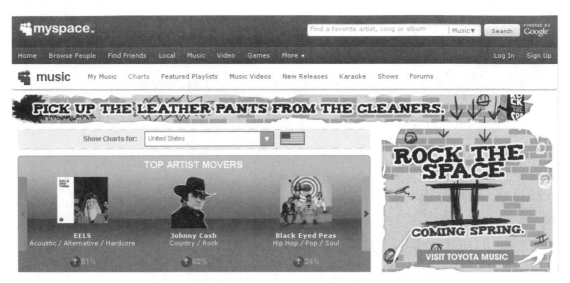

Figure 20.6   The Toyota Music ads across the top and in a square banner on the right side are paid placements.

improve it next time. Additionally, their traditional advertising services give clients the ability to target their audience much more accurately based on keywords and segmenting not available to self-service clients. This is especially helpful for niche products. Traditional advertisers are guaranteed a certain number of ad placements based on the investment.

The catch is that only advertisers with substantial budgets can use the traditional service. Typically, a minimum $10,000 investment (and that's for one flight) is needed before an account exec will work with you. If you're in the market for this type of service, contact Fox's Digital Media Group (of which MySpace's advertising execs are a part) at (310) 969-7200, 407 N. Maple Drive, Beverly Hills, CA 90210. While $10,000 is usually the minimum, times are a bit tough as of this writing, so it is possible that you can still go traditional with slightly less than that. Do keep in mind, though, that in order for advertising to really make an impact, you need to do multiple flights—repetition is key for consumers. So, plan on being able to part with a *minimum* of $25,000 in order to see consistent results through traditional advertising.

Self-service, introduced since the first edition of this book was released, allows you, the musician, to create your own banner ads, upload them to MySpace, pick your target markets, and pay with a credit card. It doesn't require a MySpace staff member to assist you, and it is a less expensive option than the traditional advertising model. Anyone, not just musicians, can use this self-service model, and there isn't a minimum investment. Most DIY musicians will fall into this category. To access the MySpace self-serve advertising portal, go to https://advertise.myspace.com (see Figure 20.7).

Self-service is a competitive area. Advertisers compete against each other for the same banner ad space, and whoever has bid more for the same keywords wins. This requires you to

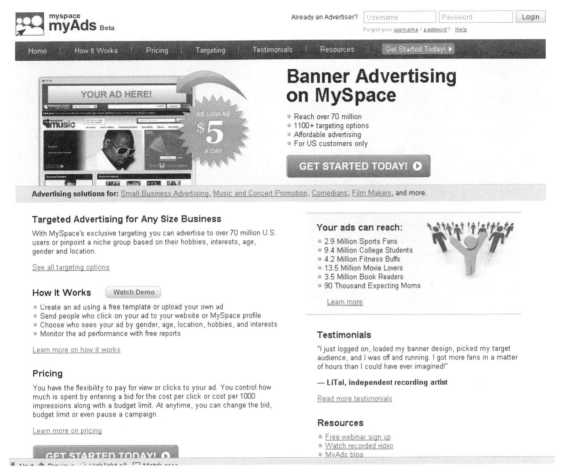

Figure 20.7   The MySpace self-service advertising portal at https://advertise.myspace.com.

monitor your advertising campaign closely so you can see how the bid amount fluctuates throughout the day or flight. Then, you can adjust your bid accordingly and in line with your goals and budget. The self-service model, while less expensive than traditional, is a hands-on endeavor. With traditional, you have an executive to handle the details. You don't need a minimum of $25,000 to make a dent, but you should see whether your advertising efforts are making a difference. If your ad is directing people to your profile, but you're not getting many clicks, friend ads, or plays, then it's time to revise your creative (graphics/text), tweak your targeting, keywords, and bidding, and/or rework your landing page so you can effectively convert clicks into consumer action.

Whichever model you choose, advertising can be an excellent way to drive traffic to your profile. And luckily, the self-service model gives you a way to try it out with a minimum dollar commitment.

Editorial

If you've spent a bit of time on MySpace, you've seen editorial all over the place. These are the front page and music features, Daily Charts (formerly Top Artists), and even the Indie Spotlight in the MySpace newsletters emailed to users (see Figures 20.8 and 20.9).

Unlike advertising, where you pay for a banner ad and have some control over who sees it, editorial is unpaid, and who gets placement is decided by a team of MySpace editors and channel managers. They choose who gets featured and where, based on factors such as traffic to the artist's profile, buzz in and out of the MySpace world, music plays, and the editor's personal preferences. I contacted MySpace for interviews with some of their editors, and they declined to comment for this book.

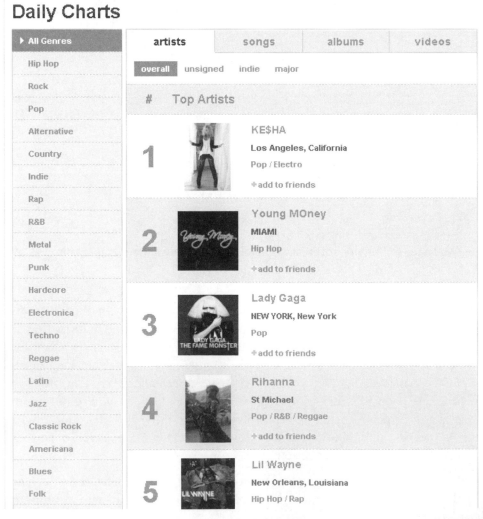

Figure 20.8   The Daily Charts (formerly called the Top Artists lists) are compiled by MySpace editors.

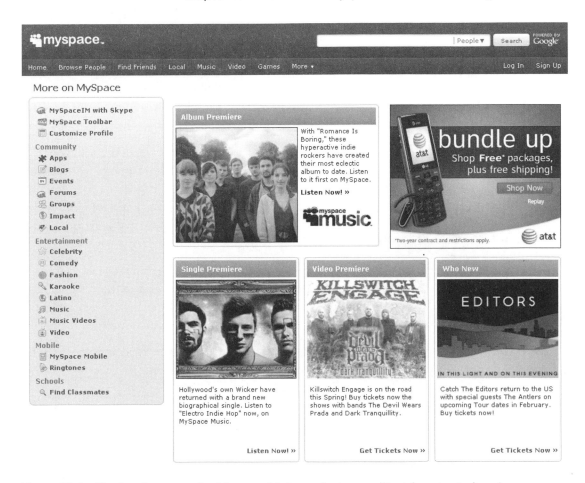

Figure 20.9   The landing page for More on MySpace features editorial content plugging new albums, singles, and more.

However, I will say that if you are determined, you can look for MySpace editorial contacts on LinkedIn.com and other business social media networks. A few web searches wouldn't hurt, either. They are usually located in the Beverly Hills/Santa Monica area of Southern California, and they have editors that handle different types of music (such as hip-hop, metal, and so on). If you can make a contact, you might be able to bring your band to the editor's awareness. And should you be playing in the Los Angeles area and you have a contact already, invite them to the show. From there it's out of your hands, but it never hurts to try to build a genuine relationship with a MySpace editor who may dig your music.

Driving Traffic

Getting eyeballs to your profile and increasing your overall fan base and media awareness requires consistency and creativity. Consider just some of the many ways you can promote and use your profile:

- **First, make a goal and a plan.** What do you want to accomplish with your profile? Start with smaller, short-term goals and then develop bigger, longer-term goals. Plan out activities and deadlines for achieving each goal. For example, a short-term goal could be adding 200 new friends this week or getting 500 people to add your music to their profiles. A longer-term goal might be to gain 150,000 friends or music plays, or even to use your MySpace to increase your email list by a certain number.

- **Schedule the time.** Treat your online and MySpace promotion activities as a job. Mark in your calendar the days/times you will devote to being online and promoting your band, as well as what you will do. If you aim to send out an email every month to your fan list, then put that in your planner. If you work at a regular job and have band rehearsals and other commitments, when will you be online to promote? Even if it's just one hour a day, write it down, make it a priority, and commit to getting it done.

- **Delegate.** For those in bands or who have management help, delegate some of your promotional activities. Strive to find a fit based on members' strengths and interests. If your bass player is already on Twitter a lot, then put him in charge of the Twitter activities for the band. Is your drummer a whiz with graphics? Let him design the emails.

- **Keep your profile fresh.** Add new content regularly, such as blog entries, announcements, banners, photos, videos, and novelty toys, such as cell phone alerts.

- **Put your MySpace URL on everything.** This includes CDs, stickers, your official website, tees and other merchandise, posters, fliers, advertisements, press releases, and press kits. Be sure to mention your MySpace page to writers and editors, reviewers, venue owners/managers, and other people with whom you are conducting business.

- **Individualize.** In some cases, it makes sense for individual band members to also have their own MySpace accounts. There they can not only promote the band's profile, but they can also discuss solo projects and even topics more personal to them. Put members in the band's Top Friends and vice versa.

- **Press links.** On your profile, insert a link to your band's press kit, which should be available on your official website. This way, if a journalist is perusing your profile, she doesn't have to try to track down your press kit on your official site.

- **Use MySpace to recruit a street team or build a fan club.** You need a big enough following to accomplish this, of course, but when you do, these are natural additions to your promotional activities. Offer street teamers free tix for promoting your shows in their area. Fan club members could have access to early ticket sales, discounts, and special merchandise not available to the general public.

- **Target local media with news about your MySpace profile.** Small newspapers and publications in your area love to cover local artists. Got a new profile? Offering streaming music on your page? Or did you add downloadable ringtones or music for purchase?

Are you launching a new album? Even bigger news qualifies, such as tour announcements and promotional partnerships. Did you just reach a profile milestone, such as 25,000 friends or 50,000 song plays? Send press release announcements to local newspapers. For tips on press releases, do a web search on "how to write a press release." Make sure to include your contact information at the top of every page and keep the writing clear and concise. Always include a headline and double-check to be sure your release is free of any spelling or grammatical errors. Call each media outlet and ask who handles news about local artists and the music scene. Post your press releases on your profile as well.

- **Aim for quality throughout your profile.** MySpace profiles can act like virtual demos, but you have to include other elements as well. Artsy photos, a great bio, and video clips show club owners and record-label execs how polished you are and how seriously you take your career.

- **Create a giveaway, contest, or competition.** For example, encourage fans to post a band banner promoting your new album to their profile, bulletin their friends, and then leave you a comment. Every fan who does this gets a chance to win the album, some T-shirts, a phone call from the band, or some other cool band prize. Promote this regularly on your profile, in emails, at shows, and so on.

What are some additional ways you can think up to use and promote your profile?

How to Target Musicians

Industry service and product providers use MySpace to target musicians. Recording studios, software and gear manufacturers, managers, stylists, lawyers, designers, photographers, and marketers go through the same process in figuring out which artists could use their services. However, simply adding friends isn't usually enough. Providers must carefully target their artists and interact with them directly. Email or chat with musicians to see what their needs are and how you can help them. And, since many businesses serve local markets only, getting a face-to-face meeting is often essential in closing a deal.

Audacity Recording in Hollywood, Florida, uses MySpace to find local musicians who could use their recording studios, video production, and DVD-authoring services. Owner Linda Thornberg monitors the company's profile at www.myspace.com/audacitystudios and uses it as part of their strategic marketing plan. She tasked freelance producer Jack Beasley with seeking out bands who would benefit from their premier facilities.

Beasley notes that to target local clientele, businesses should use the MySpace music search function to target specific genres in a suitable radius around their business.

"In any given week, I would focus on one genre. One week I would concentrate on bluegrass bands within a five-mile radius only," said Beasley. He would then listen to their music and offer suggestions on how the studio could help the artists. Sometimes he would go to gigs and approach bands personally, inviting them to the studio for a tour. Even a 10-percent return, he said, is a good investment of time.

Beasley suggests the real key to success for providers is "to develop a relationship and show [musicians] you care about their project.... MySpace has really helped us develop relationships."

Now for some final thoughts on *MySpace for Musicians, Second Edition...*

21 Last Words

While writing this book, my research and discussions with artists and other marketers kept bringing me back to the same conclusion. The key to using MySpace successfully to build your band's or company's exposure isn't about how many glittery, sparkly baubles you can add to your profile or how well you can demonstrate your programming prowess. It's about staying consistent and constantly looking for ways to market yourself on *and* off the service. The profile that sits dormant for months on end isn't the one that draws the most interest. But the artist who takes the profile and works it, scouring the community for friends, business associates, and other collaborators, and pushes the profile to media and fans in the real world is the one who gets results. Marketing yourself is time-consuming. What if you met and bonded with another MySpace artist and got to tour with that artist? Wouldn't it all have been worth it?

The only way to even get close to that point is to get out there, network, introduce yourself, find fans that fit your target, and keep applying what you know. It's that consistency that brings results. Spend an hour every day focused on improving your profile, adding new content, announcing it to friends, sourcing new friends, and getting people to listen to your music and review it. Look for opportunities to draw people to your profile, from commenting on others' YouTube videos with your MySpace tagline in the comment, to getting spins on Internet radio and inviting bloggers and podcasters to take a listen. For some artists, one day a week works best. But they do it every week and work it like a day job, or they focus that one hour a day on the task at hand.

It's not any different than the small businessperson who must network regularly to bring in customers. She goes to chamber of commerce functions, attends community events, calls on referrals, and hands out business cards. At first she wonders whether anything will ever come of it. Soon, however, she sees that continually getting her name out there and having people hear her name from various sources produces results. Opportunities come her way. That big account she called twice finally agrees to meet with her to hear what she has to say. They heard good things from an associate and decided to give her a chance.

MySpace (and online marketing in general) isn't any different really, except you're doing your networking in a virtual world. Gigging musicians and clubgoers especially see that translated into real life. They're always being asked for their MySpace address. Now they can build relationships inside *and* outside of the service.

Hopefully, this book has at least given you the tools you need to feel comfortable getting onto MySpace. My greater hope is that you are inspired to take it further than just establishing a profile. Treat the "working" of MySpace as an essential part of your music marketing plan, because it is. Fans, managers, the media, and industry insiders alike expect you to have it. Major-label artists do, so why shouldn't you? Leave any apprehension behind and dive in. Take advantage of the free web presence that MySpace gives you. You have all the tools you need to build a plan, create an awesome profile, showcase and sell your music, and maximize the time you spend on MySpace. For all the new tech developments that are sure to come your way, you have the foundation. You can make your way through, learn as you go, and tackle the ever-changing Internet marketing landscape.

As a MySpace music marketer, you have to look beyond just your profile. Regularly peruse other music profiles—major, indie, and unsigned—and see what others are doing with their profiles. You just might find some new gadgets and be inspired by how your fellow artists are marketing themselves.

So will I see you on MySpace? I hope so! You'll find me at www.myspace.com/retroisland. Send me your stories, tips, and of course a friend request. After Tom, count me as your second friend!

Appendix A: Marketing and Merchandise Resources

This appendix lists providers who can help you with marketing, web design, music services, promotion, and merchandise.

A&R and Artist Development

Find opportunities, get discovered, and be developed by the following companies.

- **KingsofAR.com (Kings of A&R).** Features emerging talent and interviews with industry veterans.

- **CrazedHits.com.** Unsigned bands are showcased on this blog, read by industry executives.

- **SonicBids.com.** Members create online press kits and can submit themselves for various promotional, festival/event, and A&R opportunities. Pricing is about $50 per year plus submission fees for some festival opportunities.

- **Taxi.com.** This A&R company gives members exclusive opportunities to pitch their music to record executives. The full one-year membership is about $300. Song critiques are also available.

Blog Hosting

The following blog hosting sites and management platforms offer free and premium services.

- Blog.com

- BlogHost.com

- Blogger.com

- LiveJournal.com

- MyBlogsite.com

- OpenDiary.com

- Squarespace.com

- Thoughts.com

- TravelPod.com

- Tumblr.com

- TypePad.com

- WordPress.com

- Vox.com

- Xanga.com

CD/DVD Manufacturing

Why wait for a record deal? Get your CD or DVD replicated and sell it on your own!

- **DiscMakers.com.** A well-known leader in CD/DVD manufacturing, Disc Makers also prints up CD inserts, posters, and more.

- **DubHubDisc.com.** With contacts across the nation, they aim to find the best price for your needs.

- **KMSMedia.net.** Located near Nashville, they do large orders and short runs, plus USB Flash Drive duplication.

- **Kunaki.com.** Great for short runs.

- **OasisCD.com.** Another respected CD/DVD manufacturer also offering many premium packaging and insert products.

- **TheDubHouse.net.** A popular CD/DVD manufacturer with no minimums and no setup fees.

Contests

American Idol isn't the only contest to recognize new talent. Below are just two of the many contests available to performers and songwriters. Keep your ear to the ground and do your own web searches for songwriting, music, talent, and other entertainment-related contests.

- **Famecast.com.** American online talent competition, awarding the top winner $10,000.

- **John Lennon Songwriting Contest (www.jlsc.com).** Songwriters could win an EMI Publishing contract, studio equipment, and more.

Email Marketing Services

While this list only begins to scratch the surface, here are a few email marketing service providers to get you started.

- **AardvarkMailingList.com.** This free web tool lets you add an email signup list to your website.

- **Campaigner.com.** This tool sets up email campaigns based on various schedules and criteria you specify, allowing you to really customize your contacts with fans. Monthly fees start at $25 and are based on volume.

- **ConstantContact.com.** A very popular web program that allows you to create email campaigns and manage lists. Your monthly fee is based on the number of email addresses on your list.

- **EliteEmail.com.** Build lists and newsletters, as well as track your email campaign to see how it's doing. Instead of monthly fees, you pay for "credits" and use them as needed.

- **EmailBrain.com.** In addition to email marketing, this site also offers text messaging services.

- **Everyone.net.** An email provider for businesses and small groups alike. You can even offer free email accounts to your fans using your own domain name.

- **FanBridge.com.** Focused on serving the band community, FanBridge also gives artists tips for making the most of their email marketing and fan relationships.

- **MailChimp.com for Musicians (http://tinyurl.com/yek3e6w).** This link will take you directly to the musician's section of MailChimp (as of this writing).

- **MyNewsletterBuilder.com.** Carries lots of email newsletter templates that can be customized with your band info, pics, video, and more.

- **ReverbNation FanReach Pro (http://www.reverbnation.com/fanreachpro).** ReverbNation offers a variety of artist services, including email marketing. Starting at $9.95, you can email your fans regularly using their snazzy email marketing templates and more.

- **SwiftPage.com.** Integrate your current database with SwiftPage and get started with email marketing quickly.

- **TextConnex.com.** Offers both email and text messaging marketing.

- **Topica.com.** Target your fans and track the success of your marketing campaigns.

- **VerticalResponse.com.** Specializing in web-based marketing and printed postcards, VerticalResponse helps you collect email addresses and create snazzy email and printed postcards to send out to your list. They charge based on the number of emails you send per project.

- **YourMailingListProvider.com.** A web-based application that helps you gather and manage email addresses and send out newsletters and e-zines. The fee you pay depends on how many emails you send in any given month.

Event Sites

Promote your gigs to your audience through these event promotion sites.

- **Eventful.com.** Create and promote gigs and events online or locate them in your area.

- **LocateBands.com.** Build a profile, offer music samples, and promote gigs in your local area.

- **TopsinAmerica.com.** Promote yourself as the tops in your area or category and see others who are tops in various categories.

Graphics and Printing

Bands often need graphic design help and good sources for printing fliers, postcards, promo photos, and other items. Below is a starter list for your graphic and printing needs.

- **99Designs.com.** You post a project (such as a CD cover), and designers submit their best designs and compete to be the one you pick.

- **AccessPasses.com.** Print up professional badges for press and VIPs at your shows.

- **ClubCardPrinting.com.** Postcards, promotional cards of all sizes, plus posters and large-format prints.

- **ClubFlyers.com.** In addition to printing your project, they'll mail it to your fans, too.

- **CrowdSpring.com.** A global creative community and design marketplace.

- **DropCards.com.** Creative music download cards and other redemption items that can be sold or given to fans.

- **FizzKicks.com.** Design your own music download cards to give or sell to fans and/or make a custom digital download store.

- **GotPrint.com.** Inexpensive, quality printing.

- **MemorySuppliers.com.** Instead of CDs, try USB flash drives in the shape of credit cards.

- **MiamiFlyers.com.** Fliers of all sizes plus posters and more.

- **MPix.com.** A great place to have photos retouched and printed.

- **PostcardMania.com.** Self-described postcard marketing experts, they also offer a whole area of marketing tips and techniques.

- **PrintClick.com.** Create your postcards and posters online in minutes.

- **UPrinting.com.** Tons of items available for printing.

- **TheFlyerLab.com.** Get thousands of postcards for less than $100.

- **VistaPrint.com.** Design your projects right on the website.

Merchandising

Musicians can make a lot of money by selling merch at shows and online. These vendors offer products ready for printing your band logo, e-commerce solutions, and distribution.

- **TheBizmo.com.** Create your free store and sell tickets, ringtones, merch, and more.

- **CafePress.com.** Create your own merchandise store by uploading band logos, photos, and designs and putting them on CafePress-provided merchandise, such as T-shirts, hats, mugs, mouse pads, and more. Basic stores are free. Premium stores are $4.99 to $6.95 per month.

- **CinderBlock.com.** A full-service merch company offering licensing, design, retail development, and e-commerce solutions for musicians.

- **CustomInk.com.** Design your tees and hats online, with lots of funky merchandise colors to choose from.

- **Disc Makers Merch (DiscMakers.com/merch). Get custom merchandise with low minimums at really reasonable prices.**

- **MerchDirect.com.** Providing merch design, production, and distribution for artists, bands, and record labels.

- **MerchLackey.com.** Run by musicians, MerchLackey offers merchandise printing, tour service, and e-commerce solutions for bands.

- **Oasis Wearables (OasisCD.com/Products/merch.asp). Printable band T-shirts, hoodies, and hats with no setup fees and low minimums.**

- **SmartPunk.com.** Catering to unsigned bands, SmartPunk allows approved bands to sell their merch and music through their site.

- **WeNeedMerch.com.** Merchandise printers whose owners are full-time musicians. They say they'll beat anyone's prices and offer quickie turnarounds.

- **Zambooie.com.** They say it best: "We build web stores for bands, screen print their products, and ship out their orders."

- **Zazzle.com.** Create custom T-shirts and other merch items.

Mobile Music

The following sites offer mobile content delivery and management for such items as ringtones, text messages, and videos. Many of them allow you to create modules to sell your ringtones on your MySpace page.

- **Bango.com.** Offers programs for entry-level mobile content providers all the way up to leading brands to analyze the success of their mobile programs.

- **BroadTexter.com.** Get fans to sign up and then send them broadcast text messages. Great for reminding fans of gigs, CDs, and other special band happenings.

- **MediaPlazza.com.** Make your content mobile. Publish your songs, videos, and pictures for fans from around the globe to download from your site.

- **Mozes.com.** Fans can sign up for your mobile mob and leave messages for each other and you. Artists can communicate with all their fans with just one text message to the mob and run mobile promotions.

- **mPush.com.** Another site to help you sell your mobile content to a worldwide audience.

- **MyMusicSite.com.** Create your own ringtones and sell your indie music to fans.

- **Myxer.com.** Earn a percentage of every item you sell through Myxer. You won't have to sign a contract or pay setup fees, and they offer a distribution widget you can use on your profile.

- **Upoc.com.** Create interest groups and interact with members via text messaging.

- **Zedge.net.** If you want to offer your pics, ringtones, or other media to fans for *free,* this is the place to do it.

Music Downloading

These are just a few of the dozens of downloading sites available. Some deal directly with artists; others deal with labels and distributors only.

- **BandSpace.com.** Artists make 70 cents per song they sell through BandSpace and can also offer merchandise to fans through an online store.

- **CDBaby.com.** An online record store where indie musicians can sell their CDs direct to consumers.

- **DiscRevolt.com.** Artists upload music for sale and then order printed cards to sell to fans at shows. Fans get credits toward the purchase of the artist's music.

- **DJDownload.com.** Catering to the electronica, dance, DJ, and club communities.

- **eMusic.com.** eMusic is the largest retailer of indie music, and consumers can find new and upcoming bands in all genres. However, eMusic works in labels online, and not directly with unsigned artists.

- **Indiestore.com.** Based in the UK, IndieStore allows indie artists to create and manage their own digital download stores.

- **iTunes.com.** Now an icon in digital downloads, Apple's iTunes offers singles, albums, and even TV shows for download for a per-item fee.

- **Mysongstore.com.** They'll host your store, which can integrate your graphics and band look. Fees are membership-based depending on how much song storage you need.

- **Napster.com.** After shedding its former life as a file-swapping service for unlicensed music, Napster has reinvented itself as a completely legit download service.

- **Rhapsody.com.** A membership-based downloading service that also offers a free program where you can listen to dozens of preprogrammed radio stations or create your own.

- **Soundation.com.** Sell your songs online by creating your own web store. You keep all of your profits and pay only an annual store fee.

- **TheOrchard.com.** A full-service media company specializing in music distribution and licensing.

- **TuneCore.com.** A service that brings your music to major online distributors, including iTunes, Rhapsody, Napster, and others.

- **TuneTribe.com.** Offering music downloads from artists and labels, plus music news and editorial.

- **Walmart Music Downloads** (mp3.walmart.com/store/home). Is it any surprise that one of the biggest discount retailers in the world also sells digital music? Their music downloads are also discounted at less than the usual $1 per track.

Press Release Distribution Services (Wires)

These sites will take your press release, such as an album release announcement, and distribute it to media outlets in categories you specify. Some also go direct to consumers and are also sent to online aggregators and search engines, such as Google News.

- **Beatwire.com.** Press release distribution service for indie musicians and labels.

- **BillboardPublicityWire.com.** Specializes in music and entertainment media targets. Also sends to opt-in consumers.

- **BlackPR.com.** Get your music news out to almost 900 black media outlets, including print, TV, and radio.

- **BusinessWire.com.** A favorite of PR professionals, Business Wire is a well-known distribution service that sends direct to journalists.

- **Collegiate Presswire (www.cpwire.com). Send your press release to college print and broadcast media nationwide.**

- **HispanicPRWire.com.** This Miami-based company sends releases to key Hispanic media.

- **Indie Media Blast** (IndieArtistsAlliance.com/PR.htm). Reasonably priced option to send your news to 1,000+ music and entertainment publications.

- **Music Industry News Network** (mi2n.com/services). Guaranteed placement on a variety of blogs, forums, and other online music communities.

- **PRWeb.com.** A well-known service used by large and small businesses alike.

- **PRNewswire.com.** A staple of the PR pro's toolbox, PR Newswire has a stellar media reputation.

- **Rapnewswire.com.** Offers free and premium services to reach the rap and hip-hop entertainment communities.

- **Send2Press.com.** Frequently used by entrepreneurs, Send2Press has many circuits from which to choose, including music and entertainment.

- **TheGospelNewswire.com.** Send your gospel and Christian music news to 1,500+ outlets.

- **TheOpenPress.com.** Offering free and paid Internet distribution in a variety of topical areas.

- **Urban Music News Network (um2n.mi2n.com/index.php3).** Submit your press release and have it sent out to urban music outlets.

- **uWire.com.** Send news items to more than 700 college media outlets in the U.S., Canada, Europe, Asia, and South America.

- **WDCMedia.com.** Specializing in Christian content, WDC Media is especially valuable for the contemporary Christian or gospel artist.

Radio

Whether you want to just listen or actively broadcast, check out these radio providers and research sites.

- **AirPlayDirect.com.** They act as a file transfer system from musicians and labels to radio DJs. Radio programmers also discover new music through the site.

- **AOL Radio** (Music.aol.com/radioguide/bb). Features XM content and more than 200 free, preset stations.

- **GoomRadio.us.** An online radio station site that mixes hits with new music, in-studio performances, and interviews.

- **Grooveshark.com.** A community for fans to discover new music and for bands to promote their new releases.

- **iSound.com.** Bands promote their music through the site. Users listen to preset radio stations or create their own.

- **Jango.com.** Pay-for-play Internet radio.

- **Last.fm.** Makes music recommendations and creates custom radio stations based on your artist preferences.

- **Live365.com.** Listen to one of the hundreds of Live365 radio stations or broadcast your own.

- **Musicovery.com.** An interactive web radio destination.

- **Pandora.com.** A creation of the Music Genome Project, Pandora helps users discover new music based on what they already like to listen to.

- **Radio-Locator.com.** Search for terrestrial radio stations nationwide. Great for deciding which stations to target in a promotion.

- **Rhapsody.com Radio.** Listen to dozens of free radio stations or create your own. Songs played are accompanied by album artwork, song info, and artist bio blurbs.

- **ShoutCast.com.** Free Internet radio stations compiled by DJs and broadcasters around the globe. Even you could be the next DJ.

- **Slacker.com.** Create your own personal radio station or listen to premade stations.

- **VH1.com Radio.** Programmed by industry DJs and execs, VH1 has bunches of hip stations to explore.

- **MTV.com Radio.** MTV's radio station selection comes mostly from celebrity playlists and themes inspired by the network's own shows.

- **Yahoo! Music Radio (Music.Yahoo.com). Take advantage of free and premium stations or create your own. Plus, you can watch streaming video stations.**

Social Networks for Music

Social networks created specifically for artists to promote their music amongst a community of music lovers are a great way to build a fan base. Here are just a few you should check out. Be sure to web search for communities that are specific to your genre of music as well.

- ArtistDirect.com

- BeatKing.com

- Broadjam.com

- BuzzNet.com

- GarageBand.com

- Hyphy.com

- iLike.com

- InternetDJ.com

- LoudFusion.com

- Mog.com

- MusicForte.com

- Ning.com (join an existing social network or create your own)

- PureVolume.com

- ReverbNation.com

- SwingVine.com

- Virb.com

Website Creation

Put together your own website or store, even if you have no programming experience.

- **Bandzoogle.com.** Build your very own band site and integrate your merch and music store in one place.

- **FourFour.com.** Created specifically for musicians, the free version boasts a host of features.

- **ReverbNation Site Builder (http://tinyurl.com/ylpy3bs).**

- **Shopify.com.** Get your online store up and running quickly. Includes shopping cart.

- **Snappages.com.** A limited, free version is available.

- **Squarespace.com.** This service is already used by major artists and comedians. Handles multimedia well.

- **Weebly.com.** A good option for a really simple site.

- **Wix.com.** Free Flash website builder.

- **Zlio.com.** Create your own store quickly.

Web Templates

Use ready-made templates to help you create your official website or blog. Hundreds of them are out there . . . do a web search for "web templates," "blog templates" or "css templates." Here are a few to get you started.

- CSSTemplates.net

- DIYThemes.com

- FreeCSSTemplates.org

- MusicMogulDesign.com

- TemplateMonster.com

Widgets

These portable little programs can be customized with your band info and music and plugged into your profile, where fans can interact with your content and spread it to their friends virally.

- **Clearspring.com.** With their advertising model, you can get your widget or video seen across many sites and social media networks.

- **eSnips.com.** Upload files and then create widgets that allow users to interact with your files (such as uploaded music, videos, and pictures).

- **Gydget.com.** Create a band widget and help fans easily spread your widget to their friends using the FanSpace application by Gydget.

- **LoudFeed.com.** Get a widget to sell your music online. Other promotional services available.

- **Nabbr.com.** This innovative company has leased real estate on sites all over the web. When you purchase an advertising package, they build you a custom, branded widget to your specification and put it on their network of sites so you can get the word out about your band.

- **Outshouts.com.** A fun way to create a video mix and then send to fans and embed it on your profile.

- **ReverbNation.com.** Choose from microsite widgets, email widgets, and more. RN also offers a host of services to help bands promote themselves.

- **SayNow.** Get a special number, invite them to call you, and send out broadcast messages.

- **Snapvine.com.** Record messages for fans. Then fans can call your special number and leave you messages as well. Put the widget on your profile for all to hear. Excellent as a voice blog.

- **Spinlets.com.** A sleek-looking widget. Add your band videos and more, and share on your social networks.

- **SproutBuilder.com.** This nifty authoring tool helps you make a completely branded widget, even if you don't know how to write code. You can make three for free; otherwise, they have subscription packages.

- **UrFooz.com.** Dubbed a "portable profile," urFooz allows you to create an avatar that looks like you to greet visitors to your widget.

Miscellaneous

These goodies didn't fit into the other categories but are still worth a look!

- **ArtistFreeMp3.com.** Get download cards to direct your fans to your own custom music channel where they can get free music.

- **Crunkbox.com.** Lots of online music tools for the indie musician.

- **Dizzler.com.** Free downloadable application to help you search for music and play media on your computer or mobile device.

- **eJamming.com.** Play and record live with musicians from around the world.

- **Fancorps.com.** Street team management and promotion.

- **FormSpring.me.** Keep the dialog open by encouraging fans to ask you anonymous questions that you can answer for all to see!

- **Go-Backstage.com.** Spread the word about your music and start building a fan list by creating your own download promotion where fans can get your music or video for free.

- **MyRecordLabel.com.** Multifaceted, this site offers digital distribution, widgets, email marketing, and other online tools.

- **Nimbit.com.** Loaded with lots of tools for the musician, from catalog and content management to marketing and ecommerce.

- **SoundCloud.com.** The fast and easy way to receive, send, and distribute your tracks.

Appendix B: MySpace Resources

This appendix lists sites that offer layout codes, generators, tweaks, tutorials, and other MySpace toys. Plus, it details hosting sites for photos, video, slideshows, and podcasting, as well as news sites and blogs that focus on social networking. Note that some of the sites may contain advertising, pop-ups, and possibly adware, so proceed with caution and run your adware scans after visiting.

MySpace Code Sites

These sites offer free layouts, code generators, and tweaks.

- Bigoo.ws
- FreeFlashToys.com
- FreeWebLayouts.net
- HotFreeLayouts.com
- KawaiiSpace.com
- MyBannerMaker.com
- MyFlashFetish.com
- MyGen.co.uk
- MySpace4pimps.com
- MySpace.NuclearCentury.com
- MySpaceCore.com
- MySpaceGens.com
- MySpace-Images.com
- MySpaceLayoutSupport.com
- MySpaceProDesigns.com
- Myspace-scripts.com

- MySpaceSupport.com

- MyTheme.com

- New.ModMyProfile.com

- PimpItOut.net

- PimpMaSpace.com

- PimpMyCom.com

- ProfilePimp.com

- ProfileTweaks.com

- Skize.com

- Zoodu.com/top-banner

Layout Editors

Use a layout editor to custom-create your profile.

- Pimp-My-Profile.com/generators/myspace.php

- www.Pulseware.com.au/site_pi.asp?p=wpa-167088

- RealEditor.com

Free Div Overlays and Generators

The div overlay will completely change the way your profile is structured.

- Chr15.net/overlay

- Divoverlaylayouts.com

- Squidoo.com/MySpace_Div_Overlay

More MySpace Profile Toys

Add more fun widgets to your page.

- Snapvine.com

- Quizilla.com

- MyFlashFetish.com

HTML and Bulletin Editors

Edit HTML for your profile, bulletins, or comments with these tools.

- Pimp-My-Profile.com/htmledit
- Zoodu.com/html-editor

Web Design Resources and Tutorials

Brush up on HTML and CSS with the following sites.

- **Basic HTML Tutorial.** www.pageresource.com/html/index2.htm
- **How to Create Special Characters in HTML.** www.tamingthebeast.net/articles2/special-characters.htm
- **Extensive CSS Tutorial.** W3Schools.com/CSS/default.asp
- **Extensive HTML Tutorial.** W3Schools.com/html/default.asp

Media Hosting Sites

This list is a compilation of photo, video, and slideshow hosting sites. Some, in fact, offer all three services.

- Box.net
- CastPost.com
- Crackle.com
- DailyMotion.com
- Flickr.com
- ImageShack.us
- MetaCafe.com
- Mevio.com
- Motionbox.com
- OneTrueMedia.com
- Pbase.com
- PhotoBucket.com
- Piclynks.com

- Pixagogo.com

- Pixilive.com

- Revver.com

- Ripway.com

- RockYou.com

- Slide.com

- Stickam.com

- VideoEgg.com

- Vimeo.com

- VMix.com

- VSocial.com

- YouTube.com

- Zorpia.com

Social Networking Blogs and Updates

Stay abreast of current topics in social networking.

- Bloggersblog.com/socialnetworks

- DMWMedia.com

- Mashable.com

- SocialNetworkingNews.com

- SocialNetworking-Weblog.com

Podcasting

The following sites offer podcast hosting, tools, and directories.

- Apple.com/itunes/podcasts

- GCast.com

- MyPodcast.com

- PodcastAlley.com

- PodcastDirectory.com
- PodcastingNews.com
- Poderator.com
- PodHoster.com

Appendix C: Music Business Resources

This appendix lists music industry organizations, companies, and other resources.

Performing Rights Organizations

Songwriters should join a performing rights organization, which helps protect performance rights through collecting and disbursing performance royalties to artists and publishers.

- **American Society of Composers, Authors and Publishers:** ASCAP.com

- **Broadcast Music:** BMI.com

- **SESAC (originally known as Society of European Stage Authors & Composers; represents U.S. artists as well):** SESAC.com

- **SoundExchange.com (collects for streaming audio, satellite, and others)**

- **PRS for Music:** www.prsformusic.com/Pages/default.aspx

- **Canadian Musical Reproduction Rights Agency:** www.CMRRA.ca

Conventions

The following conventions are some of the most popular in the U.S. for musicians.

- **Audio Engineering Society Convention:** AES.org

- **Billboard Events (for more Billboard conferences and seminars):** billboardevents.com/billboardevents/index.jsp

- **Billboard/Hollywood Reporter Film and TV Music Conference:** billboardevents.com/billboardevents/filmtv/index.jsp

- **Billboard Latin Music Conference:** billboardevents.com/billboardevents/latin/index.jsp

- **International Music Products Association Convention:** NAMM.com

- **Millennium Music Conference:** musicconference.net/mmc11

- National Association of Recording Merchandisers Convention: NARM.com

- South by Southwest: SXSW.com

- Vegas Music Conference: lvmc.us

- Winter Music Conference: wintermusicconference.com

Music Licensing and Supervision

The following providers can help you secure licenses for using others' songs or find music for your project.

- Harry Fox Agency: HarryFox.com

- JetSetIndie.com

- Mobile Business Information Group: MBIG.com

- MusicSupervisor.com

- Musync Music Licensing: www.musync.com

- PumpAudio.com

- RumbleFish.com

- The Music Bridge Music Clearance: themusicbridge.com

- Ricall Music Licensing and Clearance: www.ricall.com/home/syncsiteHome.seam?cid=31749

- YouLicense.com

Organizations

The following organizations serve as support and resources for various sectors of the music industry. Some are also trade groups and unions.

- American Federation of Television & Radio Artists: AFTRA.org

- American Association of Independent Music: A2IM.org

- American Composers Forum: composersforum.org

- American Federation of Musicians: AFM.org

- American Music Conference: AMC-Music.com

- Audio Engineering Society: AES.org

- International Alliance for Women in Music: IAWM.org

- **International Association for Jazz Education:** www.apassion4jazz.net/iaje.html

- **International Computer Music Association:** ComputerMusic.org

- **International Musical Products Association (NAMM):** NAMM.org

- **Latin Recording Academy:** Grammy.com/Latin

- **Music Publishers' Association of the United States:** MPA.org

- **Music Teachers National Association:** www.MTNA.org

- **MusicUnited:** musicunited.org

- **National Association of Record Industry Professionals:** NARIP.com

- **National Association of Recording Arts and Sciences (a.k.a. The Recording Academy):** Grammy.com

- **National Association of Teachers of Singing:** NATS.org

- **National Music Publishers' Association:** NMPA.org

- **Percussive Arts Society:** PAS.org

- **Recording Industry Association of America:** RIAA.com

- **Society for Electro-Acoustic Music in the United States:** SEAMUSonline.org

- **The National Association for Music Education (MENC):** MENC.org

- **The Society of Composers & Lyricists:** TheSCL.com

Index

COURSE TECHNOLOGY
CENGAGE Learning™
Professional • Technical • Reference

Course Technology PTR
COURSE CLIPS

Introducing *Course Clips*!

Course Clips are interactive DVD-ROM training products for those who prefer learning on the computer as opposed to learning through a book. *Course Clips Starters* are for beginners and *Course Clips Masters* are for more advanced users.

**Pro Tools 8
Course Clips Master**
Steve Wall ■ $49.99

**Pro Tools 8
Course Clips Starter**
Steve Wall ■ $29.99

**Ableton Live 8
Course Clips Master**
Brian Jackson ■ $49.99

Individual movie clips are available for purchase online at **www.courseclips.com**

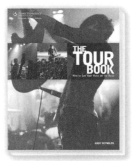
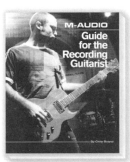